Hurling

The Revolution Years

DENIS WALSH

PENGUIN
IRELAND

PENGUIN IRELAND

Published by the Penguin Group
Penguin Ireland, 25 St Stephen's Green, Dublin 2, Ireland
(a division of Penguin Books Ltd)
Penguin Books Ltd, 80 Strand, London WC2R ORL, England
Penguin Group (USA) Inc., 375 Hudson Street, New York, New York 10014, USA
Penguin Group (Australia), 250 Camberwell Road,
Camberwell, Victoria 3124, Australia (a division of Pearson Australia Group Pty Ltd)
Penguin Group (Canada), 90 Eglinton Avenue East, Suite 700, Toronto, Ontario, Canada M4P 2Y3
(a division of Pearson Penguin Canada Inc.)
Penguin Books India Pvt Ltd, 11 Community Centre,
Panchsheel Park, New Delhi – 110 017, India
Penguin Group (NZ), cnr Airborne and Rosedale Roads, Albany,
Auckland 1310, New Zealand (a division of Pearson New Zealand Ltd)
Penguin Books (South Africa) (Pty) Ltd, 24 Sturdee Avenue,
Rosebank 2196, South Africa

Penguin Books Ltd, Registered Offices: 80 Strand, London WC2R ORL, England

www.penguin.com

First published 2005
1

Set in 12/14.75 pt Monotype Bembo
Typeset by Rowland Phototypesetting Ltd, Bury St Edmunds, Suffolk
Printed in Great Britain by Clays Ltd, St Ives plc

A CIP catalogue record for this book is available from the British Library

ISBN-13: 978-1-84488-033-1
ISBN-10: 1-844-88033-8

Hurling

To Paula, Adam and Katie with love

Contents

Acknowledgements

As I write, in June 2005, the Leinster hurling semi-finals have just been decided by an aggregate margin of 42 points. Offaly, proud tormentors of Kilkenny through the 1980s and 90s, have suffered their greatest ever humiliation at the hands of their old rivals. Ten days ago the Dublin hurlers trained by themselves as their dispute with the county board and the search for an emergency management team continued. Four matches have been played in the Munster hurling championship, producing less than half an hour of truly satisfying hurling between them. Crowds are down, apathy and despair are up. The feeling that things will never be any better is as potent and compelling now as it was around 1992 or 1993. Just before the clouds parted.

The world I re-visited in this book seems a million miles away, almost a fantasy world. The sense that it was an extraordinary period in the history of the game was not lost on any of us at the time, but I suspect that our wonder and our gratitude expired too soon.

The greatest pleasure in writing this book was to renew old acquaintances with the players and managers who made those years what they were. I am deeply grateful to all of them for their time, hospitality and candour. Without them, this book would not have been possible.

I also leaned on a battalion of generous people. My thanks to Brendan Barrington at Penguin Ireland for his expert editing, endless patience and calming presence; my thanks also to Michael McLoughlin for embracing this project with such enthusiasm. When transcribing nearly fifty hours of interviews became too much, Michael Moynihan and Gary Murphy came to the rescue and located people who were willing to share the load: Patricia Davis, Francis Sheehan and Brian Finnegan picked their way through the dopey questions and imperfect recordings with enormous professionalism.

Dave Hannigan encouraged me to do this book long before I finally had the courage to close my eyes and jump. His advice and support were invaluable, as always. Doubtcha boy.

Over the years Carrigtwohill GAA club has enriched my life and the life of those around me, ignoring the feebleness of my contributions on the field. More than twenty years ago they gave me my first break in this business, letting me loose on juvenile match reports for local papers. Ten years later they invited me to collaborate with John O'Mahony and Oliver O'Connor to produce a book on our club's history. The value of that experience sustained me in the final months of this project – though it was lonely journey without ye this time, lads. Friendships that began in the club many years ago continue to this day and are cherished still.

Some thanks are overdue. To John Horgan in the *Evening Echo*, Tom Ahern in the *Irish Examiner*, Sean Scully in the *Southern Star* and Ger Siggins in the *Sunday Tribune* for their kindness and blind faith. To all of my colleagues in the *Sunday Times*, especially Michael Foley and my sports editor Paul Rowan, for their forbearance and sensitivity over these last few complicated months. The *Sunday Times* kindly permitted me to reproduce passages from pieces which had already appeared in the paper and for that, too, my thanks.

Special thanks to my parents, Jack and Breda. My debt is incalculable, my gratitude beyond words. Thanks also to Phil who, among many other things, brought books and news-papers into my world many moons ago. Thanks to Niall and

Roma, Liz and Ger, Harriett and Tony, for all kinds of everything over the years.

Deepest thanks to my wife Paula. Without her love, patience, sacrifice and understanding this book could never have happened. This, and so much else. And to Adam and Katie, the light in our lives. Que Dios os bendiga a los dos.

Prologue

This is how it was. On the last Sunday of May 1992 a crowd of 8,000 showed up in Thurles for the meeting of Clare and Waterford in the first round of the Munster hurling championship. Tens of thousands of others who would later identify themselves as the great and faithful hurling people of both counties were elsewhere that day, subscribers to the general carelessness.

The attendance reflected a resignation that was institutionalized and accepted. Though it wasn't polite to say so, Clare and Waterford was the meeting of tuppence and tuppence ha'penny. It didn't matter who won. One of them would live to die another day. The All-Ireland would be decided without them, as it was every other year.

Whenever a head count was done of hurling counties, though, Clare and Waterford always raised their hands. They declared their passion and their tradition and their lifelong membership of the club, and because numbers were so tight hurling was grateful for their continued stoicism. Acceptance as a hurling county, though, didn't amount to status. Between them Clare and Waterford had won three senior All-Irelands in 105 years, and six Munster championships since 1932. Every picture of glory was stained by time.

They weren't alone on the bread line. Hurling was a divided society where the rich got richer and the poor were patronized with pennies of encouragement and pats on the head. The status quo was occasionally challenged but never overthrown. Offaly, in 1981, had been the only first-time winners of the All-Ireland in forty-four years. The hurling championship drifted along on the same current, as good or as bad as it always had been.

As a cultural entity, hurling was loudly acknowledged to be a national treasure, a golden strand of our identity, uniquely ours, gloriously us. Yet, beyond the rhetoric and the *plámás*, hurling was wilfully neglected in two-thirds of its homeland and half of the counties who took the game seriously were never contenders. Underneath the lipstick and mascara of Munster finals and big days in Croke Park, the hurling championship was pale and sick.

Clare and Waterford drew that day in Thurles, its significance buried for the archaeologists to find and display. It was Anthony Daly's first match as Clare captain. Tommy Guilfoyle had gashed his hand in a domestic accident that week and the wound required twenty stitches, so Daly was asked to step up. He was a young man of twenty-two, ambitious and driven beyond his station as a Clare corner-back. Not famous then. But soon.

Kieran Delahunty was marking Daly by the time he scored Waterford's equalizer from a free in the last couple of minutes. He wandered back to his position and suggested to Daly that Clare should 'stick to the traditional music'. For his lip, Daly met him with the handle of the hurley.

'You know,' says Daly, 'it was like something I'd say myself. In fairness to Delahunty I was probably roaring into his ear the whole day. I was a bold fella that time. But it really hit me. 'That's all ye're good for.' And I said in my own mind, 'You're right, Dela.'

'I remember going down the tunnel afterwards and Tuts [Fergie Tuohy] said, "Good boy, Dalyo, we'll take them the next day." And one of their fellas says, "Ye will in yer hole." And somebody else says, "We will." And the fellas from Thurles looking at us saying to themselves, "What are they on about? Nobody gives a damn."

'The replay was the following Sunday and afterwards we were told, "No drinking now tonight, lads." Sure we drank pints that night in the Queens [an Ennis nightclub] and we were bulling that there wasn't going to be any session on the Monday. There's nothing worse than a draw – it's a fierce anti-climax. We were training that night, stretching and jogging – and sure we wanted to be in the Diamond [Bar].'

Len Gaynor was the Clare manager and Ger Loughnane was one of his selectors. Loughnane had already lost eleven Munster finals as a player and mentor; that tally would rise to thirteen before the sequence was broken. In time he would frame the mentality that would make Clare winners, but back then he couldn't distance himself from their losing condition.

'I remember Loughnane fucking ate us between the drawn game and the replay,' says Daly. 'I remember he tore into me and a few more. I suppose it was a little snippet of what we were going to get used to. He lambasted us.'

It made no difference. Fewer people bothered to come to the replay a week later on a miserably wet day in Thurles. Waterford won a gripping match with two late frees, 0–16 to 0–14. They went on to rattle Limerick in the Munster semi-final, and lost. Gone before mid-summer's day.

Clare pored over the corpse of another championship. 'Will you take them again?' Gaynor was asked by a reporter straight after the Waterford defeat.

'Do you want to kill me altogether?' Gaynor replied.

Gaynor stayed for two more years and made that Clare team stand up straight against the best, shoulders back, chest out. That day in Thurles he probably couldn't have imagined such a sight.

On those afternoons in Thurles there was no premonition

of the future. Of the outlandish changes to come, of a championship reborn, of hurling's new glamour. Ten years later, in August 2002, Clare and Waterford met in an All-Ireland semi-final in Croke Park before a crowd of 58,000. Clare had won two All-Irelands and three Munster championships in the meantime; Waterford had just won their first Munster championship in thirty-nine years.

Hurling changed before our eyes.

Daly captained Clare for those two All-Irelands. When he took the microphone on the Hogan Stand after the 1995 final he remembered Delahunty.

'We love our traditional music,' said Daly. 'But we love our hurling too.'

On that dog-day afternoon in Thurles, though, the Clare captain wasn't collecting lines for a victory speech.

Nobody knew what was coming. Nobody could have known.

1. Crusheen

The 1992 championship had passed away and from Thurles to Newport they observed a respectful silence. Ger 'Sparrow' O'Loughlin drove, and with him in the car were his Clarecastle clubmates. For the fourth year in a row Clare had been knocked out in their first match, and with practice Sparrow had perfected his response. They parked the car outside the pub and as the others went ahead Sparrow turned to his old friend Anthony Daly.

'Dalyo,' he said, 'did you see me?'

'How do you mean, Gerry?' said Daly.

'At the final whistle – I waved goodbye to the Old Stand. A last farewell.'

Every year since Daly had joined the panel as a teenager in 1989, Clare's exit from the championship had been accompanied by the poignant announcement of Sparrow's retirement. It had become ceremonial, like lowering the flag to half-mast or the piper's final lament. On losing days Sparrow saw nothing in the future that could moderate his hostility for the present. He was part of the Clare condition, and he hated it. They drank a couple of pints and carried on, giddy with the concussion of another defeat.

'We came to the conclusion,' says Daly, 'that we'd never win nothing. "All I want is one Munster championship," said Sparrow, "and I'd never be seen with a hurley in my hand again."'

The thought that haunted Sparrow was that his best chance

might have come and gone. A few weeks before Clare played Cork in the 1986 Munster final he was added to the training panel, and a year later he was on the team when Clare lost narrowly in the league final. They drew with Tipperary in the Munster championship that year but lost by seven goals in the replay. In the bomb blast the good team of the 1980s was blown apart and Sparrow was one of the young players left standing in the rubble.

'In those days Sparrow used to set himself up as one of the greats because he'd played in the League final in 1987,' says Daly, laughing at the harmless conceit. 'He was on that team and like, I was never going to experience that. "You're a good player," he'd say to me, "but you've been unlucky." He'd start telling you about Ger Loughnane and Johnny Callinan and all the great players he played with. "I'm finished with it now," he'd say, "but at least I saw the good days. I'm sorry to have to say it to you, but you're wasting your time here."'

Behind the slagging the despair was real. Cork beat them by sixteen points in the 1988 Munster semi-final and Waterford beat them by fifteen points a year later. Limerick came to Ennis in 1990 and ran amok: 2–16 to 1–5 was the final score and Clare's goal arrived so late it nearly missed the wake. Clare always fancied themselves against Limerick and facing them in Cusack Park would have nourished their optimism. But at the same time such an outlook was delusional. They were just drifting, without a puff of breeze in their sails.

'There was a lot of negativity among the players in those days,' says Sparrow, 'including myself. I was genuinely calling it a day every year. I didn't see the point. It's like everything else – if you get enough thumps on the head you'll go dumb from it. If you lose enough hurling matches you accept losing at the end of the day. We didn't have it right in our heads. There were no outstanding individuals to take a match by the scruff of the neck. We didn't do it back then. The likes of myself had the potential to do it and I should have been doing it, but I wasn't. Maybe in the end it came down from the top. The likes of myself should have been shown the door if we were being negative.'

The assaults on their self-esteem came from all sides. A couple of months before the Limerick defeat they had won Division Two of the league and played off against the winners of Division Three for the prize of a weekend trip to London. Kerry beat them. Sparrow and Daly took Ennis by storm that night and met at noon the following day to do it again. On the Sunday night of desperate defeats they often drove past Clarecastle, deferring the post-mortem in Navin's bar until Monday afternoon, waiting for some of the radiation to leave the atmosphere.

Daly recalls those days with a kind of gallows humour. He remembers a tournament they played in Westmeath during his first season. 'We went up in Sparrow's old blue Fiesta, and at the time going away for a weekend was a great thing. We won our match on Saturday and we were due to play again on Sunday. Anyway, that night we took off in Sparrow's Fiesta to a party in Mullingar, real sneaky like. Christ, we walked in and half the panel was inside there. We felt pure guilty.'

When it came to Clare, though, their conscience didn't have a veto on their behaviour. They were happy to sacrifice drink for Clarecastle, but doing it for Clare was beyond all reason.

The 1990 hammering by Limerick was Daly's championship debut, and after all this time he can still show you the scar. 'I was young and I had notions in my head. I remember going home that evening and, like, our club would have been one of the stronger clubs in Clare and I remember saying, "We might win a Munster club some time." That's what was in my mind. "Fuck this Clare scene, you're never going to win anything there – but you could win a Munster club." You know, I was working in the bank and if you were on the Cork panel you were going to get promoted, no bother. But hurling for Clare they were laughing at you. It was a sad day I can tell you.'

Into this walked Len Gaynor.

In the autumn of 1990, before Gaynor's first league, a trial match was held in Newmarket-on-Fergus and about thirty-six players showed up. Gaynor introduced himself and asked them to dream. His record as an All-Ireland winner with Tipperary set him apart from everybody else in the room, but his origins didn't. He had come from an un-fashionable club, Kilruane McDonaghs, that had no tradition of producing Tipperary seniors. They were outside the elite, just as Clare were. He had overcome that; why couldn't they?

'Gaynor was a breath of fresh air,' says Daly. 'Straight away he came across as a real, decent, honest fella. His attitude was, "If you work hard enough at something in life you will achieve." I'd say that's the way he lived his life and that's the way he played his hurling. I remember there was one guy on the previous management and his big goal in life was getting Clare out of Division Two. I'd be disgusted with this. Fucking Division Two. When Len came in he said, "I'm not here to put the pride back in the jersey. I'm here to win a Munster championship." For a young fella like me, this was brilliant.'

Father Willie Walsh, who later became the Bishop of Killaloe, was one of Gaynor's selectors. Walsh knew the players and he knew the devastation better than Gaynor's naked eye could see. Years later Clare manager Cyril Lyons recalled that they didn't even play the best teams in challenge games in those days for fear of the outcome and the collateral damage to team spirit. Walsh had a word in Gaynor's ear and urged restraint.

'I remember him saying to me, "Go easy on these guys. They're not used to this,"' says Gaynor. '"What do you mean?" I said. "Their morale is very low." I found that strange. I wouldn't have been aware that their morale could be as low as that, but we did go easy on them and we worked on their confidence more than anything. It was brought on gradually. We didn't steamroll them. They were ready for steamrolling when Ger [Loughnane] took over in 1995, but that wouldn't have worked in '90 or '91 or '92. They were fragile enough. They were very vulnerable at that stage.'

Gaynor stayed for four years and changed the landscape. He didn't win anything, but Clare's failures under him deposited minerals in the soil. His training was sufficiently different for the players to regard it as progressive. Tim Crowe brought their fitness to a level that trainer Mike McNamara could later use as a platform. They went to the running track at the University of Limerick and had tests done in the lab. It was new and it was modern. Gaynor also brought Loughnane with him as a selector in his second season in charge, and when Loughnane's stock bottomed out at the county board he insisted that Loughnane return as a selector in the autumn of 1993, with a view to being his successor. There was resistance at the county board, but Gaynor was adamant. McNamara was invited to be a selector in the autumn of 1993 too, but that was a brief association. 'He has written in his book that he walked out because he didn't like what he saw,' says Gaynor. 'I remember at the time it was reported that he was charged at the stiles going into a club match in Ennis and he took umbrage against that. He never gave me an explanation, and I didn't look for one. He walked out and I said, "That's it."'

When players think back on Gaynor's sessions, the square bales of hay spring to mind. In essence it was a strength drill, though it wasn't described in those terms. Players ran at full speed carrying a bale and threw it at another player coming at speed in the opposite direction. 'Eventually we got pissed off with this,' says Fergie Tuohy, who joined the panel in 1991, 'but in principle it was a good idea. He had the foresight to see that we needed a bit of beefing up. In later years [under McNamara] something similar was done with tackle bags.'

Progress was slow. They lost with some restored honour to Limerick in the 1991 championship, but the defeat against Waterford in 1992 rattled Gaynor. 'We were expecting a bit more,' he says, 'and we got a bit less.' The players were afraid they'd lose him. They made him a little presentation and tugged at his heart strings. He stayed.

The summer of 1993 was an adventure nobody had expected. The league had ended with a thrashing at the hands of Cork in a play-off in Thurles and Gaynor discharged the panel for a couple of weeks to clear their heads. When training was resumed some players were cut from the panel. Sparrow was amongst them.

He went off and lit up the sky playing for Clarecastle, and on the week of the championship match against Limerick he was asked back on to the panel. Sparrow made them sweat over his reply for a couple of days before returning to the fold. He played golf with business clients on the day before the match and stayed up until one in the morning, not expecting to play any part the following day. After two minutes, though, Alan Neville injured his shoulder and Sparrow was sent on; he rustled up 1–5 from play and won the match. After all the planning and plotting the game had turned on an accident.

From a standing start, Clare were on a roll. They turned over Cork in the Munster semi-final and breezed into the Munster final for the first time in seven years. Everything about the day, though, was wrong. They gathered in the Greenhills Hotel near the Gaelic Grounds in Limerick, mingling with the great throng of their supporters, interacting with familiar faces and well-meaning strangers. 'I remember walking in and seeing fellas from the town that I was in National School with,' says James O'Connor, who was in his rookie season, 'and you were thinking that these were the last guys you would expect to see at a match. There was a kind of carnival atmosphere but we needed to be a million miles from that place. We had a room for our meeting but we were using the same toilet as Joe Public. We walked up to the pitch through the crowd. That was part of the naivety or innocence or whatever. I was just heading up to play in a Munster final.'

'Looking back it was a bit unreal,' says Daly. 'We were calm and we were loving it but we weren't tuned in to what we had to do.'

Clare were starstruck and deferential. For the first ten minutes they weren't even bold enough to meet a Tipp player with force. It was bloodless. They couldn't live with the pace either. With four points from play O'Connor was one of the few Clare players to enhance his reputation that day, but he can remember chasing Raymie Ryan on a long run just before half-time and he reckons it was ten minutes into the second half before he fully recovered.

'We had never played a match of that intensity before,' says Tuohy. 'That fever.'

'I remember Tim [Crowe] in particular had a cut at

half-time,' says O'Connor. 'Beforehand our attitude had been, "Look, get out and go for it, take chances, play from the front. We've nothing to lose." But we'd played conservatively, we'd played safe, we'd played from behind. His attitude was, "Look where it's gotten us." The Tipp game was a huge game for all of us who were a part of it. It was a black day. They took the piss. They just destroyed us. We were out of our depth.'

When it came to it they didn't have the inner conceit to face Tipperary as equals in a Munster final. They were prisoners of tradition, cuffed and cowed. Tipp beat them by eighteen points. Double scores. Buried. For the fifth time in seven years Clare had lost a championship match by fourteen points or more. If you want to remember what hurling was like before 1995, just think of that.

'The Willie Clancy week was on [a traditional music festival in Miltown Malbay] and I was on a week's holiday after the match,' says Daly. 'Myself, Tuohy and [Stephen] Sheedy went down there for that week and went off the rails. We drank it out. We were so bad in the Munster final it just wasn't worth talking about.'

The draw for the 1994 championship reunited them with Tipperary in the first round. For six months the fixture dominated their horizon. A part of every day belonged to that day. That winter they lost one of their teammates, when John Moroney was killed in a car crash. Moroney played corner-back, a quiet, well-respected, well-liked fellow. They absorbed the loss and took what strength they could from it.

'It brought us a bit closer,' says Gaynor. 'I felt very strongly about it, and it certainly helped us. I can remember the evening his remains were removed from the morgue. It was teeming rain, a wet, wet evening, and they all stood there waiting for his remains to come. They had their guard of honour and they were drowned to the skin. It really shook them. We spoke about it later on, a few weeks later when we were getting ready for the championship. We said that John Moroney couldn't play any more and we had the chance to play again and redeem ourselves. It really helped them along and made them stronger.'

On the day, Tipp suffered from injuries and complacency in equal measure. They had won the league and had their sights set on the All-Ireland. For Clare it was a bigger scalp than either Cork or Limerick had been the year before because nobody doubted Tipp's status as one of the three best teams in the country. In a driving finish they won by four points. More than that, they had stood up.

In one sense, though, it didn't prove anything new. Over the decades Clare had regularly beaten their superiors in the Munster championship. That wasn't the issue. The final was the thing. The Big Day. Clare had played in ten Munster finals since 1932 and lost them all. They didn't feel part of the institution. In the folklore of the Munster final an overwhelming majority of the 'truly great' matches were ascribed to Cork and Tipperary. Clare didn't have a 'great' Munster final to their name. When it came to Clare hurling, the Munster final was a giant jack-boot resting on their throats.

During his playing career Johnny Callinan lost six Munster finals with Clare between 1972 and 1986, which was a lot given that in his youth they had only reached one final, in 1967. He was away at a Gaeltacht college on the Aran Islands that summer and listened to another Clare defeat on the wireless. His father took him to Munster finals as a child, and when he died his father's friends took him, but they didn't feel included. They were on the outside, peering in.

'I can remember the routine,' says Callinan. 'We'd be

down there at eleven o'clock, eating our sandwiches and quite happy, but because Clare weren't playing it was somebody else's Munster final.'

In 1972 he was playing. Cork beat them by twenty-two points in the end, although Callinan claims, playfully, that there were thirty-two points between the teams when he joined the match. Haulie Daly, an uncle of Anthony's, sent him on with twenty minutes to go and told him to 'play anywhere. It was really weird. I was just a child – I was minor again the following year – and I'd say I didn't even get a puck. But I have a memory of shaking hands with all the big Cork names – Tony Maher, Ray Cummins, Paddy Barry, Denis Coughlan – at the end of the match, as if I was a fan who had run on in my street clothes.

'By the time 1986 came round I was well cheesed off. I remember a supporter called me over as I was leaving the field in Killarney. "Give me the hurley," he said, "you won't be needing it again." I nearly gave it to him between the eyes. There's a photograph of the incident. I flicked the hurley back at him and hit the wire. As far as I was concerned the Munster final was a bit of a sacred cow which, among other things, had stopped the arrival of the open draw in hurling.'

So, here they were again in 1994, in another Munster final, and it was as if the experience of all the other Munster finals had counted for nothing. They were beaten by Limerick, but they were beaten by the day too. The Big Day. Again.

'The pre-match stuff,' says O'Connor, 'would have been very amateurish. I remember we drove in cars to Thurles and went through the middle of the town in traffic.' Instead of distancing themselves from the buzz and the party of Munster final day they had put themselves in the way of it again, just as they had a year before in Limerick.

'The occasion got to us,' admits Gaynor. 'I didn't shield them enough from that. I didn't guard them against the pressure of the day. Again it would have been my own background. The pressure would never have bothered me when I was playing. The big game didn't bother me that much; I was able to handle it. I didn't realize that maybe these guys weren't . . . I suppose they had come from far deeper on the ladder.'

Ger Loughnane and Fr Willie Walsh were Gaynor's selectors, and in O'Connor's view the changes they made at half-time destroyed whatever lingering chance Clare had of rescuing the match. Sean McMahon was moved from centre-back to the wing in place of John O'Connell. Mike Galligan had taken two points off O'Connell in the first half; in the second he took five off McMahon. Francis Corey, a corner-back cum full-back, was put in at number six on Gary Kirby. He was lost at sea.

'Half-time was a disaster,' says O'Connor. 'We were four points down. What we needed was someone to come in and say, "Look, we played absolute shite in that first half and we're only four points down, we're right in it." We needed someone to be positive. Instead we came in, sat down and someone said, "We're not beaten yet, lads." We were beaten there and then. I just think in hindsight the dressing room was negative at half-time.

'When they announced the changes I think certainly the players themselves knew this was a disaster. "You're after making a balls of it here." I don't think anybody on the team would have agreed with the changes that were made and I think that feeds into your psyche as well. It knocked the stuffing out of some of the team. I don't think it was fair on Francis either. Centre-back is a key position and they were putting in a guy that had never played there before. You could just smell the panic. The heart had been knocked out of the team at half-time. The game was over.'

Daly did enough that day to win his first All Star five months later. Limerick finished the match with twenty-five points, but alongside Brian Lohan and Liam Doyle, Daly was part of a full-back line that conceded just four points from play, despite the constant shelling. A year earlier the full-back line had conceded 1–15 against Tipp. For Daly it was something and it was nothing.

'The 1993 defeat was bad, but the feeling of disappointment after 1994 was far worse,' says Daly. 'Jesus, like we're fucking chokers. That's what it felt like. In '93 when we were caught we were all green young fellas, but it was the whole Thurles thing that caught us in '94. As well as that we codded ourselves into thinking that because of what happened in '93 this isn't going to happen again. It was going to happen for us in '94 and we were all waiting for it to happen without making it happen. Limerick came out to win the Munster final; we went down to collect it.'

Gaynor felt the loss deeply too, and the following week he informed the county board of his decision to quit. 'I was trying to relax the situation that day but it wasn't working. They were very tense and very keyed up and over-anxious to do well. There was a lot riding on that match and I'd say it got to them all right. Yet the opposition wasn't as daunting for them as Cork or Tipperary would have been. They would have been able for Limerick over the years, up and down, in and out. I knew we were good enough to win. The year before I could accept that Tipp were ten times better than us on the day, but this was a moderate Limerick team and they had beaten us after all our great work – as we thought – in beating Tipp and getting to the Munster final. I decided to call it a day straight away. They needed something extra. I brought them so far but they needed an extra lift to go further.'

The Clare U-21s of 1992 knew that Loughnane was the future. They had lost the Munster final to an exceptional Waterford team who went on to win the All-Ireland. Only two points separated the sides, and in the last minute Clare were awarded a 21-yard free. Davy Fitzgerald was in goal, and over the course of his senior career he developed a reputation as the most fearsome striker of a dead ball in hurling; but he wasn't asked to come forward that night and the shot was saved. The Clare county board couldn't accept the defeat. Three years earlier this bunch of players had reached an All-Ireland minor final, and a Munster championship was the least that delegates demanded. Loughnane and his selectors Mike McNamara and Louis Mulqueen were sacked. O'Connor played that night and he could understand the argument that tactical misjudgements were made on the sideline, but that missed the bigger picture. 'The training was incredible,' says O'Connor. 'The organization, everything about the fella, was top class.'

Loughnane was outside the system in 1993, but a couple of weeks after the Munster final that summer he called round to O'Connor's house. 'In hindsight,' says O'Connor, 'he was sounding me out. The guy was hatching a plan. He wanted to know where fellas stood on him, how they felt about him, how they felt about the training and all that.'

With Gaynor's support, Loughnane returned as a senior selector that autumn. Loughnane sought an assurance that he would take over when Gaynor stood down, and Brendan Vaughan, the Clare county board chairman at the time, agreed to the plan. At a county board meeting to ratify Gaynor's selection committee some voices were raised in dissent, but the motion was passed. Twelve months later Loughnane didn't risk the possibility of the county board reneging on what they had decided a year before. He went on Clare FM and, in his own words, 'declared that I was the Clare manager'.

McNamara and Tony Considine were his selectors, and in the beginning the chemistry was good between them. McNamara and Loughnane came from neighbouring parishes, Scariff and Feakle, and on the hurling field their paths would have crossed. After a gap of many years their paths crossed again in 1989. Loughnane was appointed manager of the Clare minor team, but after a disagreement with Bord Na nÓg he walked away and McNamara was asked to be his replacement. Instead Loughnane managed the Wolfe Tones minor team that year and, as favourites for the county championship, they had some players McNamara wanted. 'Things were frosty between myself and Ger because we wanted the same players at the same time,' wrote McNamara in his book *To Hell and Back*. 'In the end we agreed to compromise.'

McNamara brought that Clare team to an All-Ireland final, but after Clare lost the Munster minor final a year later he was sacked. He returned as an U-21 selector with Loughnane in 1992, and a year later coached the juniors to win Clare's first All-Ireland since 1914. They had won the double in that glorious year, senior and junior, and hadn't won either of them for the next eight decades. McNamara's unstable relationship with the county board mirrored Loughnane's. Over five years he had been involved in two Munster titles and one All-Ireland, had been sacked twice and walked out once.

They developed what McNamara described as a 'strong working relationship' during the summer of 1992, and it was clear to them both that they shared a vision for Clare. Loughnane wanted the Clare players to be stronger, fitter and harder. McNamara couldn't have agreed more. During fifteen years living in south Kilkenny he had made a name for himself in junior rugby. At his peak he played junior for Munster, a hard bastard in the back row. In those days he was a fitness fanatic. Before breakfast he would go for a run – five, six, ten miles, never less than five. This was the outlook he brought to the party.

Considine brought something different. Like McNamara he didn't have a reputation as a high-class player, but during the 1980s clubs from all over the county asked him for a hand. A couple won county titles; nearly every team was lifted. 'He brought one club from absolutely nothing,' McNamara said at the time. 'From being an undisciplined, unsporting, unsociable kind of team to a crowd you'd be happy to play with or against. They didn't win any honours, but I remember being impressed with that.'

McNamara asked him to be a selector with the Clare juniors in 1993, and Loughnane came calling a year later. He wanted an antidote to the seriousness of himself and McNamara. A sugar lump when players were taking their medicine on foul nights in February. He wanted a comic, but he didn't want a clown. Considine was perfect.

Early in their relationship Loughnane told Considine that there weren't five minutes in the day when hurling didn't come into his mind. Loughnane often expresses himself in hyperbole, but the obsession was authentic. It was indivisible from his personality and from his presence. He dominated the group and everybody who came into contact with them – players, selectors, county board officers. He didn't regard Considine or McNamara as equals in the selection process; they were his advisers, his inner cabinet. The final decision on everything was his. He ruled. There was no question of Loughnane being out-voted two to one, for his vote trumped every doubt and protest. In their first year in charge they claimed that every team they picked was concluded in three minutes. They didn't even need to sit down. The clock, though, would only have started with the talking. Loughnane's contemplation didn't clock in or clock out.

At the county board's training field in Crusheen, though, McNamara enjoyed devolved power. The Clare panel gathered there in September 1994 and braced themselves for a winter campaign the like of which no hurling team had ever experienced before. McNamara told them they were training to win the All-Ireland. The words came from the trainer's mouth, but the cabinet would already have discussed the policy direction. It was sixty-two years since Clare had won a Munster championship and here they were, training to win the All-Ireland.

Crusheen is a small village north of Ennis on the way to Gort, little more than another bend in the road. Over time, though, Crusheen came to represent an idea and an attitude. It framed Clare's identity and ultimately it sponsored their mystique. Crusheen was where their power came from, their mentality, their sense of indestructibility, their aura. Before the 1990s were finished every serious hurling team in the country went in search of what Crusheen had given Clare.

Crusheen was the soul of discomfort, like a medieval dungeon in the open air. 'The dressing rooms were primitive to say the least,' says O'Connor. 'There was a crack in one of the windows and a hole in one of the other windows that wasn't repaired for four years. It was exposed and wild. It was pitch dark, pissing rain, and invariably you were being told what to do. In the middle of December and January it was as bleak a place as you could be. It was basically just a good field that could take desperate punishment and be fit to run on again the following night.'

This was where McNamara had them in his grip, where the character of every player was X-rayed. Clare needed to be fitter, but mostly they needed to be mentally tougher. The training was a test. It was Darwinian. Natural selection. The survival of the fittest. Players fell away and weren't asked back.

Michael O'Halloran joined the panel that winter for the first time. His club, Sixmilebridge, had been through a couple of long campaigns and his stamina was good. He coped in Crusheen, and he coped too when training moved to a punishing hill in Shannon later in the winter, but it wasn't handy. 'Ah, it was savage. I mean you could even call it military style. You were abused and put through the slog. Mike Mac thrived on the shitty nights in Crusheen making you do press-ups. Going down and holding the press-ups for thirty seconds, bending your body weight for thirty seconds, and if you didn't do it your sexuality was called into play. Your mother or your father or somebody was abused.' In Crusheen they lapped the field in a figure of eight. 'It was mind-numbing,' continues O'Halloran. 'You'd start at this corner, up to that corner, down to this corner, up and down for five miles. I think it involved thirty or forty circuits within thirty minutes.'

After Christmas McNamara decided that their base fitness was sufficiently good to bring the panel to the hill in Shannon. The slope rose for 130 metres and whatever mental fortitude they had gained in Crusheen was examined. 'When you look back on it now it was animal stuff,' says O'Halloran. 'I mean we did it forty times one night. Ten of them might have been 30-yard sprints at the steepest part of the hill. It was right beside one of the main roads in Shannon and the comment was passed that if you saw a fella dragging a horse up and down it forty times you'd probably call the ISPCA.'

The suffering was greater, though, than the exertion and the exhaustion. There was also the terror. The dread. Training nights clouded the whole day.

'At training you'd feel like getting sick,' says Tuohy, 'but you didn't quite because there was nothing there. You'd have nothing. Maybe water would come up. You just knew that come half twelve in the day a sandwich was the most you could eat. If you were going down to Shannon or Crusheen there was no point in eating. Maybe a cup of tea and a biscuit at five o'clock with a rake of sugar for a bit of energy.'

Sparrow reckons that the thought depressed him from about two o'clock in the afternoon. McNamara remembers getting calls on his mobile from Sparrow swearing that he was delayed on business in Cork or Kerry. 'Then he'd arrive after the first ten runs and tell you that you wouldn't believe the trouble he had getting here.' Halfway up the hill were bushes big enough to grant asylum to desperate sufferers. Daly remembers Sparrow ducking in for a quick break and jumping back in halfway through a run. 'Then,' says Daly, 'he'd turn around to the others at the top and tell them they'd want to get their act together.'

'There was craic there as well,' says O'Connor. 'Mike Mac had a great way with the players. We had great guys like Daly and Tuts [Fergie Tuohy] that would automatically have a comment to make. You might be lying down in the shit, bollixed, but you would be laughing.'

During that winter the hurling sessions were done at weekends, and that's when Loughnane took over. The reform of Clare hurling was a twin-track strategy: McNamara prepared their legs and their heads; Loughnane addressed their hurling – sternly, urgently. Every one of his drills was dedicated to speed and intensity. In his view Clare club hurling was too slow and this had undermined every Clare team in the championship. He didn't think that Gaynor or any of the other outside coaches Clare had used over the years fully appreciated the deficiencies in Clare players or how those deficiencies might be treated. They assumed that inter-county hurlers would have certain qualities and certain skills; Loughnane reckoned that for 'fourteen or fifteen' players on every Clare panel that assumption was unsafe.

There is no question that Loughnane's drills were heavily influenced by Justin McCarthy, the former Cork hurler and later Waterford manager who trained the good Clare team of the late 1970s. In an interview before the 1995 All-Ireland final Loughnane said that McCarthy was 'the best I ever saw', and after his last match as coach Loughnane gave him his Clare jersey in a gesture of appreciation. By the time Loughnane got round to writing his autobiography six years later, however, he had modified his view of McCarthy a little. 'For his time,' wrote Loughnane, 'McCarthy was a good coach.' Contemporaries of Loughnane on the Clare team of the 1970s who witnessed Clare sessions under Loughnane could instantly see McCarthy's influence. It was a greater compliment than words were allowed to say.

It wasn't just the drills, though, it was the manner in which they were performed. He drove them. All the pace came from him. 'After about ten minutes with Loughnane,' says O'Halloran, 'your legs were like jelly.'

'You would be in the middle of a line in a drill for two or three minutes,' says O'Connor, 'and you'd be fit to collapse coming out of it. Ger's hurling sessions would be every bit as tough as Mike Mac's sessions. We did other stuff as well. I remember Ger got us these heavy hurleys one time to strengthen our wrists. We were just swinging these really heavy hurleys literally until our hands were covered in blisters.'

Daly was a classy hurler and a good trainer. He was captain of the team and the only bridge between the players and the management. In his outlook and bearing and ambition he was everything Loughnane wanted. But in the hurling sessions Daly wasn't spared the acid of Loughnane's tongue. None of them was.

'He was powerful to drive fellas in training,' says Daly. 'He would really get the best out of you. He was exceptional, there was no doubt about it. The speed he put into the drills. The improvement he got in me. I was okay like, but I was slow, and he sharpened my whole game up. I mean the change he brought about in Liam Doyle. He was hardly good enough to be on the team in 1994. All right, he'd a great Munster final, but he was lucky to be on the team. It was a toss-up.

'But like he drove us demented in training. You'd be in the middle of a line doing a drill for a minute or ninety seconds and he'd keep roaring at you. "You're too fucking slow! That's why you were fucking destroyed! That's why they were laughing at you last year!" And you're there getting thick with yourself and you're getting thick with Loughnane and your first touch is getting better. He drove everyone like that. He'd be half-insulting you but in a kind of way that was right at the time.

'We had matches then that were a hundred miles an hour. He'd be roaring, "That's the stuff, give it to him, break it off his back." I'd be marking Jamesie [O'Connor] and I'd be tipping away at him, pulling him and kicking him – anything to stop him when he was in full flight. You could have a yard of his jersey and there's no way he'd blow for a free. And Jamesie would be breaking hurleys off me and I'm saying, "This isn't you, Jamesie, this is him. You're a nice fella, Jamesie, you're not supposed to be doing this." If he thought you were down then and you were sick he'd shout over, "You're being fucking cleaned!" Jesus Christ, you'd win a puck-out then or something and he'd lift you up again. He was a lunatic, but he had a way of doing it, there was no doubt about that.'

This was Loughnane's boot camp and crucible, where he built the players and formed the team. Inside the four walls of Cusack Park Loughnane created a parallel world where players were encouraged to behave in a way that would never be tolerated in normal society. Loughnane appreciated this, and by 1997 all of Clare's training sessions were behind closed doors.

'I never let anybody watch us train,' wrote Loughnane in his autobiography. 'If I had they'd be going home with stories about what I said to players. If you took what I said to players literally on the training field, not alone would all the players be offended but all their relatives would never speak to me either.'

The training matches were lawless. Loughnane blew the whistle to begin the game and then whipped them into a frenzy of aggression. Players, though, can't remember the games getting out of hand. They were forced to accept the conditions of combat and find a way to survive. Loughnane controlled the disorder so that it never threatened to become anarchy. He tested them, goaded them, challenged them not to crack. O'Connor remembers one night when Lohan was bursting out from full-back and Fergal Hegarty floored him. Loughnane fumbled for the whistle and penalized Lohan for over-carrying. 'Loughnane shouted over, "Good man, Hego,"' says O'Connor, 'and then you had Lohan going back into the square like an anti-Christ.' The referee's whistle was only useful as an instrument of provocation.

Loughnane spoke with relish about 'the poison' in Lohan

and his 'hatred' for every forward that came near him. It was a state of mind Loughnane was happy to foster. 'He felt that he needed a particular type of animal,' says O'Connor, 'and that's the type of guy he was looking for. He didn't believe in molly-coddling a guy and expect him to perform in the championship when the first thing that would happen is that somebody would plant a hurley in his ribs. He was looking for a particular type of character.

'I remember before the Munster final in '95 Seanie [McMahon] had a broken collar bone and on the Friday night before the match he more or less fucked Seanie out of it saying that there was fuck all wrong with him and he was only feeling sorry for himself. It wasn't a place for fancy dans. If you couldn't take the heat you just got out of the kitchen.'

Loughnane went in search of new blood, and the transfusion was massive. Of the twenty-seven players who had togged out for the 1993 Munster final against Tipperary only thirteen were on the panel for the Munster final of 1995. Six players – Frank Lohan, Michael O'Halloran, Fergal Hegarty, Stephen McNamara, Ollie Baker and Conor Clancy – were playing in their first Munster championship. He wanted players who were unstained by failure and he wanted players who could be shaped into winners. He found them.

With the exception of Frank Lohan, none of those players was an obvious candidate for promotion. Clancy had been a star on the minor team of 1989 and was introduced during Gaynor's first league twelve months later, but he was dropped from the panel before the 1991 championship and four years later he still hadn't made a championship appearance.

Others came from further back. When St Flannan's of Ennis won the Dr Harty Cup in 1991, Hegarty and Baker were numbers twenty-five and twenty-six on the panel. Old enough but not good enough. Baker went on to be a Clare minor and U-21, but his hurling was coarse and patently short of senior standard. He came on as a sub in the '95 semi-final against Cork and played so badly that he was shifted from centre-field to wing-forward to full-forward. If Clare hadn't already used all their subs Baker is certain that he would have been taken off. But an injury to Stephen Sheedy meant that he started the Munster final, and he was outstanding. He was precisely the kind of player Loughnane was looking for with his lack of inhibition, his nerve for the big day, his power, his lust for contact.

O'Halloran hadn't even been a Clare minor. During the five years he spent in Shannon Comprehensive he didn't make any of the school teams. When they reached the Dr Harty Cup final in 1989 he sat on the bench alongside his great friend Brian Lohan. Injury had cost Lohan his place on the team and he couldn't regain it; O'Halloran didn't have a place to lose. He was called on to the U-21 panel in 1992, but he didn't stay long. 'I dropped out. I got roasted by James [O'Connor] in training one night and I said, "I'm not of the required standard." They would have said "Hang in there," and all that but there was no point in being a sub as far as I could see. I probably would have been establishing myself as a senior club player with the Bridge [Sixmilebridge] at the time so I said I'll go back and if I'm good enough in a couple of years, I'm good enough.'

O'Halloran was intelligent and athletic, and he was aggress-ive. Clare didn't need him to clear the ball 60 yards from corner-back; all they needed was for him to tie down his man and stand up to the heat. The league final of 1995 against Kilkenny was his first real test. Like a good few others that day he failed to pass. After scoring three goals against Offaly in the semi-final D. J. Carey was held scoreless by Brian

Lohan, but the Clare corner-backs leaked 2–3 – exactly the margin of Kilkenny's victory. O'Halloran was marking Denis Byrne on the day he made his first big noise on the national stage. Clare had not just lost another big match, they had suffered another public failure. The hurling world didn't bat an eyelid.

'I felt that you could survive the league in winter conditions as a corner-back,' says O'Halloran, 'but then we went out on a summer's day in Thurles against Kilkenny and I got a bit of a roasting. You kind of went, "Right, this is what it's all about." You know, I was up in the terrace watching the Munster finals of '93 and '94 and you're an expert on the terrace. When you get down there it's a giant leap to make. After the match myself and Frank [Lohan, the other corner-back] were sitting together in the dressing room and we got up to leave around the same time, and Ger just called us back. "The two of you," he said. "Forget about it. That will never happen to ye again." '

In the Munster final two months later the full-back line coughed up only a single point.

Before the players dispersed from the dressing room Loughnane told them that they would win that Munster championship. Maybe they believed him; maybe they weren't even listening. In the days and weeks that followed Loughnane convinced them that they hadn't surrendered, their hurling just hadn't been quick enough. That difference was the key to everything.

For the next month all they did in training was ball work. By the time they met Cork in the Munster semi-final they had 150 sessions under their belt in nine months. They won by the skin of their teeth. In a hectic endgame Ollie Baker scrambled a sideline cut into the net at one end and Frank Lohan made a brilliant block at the other. Unlike '93 and '94 they had reached the Munster final under cover of mediocrity.

Only 14,101 people turned up to that Munster semi-final. The Cork crowd would have been dissuaded from travelling by a mixture of disdain for Clare and indifference to a Cork team clearly going nowhere. The match, though, was played in the Gaelic Grounds, only a couple of miles from the Clare border. Where was the Clare public? At home. Disbelieving.

But 1995 was different. Clare won, and in victory hindsight invests so many details with significance. O'Connor remembers a weekend in Killarney during the spring. It was the Sunday of the league quarter-finals and Clare had already qualified automatically for the semis. They trained and drank and sang. 'That was a super weekend in terms of bringing us together,' says O'Connor. 'I remember Ger singing "Waltzing Matilda" in the pub one of the nights and, no question about it, the hairs stood up on the back of your neck. You really felt that this was something special. There was just a great buzz about things. You could really feel that management were setting high standards and making demands from us.

'The quality of training was unbelievable, and the variety. Everything was structured, organized. You could have a hundred sliotars on the field at training – seventy or eighty minimum. You just felt, "This is professional." Everything was laid on. Early in the year we were measured for our suits. We had worn our suits to the league final against Kilkenny. There was certainly a sense of upping the stakes. This was a team that was going places.'

Before they went to Killarney that weekend the owner of the Rocks Bar in Ennis, Eamon Fitzpatrick, sent Tuohy a cheque for £250 to buy the players a drink. Tuohy passed it on to Daly and the captain found a better purpose for the money: he wagered it on Clare to win the Munster championship at 7/1.

Did they know they were going to win? How could they have known? All they knew was that things were different. Better. At half-time in the Munster semi-final against Cork James O'Connor told the others that Barry Egan had asked him to 'slow down'. They were happy to accept this as confirmation of their fitness edge over Cork, even though that match still went down to the wire.

Empirical proof wasn't what they sought in any case. They only needed to convince themselves.

'We'll say Len [Gaynor] was good in the dressing room before games, but if you haven't done it in training it's not worth a shit to you,' says Tuohy. 'You won't be able to call on something that's not there inside. That was the difference in '95. We did a few early-morning sessions. We'd do two sessions in a day. We'd have one with Mike Mac in the morning and one with Ger in the evening. Next thing you're in a Munster final saying, "What the fuck did we train twice a day for?" You can call on it. You can't say things like that if you haven't done it.'

It was obvious, too, that Loughnane had them under his spell. 'He was a great man for saying the way a game would go, even if it never went like that,' says Tuohy. 'I remember the weather was excellent that summer. Every day the ball was hopping. We were getting faster and faster, controlling the ball at speed. The next thing a downpour came at four o'clock on a night we were training and Ger came in. "Jesus, yes, I was hoping for rain. This is what we need, a greasy ball. Control it!" It made all sense and logic at the time. Next thing you'd come away from training thinking, "I can do it in the dry and I can do it in the wet."'

Daly doesn't doubt the difference that Loughnane made, but he wouldn't wish to overstate it either. 'Everyone says that Ger Loughnane came in and waved a magic wand. I don't agree with that. It was the same bunch of players in general that had lost two Munster finals, and by Jesus if you were any kind of a man you were going to stand up the third time. Loughnane was genius enough to have us primed once we scraped past Cork. "Are ye men or are ye going to run all yer lives?" kind of thing. He got rid of all the hype about the Munster final and tickets and all that. He banned all that. It was nothing but the match. You have to give him credit for doing that, but at the same time if we hadn't had the previous two Munster finals I don't believe that team would have come along and won a Munster final.

'Were the players he brought in better than the players that were there before? You can say in hindsight that they must have been better because they won two All-Irelands and three Munster championships, but at the time I would have said, "Ollie Baker can't even rise the ball." Baker would never have got a chance in '95 only for [Stephen] Sheedy bursting his knee. In a club match at that time Sheedy would run rings around Baker. We all knew that Frank [Lohan] was up and coming, but Michael O'Halloran? As it turned out he was a man, and maybe he picked fellas with a stronger character rather than better players on the club scene. He went for fellas that wouldn't lie down on the day. But I still believe that we wouldn't have won without the other two Munster finals, and I know that's the way Sparrow and Tuts [Fergie Tuohy] think as well.'

Unlike in '93 and '94, they managed the day and excluded the event. They planned their pre-match puck-around and meal for Cashel, on the opposite side of Thurles from all the match traffic. It was one of the hottest days of the summer but they believed they were built for heat, built for battle. Any battle. As they neared Semple Stadium on the team bus, a Limerick supporter shouted at them that they were wasting their time. Daly picked it up and ran with it. 'Are we wasting our time?' he said. Then another player said it aloud. Then another. Around the bus it went, like a mantra. 'Are we wasting our time?'

Daly had got tickets for a couple of old friends who were home from overseas and they arrived at the ground just as the team did. One of them hadn't seen Daly for three years and he wanted to go over and wish him luck. He took one look at their faces and backed off. 'He said it to me in the pub that night,' says Daly. '"Jesus Christ Almighty, ye were like fucking lunatics."'

Micheál Ó Muircheartaigh was waiting in the Clare dressing room to check for any late changes to the line-up. In his autobiography *From Dún Síon to Croke Park*, he painted the scene: 'Ger Loughnane was first in, walking with that jaunty stride of his. He came straight to me and in a most convincing voice spoke at me rather than to me with words I will never forget: "Don't say a word – just look at them. We cannot lose." I said nothing; I looked. A band of athletic-looking and focused young men, with chests forward and eyes straight ahead as if looking into the future, entered the dressing room and took up their places. There was something about their presence that I had not witnessed before.'

'There was a desperate focus on the match,' says Daly. 'That's what I will say. We were going out that door that day and we were going to hurl for seventy minutes. If we were beaten we were beaten, but at least we weren't going to come off the field saying we choked. If we were beaten by Limerick we just weren't good enough. There was going to be no more saying that we shitted ourselves again.'

By half-time they were a point up with the breeze to come in the second half. It was there for them. To Clare supporters of a certain generation it was like the 1978 Munster final all over again. Except that this team had no stomach for failure any more.

'I remember it was so positive in the dressing room at half-time,' says O'Connor. 'There was a real feeling that this is our day, end of story. The last words from Loughnane before we went back out were, "No surrender." Fellows were roaring. We were going to go out to blow them away.'

They blew them away.

Nothing had been planned for a homecoming. History didn't permit such a presumption. The team bus pulled up outside Clarecastle and Daly stepped off with four of his clubmates and the cup. They could see the light of a little bonfire but there was no sign of a crowd. They walked past the house where Johnny Callinan was reared, over the bridge and along behind the castle.

'There was hardly anybody there,' says Daly, 'and one of the lads says, "Will there be anyone out at all?" Kenny Morrissey said, "Don't be codding yourself. Wait till we turn this corner." We turned the corner and there was this crowd of people came against us. Thousands of people, and they just lifted us up. Victor O'Loughlin [Sparrow's brother] was under me and my cousin Gerry Murphy and Brian Hayes were under Sparrow. Leonard Mac was there and my brother Martin. Big GAA men. And we walked up the street, myself and Fergie holding the cup and the other three outside us. Jesus, it was the best feeling ever.'

There wasn't time to arrange a stage so they bundled Daly on to the roof of a bus shelter. One of the pubs filled the cup with Guinness and champagne and passed it up. For this banquet, only the finest wine. Daly looked down at the faces stretched out before him, a living tableau of euphoria. People he'd grown up with, people he'd played with, neighbours, friends. Then he picked out his mother. 'I said to myself, "There must be a good Sunday night here when my mother isn't gone to bingo in Ennis."

'The Munster final night was magic. All the times we went down that road and over the bridge to come back beaten, failed again. That night I was saying in my own mind, "Well, here it is for ye. Take a good look. We brought it back."'

The cup toured the county and the celebrations continued until training resumed on the following Friday night. A huge crowd turned up to watch and the session turned into a farce. The hurling was a confection of flicks and tricks, and after a short while Loughnane called a halt. He put the word out among the crowd that training was over and assembled the players in the dressing room.

'He fucked everyone out of it,' says O'Halloran. 'He started with Daly, saying that he was setting a bad example, and had a word for everyone. Stephen Mac[Namara] was sick the same night after a week of celebrating. He struggled in and he was sitting on the bench with his head down. Loughnane came over and caught him by the head. "You," he said. "Do you know what fucking sick is? Sick is coming out of Croke Park with your head between your legs." And he grabbed his head and pushed him nearly down into the ground.'

The party was over. Loughnane wasn't satisfied with a Munster championship and he wouldn't allow anybody else to be either.

There were complications, though. Clare had reached the Munster U-21 hurling final under Mike McNamara's management and the game was fixed for a Wednesday night in Thurles, a week and a half before the All-Ireland senior semi-final against Galway. Three of the senior team – Frank Lohan, Ollie Baker and Fergal Hegarty – were also on the U-21 team along with two subs on the senior panel, Stephen

O'Hara and Eamon Taaffe. Clare appealed to Tipperary and the Munster Council for the U-21 game to be postponed until after the senior semi-final but both requests were knocked back. McNamara sat down with Loughnane and Considine and they decided to play the match without the senior players.

What's more, they decided to turn their displeasure into a fireworks display. McNamara rang Clare FM and Tipp FM just before noon on the day before the match and announced that Clare wouldn't be appearing in the U-21 final. A day later he rang both stations again to withdraw the withdrawal. His stated plan was to mess with Tipp's preparation. Clare arrived ten minutes late for the throw-in, reportedly caught in traffic, and the Clare players were told not to swap jerseys with the Tipp players after the match. It was the first time that the Clare management consciously slighted the GAA authorities in public. It wouldn't be the last.

'Ger was totally blind towards winning an All-Ireland,' says Baker. 'That was it. Nothing was going to get in his way. You'd have to admire the man. He put his neck on the line. The way it was put to us was, "Well, lads, the U-21 match is on and there's an All-Ireland semi-final in Croke Park. Now make up yer minds." You had a choice – you always had a choice with him. It is a little regret for me given that we went up to Croke Park the night the game was on and hammered the shite out of each other in a training session. It was far more exerting than any match would have been. It was a big risk pulling the players out of that match. You don't turn your nose up at finals, but that's the chance he took.'

Clare lost that U-21 final by six points. A forgotten footnote now. Ten days later they beat Galway by five points in the senior semi-final. The juggernaut kept going. Straight ahead.

In an important sense Clare had already done the hardest thing. In their psyche, in their race memory, the Munster final had set a limit for everything – their ambition, their status, their dreams. After winning a Munster final everything was suddenly possible. That's what Loughnane saw, and that's what he made everyone grasp. Winning the Munster final was the giant, death-defying leap. Winning the All-Ireland simply couldn't be as daunting or as far-fetched.

'I hate people coming up to me saying, "Ye've done great,"' Loughnane said during the week of the All-Ireland final. 'I hate that. The satisfaction for me in hurling is measuring yourself against the best. It's not about people shouting down from a stand or clapping you on the back afterwards, or speeches or presentations. The thrill of sport is competing against the best. When I was playing I used to love marking the best that was on the other team. The better the player you were on the better it was. It's marvellous that we're playing Offaly because they're the best team around at the moment. There's a feeling out there that they could demolish us, but by Jesus I still think we can beat them.'

And so they did. The details are unimportant now. The misses, the lapses, the breaks are all devoured by the bottom line. For most of the second half and right down to the dying minutes Clare looked like losing, but they didn't. By sheer force of will they made it happen. They weren't the most gifted team in the country but they had become All-Ireland champions. To win, they had bucked every convention and cosy assumption. That such a thing could happen made everyone wonder what might happen next. The chains were off.

That summer Clare changed hurling. Deeply, profoundly, radically.

2. Purple Hearts

It was late on the Wednesday night before the 1996 Leinster final when the Wexford manager, Liam Griffin, surrendered wearily to the day and sat with a cup of tea in front of the television. His wife Mary had gone to bed and he was just flicking through the channels for company when he came across somebody he hadn't expected to meet: Alain Mimoun. The great French athlete was grey by then, in the mid-winter of his life, but the story he related to the interviewer was a timeless parable, a little bit about glory but mostly about struggle. Griffin had read about it for the first time as a young kitchen porter in a Zurich hotel thirty years before, but it hadn't struck him then in the same way that it did now.

Mimoun was a contemporary of the peerless Czech runner Emil Zatopek, who beat him time and again. At the 1948 Olympics and twice at the 1952 Games Mimoun had won silver to Zatopek's gold, and in two World Championship races the same pattern was repeated. Zatopek had won an astonishing three gold medals at the 1952 Games, the last of them in the marathon at his first attempt in the event. By the time the Melbourne Games came round in 1956 Mimoun decided that the marathon would be his battleground for one last tilt at Zatopek, even though he had never attempted a marathon before. On the day he was inspired. At halfway he kicked away from the leading pack, at 15 miles he was clear, and at the finish he was a minute and a half ahead of his closest pursuer.

Hearing the story again, Griffin embraced it like an old

friend. 'He started speaking about Zatopek and his reverence for the man and how he was the greatest man that ever lived and how he'd beaten him. He starts to rise up in the chair describing the last 100 metres of the marathon and saying, "I have beaten Zatopek," and the tears started flowing down his face at eighty years of age. Then all he could think about was celebrating with Zatopek. And Zatopek ran up to the line and he put his arms out to grab him and say, "You've beaten me at last." And they hugged and they danced around the place.

'And I thought, all of a sudden, this story was a divine inspiration. We can do this, you know, I said to myself. We are the Mimouns of hurling. Offaly have beaten us every time but this is the chance to get the ghost off our backs and be somebody. And if we don't we'll be forever in the shadows. So I told the players the story of Mimoun . . .'

Wexford's hurlers had been called many things; Mimoun was a new one. It was once said that like the Czech tennis player Ivan Lendl Wexford couldn't win on grass, but usually the cruelty was expressed in harsher terms: losers, chokers, wasters. Wexford had joined hurling's elite in the 1950s but that didn't necessarily mean much; once you had your peerage nobody was going to contest your seat in the House of Lords. The painful reality was that Wexford hadn't won a senior or minor All-Ireland since 1968, or even a senior Leinster championship since 1977.

Losing was a dead weight on the psyche of the team, manifesting itself year after year as accident or tragedy or farce. They lost so much, though, that almost by the law of averages defeat was obliged to ennoble them once in a while. During 1993, for example, Wexford were miraculously spared any shame in defeat. When they lost the league final to Cork it took three epic matches; when Kilkenny forced a draw against them in that year's Leinster final it took one of the greatest points ever scored in Croke Park to bring the sides level. It seems superfluous to say that Kilkenny won the replay.

However, a trace of haplessness was never far away. Before the drawn Leinster final against Kilkenny in 1993 they had planned to issue a dummy team to the press, years before Clare popularized the practice. The team that came out, though, was the line-up they intended to use on the day. They tried to fumble the genie back into the bottle but it only made the original clumsiness look worse.

When Griffin took charge in the autumn of 1994 the Wexford county board couldn't pretend that he was their first choice. He stood for election as manager of the minor team that October and was beaten in a vote. Others were approached to take the senior job, and though Griffin had his supporters on the committee only refusals by others brought them round to his door. In his youth he had hurled for Wexford and for Clare, and in business he was a hugely successful hotelier. But he had never faced a challenge such as this.

'We had a very good team in 1993 but it failed and it had collapsed,' he says. 'The team was in absolute free fall in 1994, but what I found most depressing was that the supporters were in absolute free fall as well. Like, everyone said to me that I was out of my mind to take the job. We'd gone beyond winning. There was a terrible inertia. When I met the players I was the most enthusiastic person in the room because I was fresh. I went to the players with this fiery enthusiasm and I'd love to tell you they were jumping up and down but they were probably saying, "Ah, Jaysus, the poor old creature." They'd gotten used to a system; they'd gotten used to being down. They were playing because they were just going through the motions. But these guys had been bludgeoned to death by their own people. They'd probably been bludgeoned to death by their own families for all I knew. These fellows had taken an awful hiding.

'Some of the things that the Wexford supporters said to some of the players during my first league, like, there were times I was going to jump the wire. I remember choking back the tears one day with someone saying something about Billy Byrne. I remember saying to Rory Kinsella [one of Griffin's selectors], "Jesus, I'll get that bastard," and Rory saying to me, "Don't lose your head for Christ's sake." Here we had a team that were the butt of ridicule by their own supporters, who the smart arse in the crowd is able to get a laugh at.'

Clouded by defeat, 1995 was a year like any other in the bad times. Meath, a team from the next tier down in hurling's stratified society, beat them in the league and Wexford followers spat at Griffin. More abuse came in the post. In his first meeting with the players the first word he wrote up on the flipchart was Honesty. It was what they would get from him and it was what he demanded of them. In return he received the kind of insidious dishonesty that had contributed to Wexford's oppression for years.

He gave the players a fitness schedule to follow over the winter, presuming that as inter-county players they would be self-motivated and faithful to his instructions. He presumed too much. Liam Dunne was in his eighth year on the panel and he knew the lie of the land better than the rookie manager. 'There was a programme there for us to go and do ourselves and to come back together with a certain level of fitness after Christmas. I'm sure lads didn't train at all, some of them. We came back in as typical Wexford lads. "We'll start now, it's time enough." I'd say he got a bit of a shock himself. He had to keep on at lads the whole time, which he did in '96.

'During 1995 you'd be thinking that Griffin was half-mad in ways. You'd be getting literature and stuff on mental preparation and all that. Three-quarters of the lads wouldn't be reading it. They didn't really understand it. I wouldn't think he had the respect of the whole dressing room in '95 because lads were doing their own thing. Our preparation just wasn't good enough and our mentality wasn't right. We were so close but at the same time when the pressure came on we didn't know what it was like to win. The players learned a lot that year, but Liam Griffin learned a lot as well. It was his first year with Rory Kinsella and Seamus Barron [another selector] and they were all different men the following year.'

Days before Wexford's Leinster semi-final against Offaly in 1995 a storm broke over the team. Club league matches were fixed for that week on the understanding that county players wouldn't play. Liam Dunne's club, Oulart-the-Ballagh, had won the senior championship for the first time in 1994 and a week after the Offaly match they were due to play against St Martin's, the team they had narrowly beaten in the previous year's county final. As far as Oulart were concerned it had been seven weeks since they had had a complete panel together for a match, and if the club league game was going ahead they were going to field their strongest team.

As county champions Oulart were allowed to nominate the Wexford captain for the first time that year, and Dunne was their choice. He made no secret of his intention to play the club match; his brother, Tomas, was also on the Wexford team and he played too; so did Paul Finn. Martin Storey was carrying a knock and saved himself. Dunne went home from the game and mended hurleys for four of the club's U-14 players heading off to Feile Na Gael that weekend. He didn't leave the shed until twenty past one in the morning and the thought crossed his mind that he'd be crucified if the selectors knew he was up so late. They never got to hear about that; only the club match.

At the time the whole affair seemed just like another Wexford cock-up, but in hindsight it was a watershed in the life of this team. Griffin could have copped out and just issued a rebuke for the sake of peace, but he knew he had to confront this situation and make a hard call. He needed to be seen to be strong. At training on Wednesday night he told Dunne that he was going to take action. He said he didn't know what yet but he couldn't let it pass. A day later Dunne was stripped of the captaincy.

Their personal relationship was a complication on one level and a fire blanket on another. Even before Griffin became Wexford manager the two had been friends. When Dunne wanted a career change he turned to Griffin for advice, 'and he spent a lot of time trying to help me out. I just said, "Whatever action you take I'll back you 100 per cent." I always did. I never said a word. Everyone was giving out about it and going mad about it. I just kept my mouth shut. I owed the man too much to blow my own trumpet. I was glad afterwards that I did, and I like to think that I came back and repaid him in '96.'

Once the story was released it combusted into a blaze. Callers to phone-in shows on local radio bristled with outrage, and Oulart were furious. The club met on Wednesday night and again on Thursday night. On Friday night they had a three-hour meeting with the Wexford county board management committee, and on Saturday their chairwoman delivered a statement on local radio, unchallenged and without any response from the team management. They argued that if the captaincy had to be taken from Dunne it should have been transferred to Storey – not that they agreed with it being taken from Dunne in the first place. But just transferring the captaincy would have defeated Griffin's purpose. He wanted to punish the club too.

'It just shows you how bad people felt Wexford were going,' says Griffin, 'that a club would chance putting fellows out in a league match on the Tuesday night before Wexford played their championship match. When I heard they were playing I was really upset. I was actually in bits about all of this. I was almost child-like, on the point of sobbing. I'm doing my best, I'm trying hard, and Oulart are doing this to me? Why are they doing this to me? At least give us a chance to get up off the ground. I said to myself, "Walk away. What do I need this for?"'

'There were people writing me letters wishing there was a death in my family and that my father was an illegitimate man from Clare. I got stuff you wouldn't believe from people over that incident. People saying that I was a disgrace and who was I? Look at what Liam Dunne had done for Wexford – who did I think I was? People said I was just a big businessman on a power trip. I got all sorts of abuse from people and I knew the pain of that. The pain of that was savage. My family and my youngsters had to listen to a lot of abuse from people as well, or purposely let overhear abuse in that typical sly GAA fashion.'

While the storm rumbled in the media Griffin went to ground. Brian Carthy of RTE Radio finally smoked him out and convinced him to give his side of the story. Carthy said he would record the interview, play it back to him, come back in an hour and play it for him again before seeking his clearance to broadcast it. Griffin agreed. 'I was trying to hide.

We've a few horses in a stable at home and that's where I was hiding. I was afraid to meet somebody and I was afraid somebody would come down the road. Anyway, Brian persuaded me to do it and he played me back the interview. I said, "It sounds reasonable," and I was happy to let it go. From that moment on I probably changed my whole attitude to management. I had done something honest. I said it straight [in the interview]. What I said to Brian I said to everybody afterwards and I suddenly felt, "No, I'm right to do this." '

Wexford played poorly against Offaly and lost by seven points. The margin of the loss couldn't convey how far they had been from winning. 'In those days,' says Dunne, 'it was only a matter of Offaly turning up and they beat us. Our performance that day was absolutely dire.' When the dust settled Griffin was summoned to an emergency county board meeting to explain the defeat and everything that had surrounded it. He knew he was walking into a sniper's alley. 'This meeting was called to get rid of us,' says Griffin. 'I don't think it was unreasonable in view of what happened. Liam Dunne got the sack, Offaly beat us, so they were entitled to ask, "What's going on here?" At least they were open and above board. The worry was that you'd get shafted before you got a chance to move on your plans, but in fairness to Paddy Wickham, the chairman, he stood by me at the time.'

Griffin survived. The dawn was coming.

Griffin was very conscious of his father's roots in Clare, and in his early twenties he lived there for a while. He lined out for Newmarket-on-Fergus, won a couple of Clare championships and made it on to the Clare U-21 team. His father was there to see it, and when Griffin reflects on his playing career he ranks it amongst the proudest days. Three weeks after Wexford were dispatched from the 1995 championship

Griffin was in Thurles to see Clare win their first Munster championship in sixty-three years. All of the taunts and sneers that applied to Wexford hurling applied to Clare too, though their suffering had been even longer and more tortuous. On this glorious day in Thurles, though, the age-old losers had won.

'Clare came and I thought, "This is fantastic." I thought, "Jesus, the team I have are as good as these," and I went through them man for man. There's no way we're not as good as they are. Then Clare won the All-Ireland and I went straight to Clare the following morning because I wanted to see the homecoming, and now I understand why: I wanted to drive it into my own psyche.

'I went to Newmarket and they wanted me to go up on the platform. Every Newmarket player that ever played for Clare was put up on the platform. I sat in the back and the Clare team came and they stood up and all the speeches were made, and when it was all over Loughnane turned to me and said, "It could be you next year." I got into the car coming home and I said, "We can do this. We can do it."'

Wexford training was called for that week, twelve months before the next All-Ireland final. For the coming year Griffin was taking no chances. He wasn't going to give the players a personal fitness programme and trust in their good faith. He was going to stand over them and make them do it. Everything had to be different.

'I didn't feel that any of them were really on board with me in '95. I didn't feel that they wanted to know me; I always felt they kept their distance from me. Nobody wanted to be seen to be too close to me, which was a very difficult thing in the first year. They didn't want to be seen to be mammy's boys. But the minute I came back in September '95, the minute I walked in, I felt they were all on board. It was the strangest thing. When I walked in I felt they were glad to see me and I felt these fellows were going to go with me.'

'Griffin was a different man altogether in '96,' says Dunne. 'It was either his way or no way. He was ruthless.'

It was known that Clare had leaned heavily on a savage physical fitness regimen in their breakthrough year. Ever since Dublin and Kerry in the 1970s Gaelic football had an established relationship with hard physical training, but a hurling team had never explored that route before. Griffin could see the value of that approach but he wanted the hardship to be underwritten by sports science, something that had always fascinated him. He acquired academic journals from universities around the world and consumed the texts from cover to cover. He studied the training schedule of the British hockey team, world champions at the time, and consulted the dietician for the British Olympic team. Then he chose somebody to bring the plan to life: Sean Collier, a kickboxer from Wexford.

Oulart-the-Ballagh won the Wexford championship again in 1995, and during their Leinster club campaign that autumn their players were excused from county training. When they rejoined the panel in January 1996 the others already had four months of hard slog deposited in their system. 'We went in after Christmas,' says Dunne, 'and it was the greatest shock I ever got in my life when I went into the gym to see what was going on in there. To see lads like Adrian Fenlon and others – they were different men to the men I'd seen before. They'd been pumping iron since September. Fenlon was nicknamed the Iron Man. We were sore for six weeks trying to catch up. I used to be complaining to my mother, and Martin Storey was the same. It was violent. We couldn't catch up, really. But just to see what was going on in there – Griffin pushing lads on. It was serious stuff. We didn't understand that really because we'd never been involved in anything like that.'

When the running started the Wexford management chose their locations carefully. One was a hilly, disused golf course in Bunclody where a route was staked out to take the players over the worst of the undulations. A lap of the circuit would take over ten minutes, and they learned to expect four laps at least. There is one night, though, that has been branded into the memory of all those Wexford players. One of the hotels Griffin owned was in Rosslare and from the harbour up to the hotel was a climb of 101 steps. For one hellish evening that was their circuit. 'Four of us got up the steps seven times,' says Dunne. 'Dave Guiney, Tommy Kehoe, Larry O'Gorman and myself. Some lads got up six times, more lads got up five. They'd lads planted in different places to drive you on. I was practically crying when I got up to the top of the steps on the last run. For the last fifteen or twenty steps there was nothing left. I could hardly breathe when I got up there. Lads were coming over to give you a drink and you were just pushing them away.'

The physical hardship, though, wasn't an end in itself, it was just part of Griffin's holistic treatment. And as with Clare, it wasn't just for their bodies; it was for their mentality too. Griffin knew that he had to invade their minds and colonize that territory. There had been regular team meetings during Griffin's first season in charge but in his second season those meetings were one of the group's biorhythms. They trained, they showered, they talked. In that meeting room the players were on Griffin's turf.

He had to win them over, and they didn't come quietly. Martin Storey led the dissent. When Oulart retained the county championship he was nominated as Wexford captain for 1996, but even without that status he was one of the strongest personalities in the dressing room and one of the best players on the team. He was sceptical about Griffin, and in team meetings he plainly stated that position.

'The thing about Griffin and Storey,' says Dunne, 'is that them boys didn't get on very well in '95. Griffin didn't really like Storey's attitude and Storey didn't really like Griffin's. Storey had his own way. And then the two of them ended up like glue from '96 onwards. Griffin turned a corner for Storey. I don't know whether he'd like me saying that or not, but he definitely did. Whatever bit of talking Griffin was doing to me he was doing ten times more to Storey.'

A lot of the tough talking took place in front of the others. Griffin knew that if he won the battle for Storey's mind, he could control the room. 'It was important,' says Griffin, 'to get inside everyone's head. Looking back, it was like the Good Friday Agreement: until I was inside everybody's head nobody was coming on board with me. George O'Connor and John O'[Connor] would be cousins of mine but they would be sitting there silently at meetings looking at me. They wouldn't have helped me to get people's respect. It wasn't up to them to go around doing politics for me.

'Storey was pushing me, and that was good in a way because if you didn't get over Storey you weren't going to get over the rest of them. He was making things a bit difficult because he could challenge any fecking thing. At the end of the day my tactics were dirty. I'd say, "Well, if you're so good, show us the money. Okay, maybe I'm wrong, but hey, what have you ever done? Why don't you try it my way because you tried it your way and it didn't work." Now that was nasty, and I didn't like doing it, but I had to do it a few times in the end.

'The other thing was they will never know the depth of thought I put into every single meeting. At the start I thought out the answer to every thing they might say to me. I wound up with a little system that I found worked for me with fellows who had not done as much in-depth thinking as I had done. I would have had lots of discussions with Rory [Kinsella]. I'd do Rory's head in because I'd ring him up and say, "Listen, I was thinking of this and thinking of that," and I was working like a savage at this thing so you get the credibility by degrees.'

Griffin was smart enough to know the value of consultation. For advice and second opinions he canvassed widely: Eugene McKenna, the Tyrone football coach; Mike McNamara, the Clare fitness trainer; Liam Hennessy, an athletics coach who would later co-ordinate the IRFU's fitness programmes after rugby turned professional. And then he decided to make a leap. He realized that he had taken sports psychology as far as he could with the group. They needed an expert.

Within the GAA Griffin knew that the formal application of sports psychology had image problems, all of them founded on ignorance. Three years earlier Derry had won their first All-Ireland football title making no secret of their sports psychologist, Craig Mahony, but such openness was exceptional. Both teams in the 1995 All-Ireland football final, Dublin and Tyrone, had used a sports psychologist – Tom Moriarty and John Kremer respectively – but the counties would have been surprised if you knew and you wouldn't have heard it from them.

Griffin was aware of the people other counties had covertly employed but he wanted somebody fresh. Hennessy suggested Niamh Fitzpatrick, a sports psychologist in her mid-twenties whom Hennessy knew from her work with the Olympic Council of Ireland. Fitzpatrick had no background in Gaelic games but that didn't bother Griffin. He rang her and they chatted, and after a while Fitzpatrick realized she was being interviewed for the position, without any declaration from Griffin that the conversation had crossed that line. For Griffin's purpose she was perfect.

'To this day,' says Fitzpatrick, 'Liam says to me that he said to himself he knew the athletes would be serious if, one, they went for having a psychologist, and two, if they went for a female. Because, he said, the idea was in some ways so ludicrous. As far as he was concerned if they would accept a girl coming in to try to help them get their heads ready to perform he knew they were deadly serious.'

For the enterprise to work the players needed to accept her. Griffin took care of that. Ultimately the players were made to believe that it was their call; the reality was more complex and cunning. 'Griffin dealt with it the way you'd deal with a young horse terrified by a white bag on the road,' says Fitzpatrick. 'You wouldn't push the horse, you'd gently cajole and find a way for the horse to believe that it was his idea to go past.'

The players were worried about the news reaching the papers and exposing them to more ridicule. This was only March 1996 and in the public perception nothing about Wexford had changed: they were still losers, going nowhere. Everyone agreed to secrecy. Later in the year, on match days in Croke Park, Fitzpatrick was identified to the relevant authorities as a physio. One night, when members of the media turned up at training, Griffin told her to go over and rub one of Larry Murphy's legs. Fitzpatrick was still living with her parents and she told only them in strict confidence, just so that they wouldn't worry about her long nights in Wexford or wonder about the phone calls from Griffin at midnight, and later.

'The players were working around the county,' says

Fitzpatrick, 'and they were meeting people in the jobs they did. From that point of view it was a case of "don't add something else into the equation". You don't want people saying to them, "Ye're a bunch of nancy boys – ye need to have some bird looking after yer heads," that sort of thing. And we also felt it was nobody's business. The only thing it might do is put further pressure on the athletes.

'With the players I had to break it down. The first night I met them I went through what I would do. There wouldn't be any chanting or tree hugging or talking to their inner child. It would be practical exercises that would train their minds in the way that Sean Collier would do practical exercises to train their bodies. I told them that just as you must have physical skills such as speed and endurance and hurling ability, you must also have mental skills: the ability to concentrate, the ability to be confident, the ability to handle nerves.'

Her commitment was enormous. To get to know the players she met them all individually for half an hour in the Ferrycarrig, a hotel Griffin owns outside Wexford town. She started at seven o'clock one Friday night and finished four hours later, and the meetings continued all day Saturday and all day Sunday. Every three weeks that process was repeated. 'You had to go,' says Dunne. 'Everyone went. Even macho fellas that felt they wouldn't need to do it, they went. Lads knew it was helping them. It helped them off the field as well as on it. I'd say she was hearing about more problems now than just winning matches.'

Such openness was the pay-out from Griffin's gamble. 'She came in like an apparition,' he says. 'She was such a bubbly person – a warm, caring, loving woman. One of the people on this earth that I'd trust more than anybody alive. You know, with the players, there was obviously a man–woman thing sometimes, a sexual chemistry I suppose, but it never came to anything like that. I feel that fellas are babies deep down and they need a shoulder to cry on. They're not going to cry on each other's shoulders and I always felt if I'd a woman there and if a fella felt afraid or if he had a problem he could actually say it to her. And I think they did.'

The life of the group was taking shape. Structure first, then order. A simple vocabulary signposted their shared path. In training and during matches they relied on key words that were designed to cue certain thoughts – Drive, Hassle, Next Ball. Whatever the specific game plan these words framed the team's fundamental outlook, so that in any given situation the players should never be lost for a positive thought. Griffin's favourite was Calm Controlled Aggression, which he repeated over and over again, but he gave the players plenty of other lines to suck on. Fitzpatrick remembers one above the others: Do what you've always done and you'll get what you've always got. For Wexford this was the essence of 1996: leaving behind the things they had always done.

To make themselves winners they had to be aware of the things that had made them losers and to learn to control those things. Griffin banned the players from speaking about the past in media interviews, believing that reflecting on old defeats only served to keep those defeats alive. And they had to learn to control their minds outside team meetings and beyond the direct influence of Griffin and Fitzpatrick. For match days and the build-up to games they worked on a colour code, each colour meant to stimulate a certain response. 'When you're at home and you're chilling out,' says Fitzpatrick, 'you're on red. You have nothing to do with your game. When you're training, or going to training or going to a match, you're on amber. You're getting ready to perform, bringing the brain up a gear. When you're on green, that's go.'

Griffin knew that his trust in the players had a much better foundation in 1996 than it had in his first year, but he still wasn't inclined towards blind trust. 'A big thing,' says Dunne, 'was your activities off the field. There was a total drink ban from a certain stage before the championship. Lads weren't drinking a lot anyway, because training was so hard, but he'd know if you were. He had owls everywhere. He'd hear things back, plus he was a cute fucker. He'd be talking to a lot of the players, including myself, and he was getting information the whole time. We'd be squealing on each other without really knowing.'

Griffin made them take responsibility for their behaviour off the field and he made them take responsibility for their actions on the field. He enlisted a statistics man called John O'Leary, who dissected the video of every Wexford match and processed the information. These stats had been available to the players in 1995 but they were ambivalent about it then and Griffin hadn't done enough to challenge that ambivalence. In 1996 the post-match stats were prescribed reading. At nine o'clock on a Monday morning the fruits of O'Leary's labour would be delivered to Griffin's office and he'd make out an individual report for every player: how they used the ball, how they misused the ball; scores, wides, frees won and frees conceded. It didn't matter how the players felt they had played, these statistics had the final say.

The thing was that Wexford were not known for playing smart, or having a game plan, or sticking to a game plan if they happened to have one. Since their breakthrough in the 1950s they had been comfortable with a simple pattern of playing the ball high into a big full-forward and feeding off him. In the modern game such an approach was outdated. Griffin had to teach them the sanctity of the game plan. Not all of them learned quickly.

Larry O'Gorman ended 1996 with two of the three Hurler of the Year awards on offer, but he was one of the players Griffin needed to reform. Because he was so talented and because his talent was so misdirected he was a vivid metaphor for Wexford's flaws. On big days in Croke Park he would take a spectacular catch over his head and launch the ball back into the skies to the acclaim of the crowd. You never knew if he was just suddenly overcome with adrenalin or consciously playing to the galleries. Either way, such behaviour had no place in Griffin's game plan. In a league match against Meath he was taken off at half-time for 'messing with the ball', and for the league quarter-final against Offaly he was dropped. For O'Gorman, nothing exceeded the terror of not being on the team. It was the most brutal and direct route to his senses. He learned.

Tom Dempsey was another gifted player who needed to be tackled. Dempsey remembers the league semi-final against Galway in 1996. Wexford were well beaten; Dempsey had played poorly and was substituted. In his eyes it was his first bad game of the year. No matter. As he left the Gaelic Grounds after the match he passed a group of supporters, and from among them an old man lunged at him with his walking stick in a gesture of condemnation. 'Tom Dempsey,' Griffin said once, 'is blamed in this county for everything from hurling to bad spuds.'

The only thing Griffin blamed him for was not sticking to the game plan, but in his court that was a capital offence. 'I'd say there was always a tetchiness with Tom and me,' says Griffin. 'I'd great time for Tom and I think Tom would tell you that he had good time for me, but Tom was always wary of me and that was our relationship. Tom was very single-minded, very Tom-orientated – which is a good thing – but Tom is a sensitive soul and he'd feel that you're getting at him sometimes. Tom was inclined to have pot-shots, and I was trying to make the point that if you send a stupid wide the puck-out was like an 80-yards free to the other side. I took him off against Galway in the league semi-final. The last ball he got he tried for a point from the sideline by the corner flag. I wanted to explain to him that some day in Croke Park a ball like that will be golden – we can't afford to waste them.'

Dempsey was dropped for the first round of the championship against Kilkenny. He rang Griffin looking for an explanation. As Dempsey remembers it, an hour into the phone call he despaired of getting a word in and cut his losses. The bottom line was that he was dropped for offences against the game plan.

Dempsey finished the year as Wexford's top scorer.

In the laboratory of team meetings and the training field, the Wexford management were systematically tearing down one mindset and building up another. But it had to work beyond the lab, and initial field tests were encouraging. In reaching the play-off stages of the league their only defeat was to Limerick in Kilmallock. They beat Offaly in Birr in the semi-final of the Walsh Cup and beat them again in the league quarter-final. Offaly's hurt at those defeats wouldn't have been as great as Wexford's gratification, but Wexford couldn't even consider the mountains until they had scaled the foot-hills. For this Wexford team, beating Offaly in any arena counted for something. It added something to all of them.

They lost by eight points to Galway in the semi-final of the league, and to outsiders it appeared to be a bad beating. On the inside Griffin had to manage its appearance firmly. The first person he convinced was himself. He reasoned that they hadn't played their championship team: Damien Fitzhenry, the goalkeeper, was playing wing-back; Ger

Cushe, the full-back, was at number six; and Liam Dunne, John O'Connor and Rory McCarthy would all be in different positions for the championship. After a good first half they had abandoned the game plan, but the game plan had looked good in full flight. Griffin sucked up all the positives and drove on.

A couple of weeks later they hammered Cork in a tournament game and beat Kilkenny in the final of the same tournament. Both teams fielded nine of the players that would line out in the championship, but Griffin invested the game with a greater significance than its face value. Early in the second half he took off Seanie Flood and Larry Murphy, their two best players on the night. 'It was a big gamble but it started a feel-good factor,' says Griffin. 'It was a kind of arrogance, but it sent out a message [to Kilkenny] that we weren't afraid.'

There were only 18,000 people in Croke Park for the championship match against Kilkenny. The assumption that Kilkenny would win discouraged the Wexford sceptics from travelling and the apparent absence of suspense about the outcome deterred the neutrals. In coded language Griffin could suggest to Kilkenny that his team were now fearless, and in team meetings the players could tell themselves that this was now true. But it wasn't the whole truth. In Croke Park that day Wexford had to beat Kilkenny and conquer their doubts. Both contests were a close call.

'Kilkenny were terrible that year,' says Dunne. 'DJ [Carey] and John Power were both carrying knocks [DJ was taken off, Power came on as a sub]. We were the whole time hearing about 1993, when we should have beaten Kilkenny the first day. That was coming at us the whole time. Then DJ in 1991 [when his late goal beat Wexford]. You were sort of believing something like that would happen again. Griffin had us believing that we would beat Kilkenny, but still, at the back of lads' minds, we weren't 100 per cent convinced that we would beat Kilkenny. We were going up with a certain amount of hope.

'We got them on a real bad day and yet we only beat them by three points. Struggled as well. But it was just the fact of beating them.'

That was the thing. They hadn't beaten Kilkenny in the championship for eight years, and in that time defeats to Kilkenny had played hell with their peace of mind. Fitzpatrick will never forget the elation. 'I can still see the faces back in the dressing room. I remember Liam [Griffin] coming over to me and saying, "I just want to say, thank you." It was as if Liam knew they'd crossed the biggest hurdle. He knew if these guys could believe they could beat Kilkenny it was like going up Everest. If they could believe that then anything else was within their capability.'

They beat Dublin by six points in the Leinster semi-final but they played poorly. In one sense it was immaterial. No matter how well Wexford had played Offaly were going to be overwhelming favourites for the Leinster final. Offaly had been in the previous two All-Ireland finals and were accepted as one of the two or three best teams in the country. Wexford hadn't beaten Offaly in the championship since 1979; six defeats spread over the following seventeen summers expressed the difficulty of Wexford's relationship with Offaly. What's more, Wexford had lost eight Leinster finals since they'd last held the title in 1977. The Wexford players thought that the Kilkenny game was their Everest, but when they returned to base camp they realized that the peak was somewhere in the clouds.

Griffin was worried that his players would freeze and he agreed with Fitzpatrick that on Leinster final week they would blitz the minds of the players like never before. At their

Wednesday-night meeting before the match they decided to ask the players why they were going to beat Offaly. Every player was asked to give one reason why Wexford would win. They had never attempted such a direct approach with the players before and they had no idea if it would work.

The room was suddenly gripped in a chilling and paralysing silence. Not a word. Not even the suggestion that words could survive in this climate. Griffin and the other members of the management team were sitting together and Fitzpatrick prayed that none of them would crack and say something. She caught Griffin's eye and sensed that he grasped the importance of biting his tongue. Silence flooded the room and hardened into ice. 'And I thought,' says Fitzpatrick, '"Oh Jaysus, I've blown it. They're going to be deflated now."'

Fitzpatrick reckoned it was five minutes before the silence was pierced. It felt like eternity. But then one word led to another, and before the session ended every member of the panel had made a contribution. Recorded on a flipchart at the top of the room were thirty reasons why Wexford would beat Offaly. Neutrals far beyond the room were still struggling to think of one.

'If you were to paint that room a colour,' says Fitzpatrick, 'it started off insipid green. It was kind of, "Aw, I don't know – I'm feeling a bit sick." And it turned into a vivid, vibrant red to the point where Liam Dunne went home and said to his mother, "We decided today that we're going to beat Offaly." That wouldn't have worked by the Kilkenny match. It reached a point where these guys knew you have to have your fitness level right, you have to have your diet right, you have to be a skilled hurler, but more than that you have to have control over your mind and emotions rather than have them control you. It took them that long to realize that we can control it, we can decide it. We had no control over the result – of course you don't. But you have control over how much you're prepared to fight to get the result you want. To do that you have to face your fears and push aside your insecurities. You have to take complete control over the focus of your attention. That had to come out that night. Anything less than that wasn't going to beat Offaly. If they come at us we can go at them harder. It's like a game of chicken.'

Griffin, though, wasn't prepared to leave it at that. His restless mind never stopped probing, reaching. While driving from Wexford to Dublin at five o'clock one morning, ten days before the Leinster final, Fitzpatrick noticed the sign welcoming the traveller into Wicklow. She had passed that sign many times that spring and summer but this time it triggered a little flight of fancy. She allowed herself to imagine for a minute what it would be like to pass that sign back into Wexford with the Leinster trophy on the team bus. With no purpose in mind she mentioned it in passing to Griffin, and his subconscious went into overdrive. Probing. Reaching.

While watching the television news on Friday night, a few days before the match, inspiration found him. The Fianna Fáil TD Brian Cowen was standing in a pub in his native Offaly singing 'The Offaly Rover', the county's anthem. Punters were asked for their view on the match, and with the usual hammed-up bravado the opposition were dismissed. Griffin could feel his blood simmering to the boil. 'I suddenly thought about what a great county Wexford was and – what the hell – we were brilliant before Offaly ever were, and here was Brian Cowen in the pub singing songs and I suddenly started thinking about what Wexford meant to all of us. Then I started thinking about George O'Connor's father [Griffin's uncle] who was dead and my own father who was dead, and I started thinking about the great Wexford teams that were gone and the way of life I'd grown up with, and that hurling was synonymous with the people I felt we were. I said to myself, "I'm going to write this."

'I got up the next morning early and I wrote what I wanted to say because I didn't want to have wasted words. I said to myself, "We need something monumental, something that's going to be mind-blowing, something to raise the whole thing on to a different plane. Something that's going to make them really believe that this is so important. A level where it's much bigger than the match. It's not just a game, it's about our life, it's about who we are." I felt, we've got to transcend sport. This thing, "Ah it's only a match" – that's only for county finals. This was about freedom. This was about striking out from this terrible place where we'd been for so long. So I wrote that speech.'

His plan was to stop the bus just before the sign welcoming them to Wicklow, evacuate the players on to the side of the road, deliver this speech about history and place and identity, and walk them over the county bounds. Fitzpatrick was the only one who knew that Griffin had cooked up something, but he hadn't even given her a spoonful to taste. Nobody else knew.

'I didn't tell Rory and Seamus because I was afraid they'd stop me. It was a bit of madness and I thought they might talk me out of it, because anything we did we would always discuss it. At home I thought about the consequences if this went wrong, and I said to myself, "Listen, what does it matter now? It's all or nothing." In a way I was putting it all on the line. If it went wrong I'd be ridiculed for ever. But I was going to take that chance. I read a book by Susan Jeffers called *Feel the Fear and Do It Anyway*, and I'd been preaching "feel the fear and do it anyway" to the players. What I was trying to say was, "To hell with being afraid any more. Fear is not an option. Let's throw off all our chains and let it happen."'

Supporters' cars flew by, blowing their horns, assuming that the bus had broken down. Griffin stuck to the plan. He delivered his speech and finished it thus: 'Today we are playing for a way of life. Breathe in now, long and hard, and as you walk, think of yourself since childhood. All of the matches you played. All of your friends, both alive and gone. And make this promise to yourself: today is the day we will be proud again. And remember, "We are the Boys of Wexford, Who fought with heart and hand." That's real tradition. Let's go.'

He walked the players over the county bounds and the bus drove up to meet them. 'I knew I got through to them. As we got back on to the bus there was hardly a word out of anybody.'

The match was something else. If you were to rank the best matches of the 1990s it would appear at or near the top of the list. Offaly picked up a hand of picture cards and opened the betting with a stack of chips; Wexford saw them and raised them. The outcome was a classic.

Wexford had a plan to beat Offaly, and they played the way they had planned. For the new Wexford, that was the greatest leap. They played with clear heads, fluency and economy, precisely the things on which Offaly and Kilkenny had sustained their rule over Wexford. Key Offaly players were targeted. The Offaly corner-back Martin Hanamy wasn't allowed to dominate his patch; he was drawn out into the field, an unwitting pawn in Wexford's puck-out strategy. Brian Whelahan at right half-back was the best source of ball to the Offaly forwards, and John Troy at centre-forward was the pulse of the attack. They were handcuffed and gagged.

'Larry Murphy had a job to do,' says Dunne, 'and that was not to let Brian Whelahan come forward. He was to drive him back – and he drove him back. Whelahan came out with

the first ball and he got hit. Then he went to turn and hit it
and there were two Wexford lads on him. He ended up
running about 20 yards back to his own goal and he was
blocked down. The precedent was set then, seeing that happen. I was told to take care of Troy. The plan for him was
for me to just stay with him. One man, one job. Over the
years he was the playmaker. I could nearly hear his heart
beating that day I was that close to him.'

Wexford led by a point at half-time, 1–10 to 1–9. They
pulled further clear in the third quarter, and a Dempsey goal
made it 2–16 to 1–13. But Offaly's reply was instant. The
real test had arrived. 'They came straight back up the field
and got a goal,' Dunne recalls. 'But Griffin had said to us,
"We'll score a goal in the Leinster final and Offaly will come
back up the field and score a goal within two minutes." He
said that to us. We said to ourselves, "Well, that's not going
to happen." But it did. They had a goal within a minute. Not
two minutes – less than one minute. And I remember Cushe
was on the ground and I just gave him a tap on the arse, and
thinking about it afterwards, there was just no panic. We
were just going to go back down the field again. It wasn't
typical Wexford, but it was the preparation we had done.
Their goal didn't make any difference to us.'

In the time that remained Wexford outscored Offaly 0–7
to 0–2 and by the final whistle they were eight points clear,
2–23 to 2–15. To win was an affirmation of everything they
had come to believe about themselves; to win with style was
a rejection of everything the hurling world had come to
believe about them.

The Mimouns of hurling had breasted the tape.

Euphoria took many different forms, but outside Wexford
George O'Connor was its brightest face and biggest smile.

In the days when people paid little attention to losing Wexford teams, he was the name they were most likely to know. Every year he came back, carrying the flame and helplessly burned by it. For O'Connor, beating Offaly was a glorious vindication of blind faith and endless hope.

At thirty-six years of age he had seventeen seasons in a Wexford senior jersey behind him. Six Leinster final defeats, five league final losses. In his pomp, high catching was his signature. Under dropping balls his left hand went up like a clay pigeon and the assassins pulled so that by 1996 his hands were crippled with arthritis. To hold the hurley he needed to coerce his hands into a grip and clench his teeth for five minutes while their protests subsided. Sitting in the dressing room afterwards, the others could see the pain on his face as the feeling surged back into his fingers.

At a tournament match at the end of 1995 Griffin had asked him for one more year. 'I was dead straight with him,' says Griffin. 'I said, "I couldn't say that I'll be using you all of the time." "Griff," he said to me, "I'll wear number five, number fifteen or number twenty-five. I'll carry the water bottle if you want." I went across the other side of the room and I said the same thing to Billy Byrne, and in different words I got the same answer. I got abusive letters about keeping them on. At matches, when the crowd goes quiet, a buffoon might shout out, "Griffin, where are you going with George O'Connor and Billy Byrne?" They heard those shouts too and they couldn't give a shite. Words can't express what I think about those guys.'

O'Connor had started against Kilkenny and Dublin, but for the Leinster final he'd urged Griffin to pick one of the younger lads. O'Connor and Byrne came on in the second half, the only two substitutes Wexford used. Their presence made the day complete.

On the bus back to Wexford that night Niamh Fitzpatrick sat next to O'Connor's wife Ellen. 'We were coming down into Gorey and we saw this sea of people and people crying on the streets. The bus stopped and the lads got off the bus, and I remember Ellen said to me, "I can't believe this." The amount of people who crossed over to the other side of the road when they saw George or Martin or some of the lads coming down the street at the times of their less than brilliant performances. People were horrible.'

People were funny too. On the night of the Leinster final Dunne finally ended up at home in Oulart. He left while the party was still swinging, not long after the exuberance of the parish had burst the seams of their local pub and spilled on to the street. 'You should have seen it — normal people doing ten-hand reels across the road. People I never saw doing a step before were doing the greatest dancing you ever saw.' A couple of days later the father of one of his closest friends, Bartlett Sinnott, passed away. Dunne went to the removal as a mourner but others couldn't separate him from his Wexford jersey. While his friend carried his father's coffin into the church, well-wishers were coming over to shake Dunne's hand. He knew they didn't mean any harm but he was struck by the incongruity of it. On the previous Sunday in Croke Park the world had tilted a little bit and a county had been left unbalanced.

On Wednesday night the players gathered on Curracloe beach for a run. That wasn't the night Griffin chose to chase three days of celebrating out of their bodies; he just prepared their minds for the purge. 'Griffin got us all together,' says Dunne, 'and he said, "We're training in Wexford Park tomorrow night. I've only one question to ask ye lads: how many more All-Ireland semi-finals are ye guaranteed to play in?" No one answered him. "Well," he said, "ye've one coming up and it might be the only one ye'll ever play in. We can carry on now and celebrate a Leinster final or we can knuckle down tomorrow night."'

He allowed them a few more pints that night, and on the following night he murdered them. Training returned to the level it had been at all summer. New motivations came easily. Galway were their opponents in the All-Ireland semi-final, just as they had been in the league semi-final. Galway had gone on to win the league title and all summer they had figured at the top of the betting for the All-Ireland. Their manager, Mattie Murphy, was giddy about his team's chances and wasn't inclined to be either silent or modest. 'Mattie Murphy had said the week before that match that he felt he had the best fifteen hurlers in Ireland,' recalls Dunne. 'That wasn't taken kindly in the dressing room at different times. Storey brought it up. Who do they think they are? Who does he think he is? This was our chance.'

Wexford didn't hurl as well as they had against Offaly but they endured and they survived – a new trick they'd learned. 'We rode our luck too in '96,' admits Dunne. 'Galway had four or five free-takers that day. They were missing 21s and everything. We couldn't believe the shots that were going wide in the second half.' In the third quarter, with Wexford two points in front, Galway were awarded a penalty that was blocked and cleared, and in Dunne's mind that was the turning point, though it wasn't the end of the story. 'Billy Byrne came on, got a goal, and that was it. Roll on September.'

The little comforts of routine had come to underpin their life together. On the bus to matches, for example, they watched the movie *Braveheart*. Rory Kinsella had introduced it for the league quarter-final against Offaly, and though it wasn't on the bus for the league semi-final it was there for every championship Sunday after that. They were never allowed to watch the movie to its grisly conclusion, however, when the Scottish patriot William Wallace played by Mel Gibson is hanged, drawn and quartered; such an image might transmit the wrong message. In the race memory of Wexford hurling there had been too many bloody endings. Instead, the tape was stopped at Wallace's speech on the battlefield, calling his countrymen to arms. By the end of the summer the players knew it word for word.

An overnight training camp on the beach was another innovation to which they became accustomed. Before all of their big games from the Leinster final onwards that summer they were housed for a Saturday night in a tent put up by the army; they ate from a barbecue, slept on camp beds, trained, talked and had the craic. The camp before the All-Ireland final clashed with the wedding of Larry O'Gorman's youngest sister Theresa, a story O'Gorman is fond of telling. He gave a reading at the mass, walked down the aisle and headed straight to the army camp. He returned to the reception later, stayed for an hour and a half, and then left again. 'I just told them I wasn't going to annoy myself any longer.' For any of them, missing the camp would have been unthinkable.

On that weekend Griffin showed them a video of Clare's homecoming from the previous September – just a glimpse of what might be theirs to savour. When the tape stopped the players pleaded for more but Griffin had deliberately kept it short, as a tease. They went through every Limerick player individually and discussed how best they might handle them. Then they rose the following morning to train at dawn.

'We were down the beach that Sunday morning at five o'clock,' says Dunne, 'pulling on tyres, lifting weights, lads doing sit-ups, lads doing press-ups – whatever they were doing. Griffin was on about the Limerick lads. They were after going to Dublin that weekend to have a run through the hotel, and Croke Park and their routine for the All-Ireland final. And he just said to us, "Lads, they're still in their beds up there tucked away in a hotel, and look at us." '

The league defeat to Limerick in Kilmallock had left a scar that was still tender. Beating Galway in the All-Ireland semi-final had avenged Wexford's only other defeat in a competitive match that year, but the Limerick defeat was different because, more than beaten, they felt they had been bullied. Wexford were a big team with a handful of players who had a reputation for aggression. At times over the years that aggression had been taken to excess; Griffin confronted that tendency and insisted on control. When Ger Cushe stepped out of line in the Leinster final Griffin nailed him about his behaviour. But that day against Limerick they hadn't been hard enough as a team.

One night, a couple of weeks before the final, the panel trained in the gym and Griffin called the players into a circle. The only theme was Kilmallock.

'It was a fairly hot game,' recalls Dunne, 'and there were some desperate shots in it. Tommy Kehoe got murdered in it. Sean O'Neill nearly killed him before the ball was thrown in. The crowd were cheering – they were loving this – and Tommy was getting absolutely hockeyed out of it.

'We were in the gym and everyone had their arm around one another. It was serious stuff now. As Griffin went by he was hitting everyone on the chest as he was talking. Two or three thumps on the chest. And then, every so often, he'd say, "No intimidation." And he'd go on a bit further and say a bit more, and he'd stop again and say the same thing: "No intimidation." The whole way round. The hair was standing on the back of your neck. For the All-Ireland final we weren't going to be intimidated the way we had been in Kilmallock.

'He stopped at Tommy Kehoe, and to tell you the truth lads were nearly crying. He said, "As long as I live and am involved with teams, what happened to you in Kilmallock will never happen to another player that plays under me." And he gave Tommy a hug. We were there, and the bond was squeezing harder and harder.'

In the last days before the final the emotional focus switched to Seanie Flood. He'd been hurt against Galway, but in the following weeks hope that he would recover in time for Limerick was kindled by a misdiagnosis of his injury. It wasn't discovered until after the All-Ireland that Flood had suffered a cracked bone in his shin, so on the week of the final he returned to training and tried to prove his fitness. On Wednesday night the Wexford management knew he wasn't going to make it but they decided to leave him to arrive at that conclusion himself. On Thursday night Flood's phone was off the hook. On Friday morning he called Griffin to confirm what they already knew. He was out. George O'Connor was in.

The year had been founded on planning, and for the final Griffin shone a flash lamp into every chamber and recess of his mind. On the week of the final he wrote down a list of things to do which stretched into hundreds of items. He went for a walk on the beach and interrogated himself one more time. Then his critical omission dawned on him: what if a man is sent off? One of ours, one of theirs. He called Rory and Seamus and they met to thrash out every permutation and what their response would be.

Nothing was considered too peripheral. They decided to embrace the pre-match pomp and ceremony rather than be distracted by it. They discussed how they would greet the president, what they would do in the parade, how they would stand for the national anthem: 'We stand like soldiers, chest out, heads up.' They even practised it. That summer teams had been breaking early from pre-match parades. Griffin suggested that Limerick mightn't go the whole way round. They didn't, as it happened. Wexford resolved to follow the band to the end. 'You don't even look at them,' said Griffin. 'March on.' They had decided too that they would parade around the outside so that they would be closer to their supporters. At some point in the puck-around one of the Wexford players noticed that the band member carrying the Limerick flag was lining up in the outside berth. Discreetly, an approach was made and that band member moved to the inside.

On the morning of the final the players were left alone, as usual, in the team room at the hotel. Flood had asked to say a few words. He opened his heart. 'When he was finished,' says Dunne, 'Seanie went over to a corner and started crying. One by one lads went over to him. I was beside George and I had my head down crying. Then George hit the table a box and said a few words, and after that there was complete silence. There was more than me shedding tears now, I can tell you that.'

Whatever fuel was stored up in their hearts, the game was all about their heads. 'We thought they were going to come at us,' says Dunne. 'They had done that and got away with it in Kilmallock. Then Sean O'Neill hits George instead of shaking hands with him before the throw-in. What a serious mistake that was. Of all the lads to hit . . .'

Limerick blasted into an early lead, 0–5 to 0–1; Wexford held tight. Already key moments were shaping the match. Dunne and Gary Kirby had clashed under the first high ball that dropped between them and Kirby went down injured. He was Limerick's strike-forward, their free-taker, the most important player in their attack. It later transpired that Kirby had broken a finger and Dunne was accused of pulling dangerously. Over the years Dunne developed a reputation for playing hard, and towards the end of his career he was sent off in three successive championships; but on that incident his defence remains strong. 'I didn't go out with any intentions of breaking his hand, or whatever. I went out with intentions of hurling him. Lads were saying to me, "He stuck up his hand." He didn't stick up his hand. The ball broke behind us. I reckon myself he was pulling with fear.

'The big battles were going to be Kirby and Ciaran Carey against myself and Storey. Storey was under an awful lot of pressure for the first twenty minutes. Then he scored what I would put down as one of the great points in Croke Park. Storey caught the ball and was running away from the goal and struck it on his left. For a fella who had been under pressure, to pull out a point like that . . .

'One of the turning points in that game – which we were expecting – was for Mike Houlihan to do something stupid. And he did. Larry O' [Gorman] was coming out with a ball and he actually broke a hurl across Larry O'. Then John O'Connor and Owen O'Neill had a confrontation in the corner at the same time. To this day I don't know what happened there. We ended up getting a free and John O' put it over the bar from about 90 yards. Then we got a goal straight after that and it broke Limerick's momentum.'

Three minutes before half-time the game took its most violent twist. A ball was thrown in between the Limerick corner-back Stephen McDonagh and the Wexford corner-forward Eamon Scallan. They both pulled wildly, and then Scallan pulled again. McDonagh tried to make a second swing too but he was hooked by the Wexford full-forward Garry Laffan. Scallan made contact with McDonagh and in a game that was starting to heat up referee Pat Horan decided to take action. Scallan was sent off. 'I feel a little bit guilty about

Eamon Scallan,' says Griffin. 'He hadn't stood up for himself against Galway and we'd taken him off after thirty minutes, so I'd say he felt under pressure not to be intimidated.'

In any case he was gone, and Wexford faced the second half a point up, a man down and with the wind in their faces. They reached for the plans they had made in the event of a sending-off and depended on their self-control. Limerick had made no prior arrangements; they were ad-libbing. 'Limerick made fierce mistakes,' says Dunne. 'Their loose man [Dave Clarke] was a disaster. They should have been moving Carey up. In the second half we had them under control. It was down to discipline too. In the second half the backs conceded no free. That was fair going in an All-Ireland final, down to fourteen men. Gary Kirby was going to clean us if we gave away frees.'

The final turned into a wrestle to the death. It was the opposite of the Leinster final, an anti-spectacle. No matter. At the final whistle Wexford were two points clear, 1–13 to 0–14. George O'Connor fell to his knees and joined his hands in prayer. Larry O'Gorman was swept up in a flash flood of Wexford supporters, the match ball in his fist. Somehow, Dunne met his mother.

Dunne's father was an engineer working on a project overseas and he couldn't arrange leave to be in Croke Park. Before the Galway game Dunne's mother had been very sick in hospital, but she was well again and strong enough to be at the final. On the bus to the ground Griffin had read out a letter that had been sent to him, not identifying the sender until the end. Dunne's mother had been the author.

'After the match,' says Dunne, 'I just remember I was bawling – roaring crying. I remember seeing my mother on the field. I just said, "Ma, I've no tears left for you." "I don't want any tears," she said. "I just want a hug." We went in under the stand and I remember myself and Tom Dempsey, arms around one another, nose to nose, and the two of us shedding a few tears. An Oulart and a Buffer's Alley man. Normally we'd be cutting one another's throats.'

The year had been full of little miracles.

In his acceptance speech, Martin Storey made all the usual thanks. When he came to Niamh Fitzpatrick he described her as their 'special friend', like a character from a Charlie Lansborough song. That secret had held. In Croke Park we saw the flower in bloom. The roots remained underground.

Griffin knew it was his last game in charge. He had known since the previous Christmas that this would be his last year, though he didn't tell the players. His wife Mary had been diagnosed with multiple sclerosis. His first thought was to quit straight away, but she persuaded him to see out the year. 'I knew the minute we were beaten I was gone and that was it. That became a massive motivation. It probably made me work that extra 20 per cent harder.'

Griffin is a spiritual man, and that summer he believed they were all on a journey together. He prayed for strength. He prayed that they would win. He wouldn't say that God has favourites, but he believes his prayers were answered. On this point we were unable to secure a confirmation. 'I prayed myself to death. I prayed to Matt Talbot. I prayed to John Paul and to the Blessed Virgin. I prayed on Lady's Island, which is a place of pilgrimage here in Wexford. You go around and say three decades of the rosary and then there's a statue of the Blessed Virgin at the very end and I sat down and I begged that woman. If you do the island nine times between the sixteenth of August and the ninth of September there's a special indulgence, and I did it with my mother.

'But do you know something, the night before the All-

Ireland final I went around the island and I did it at dusk so very few people would see me. I wanted to do it quietly, and I sat on the bench that night and that God would strike me dead I knew we were going to win the All-Ireland. A sense of calm and peace came over me. You can call it transcendental meditation – I don't care what you call it. I looked over the lake and the lake was still and it was a beautiful evening and I just said, "We're going to win." I knew we were going to win. I wasn't even nervous. I'd no butterflies. I knew we were going to win.

'It was probably a spiritual journey for me, the whole thing. It was uplifting and joyous, and I knew it was going to be good for the county and I was proud of that.'

On the morning after the All-Ireland final the players gathered for mass in the team hotel. Not all of them made it, mind you. The celebrations would be the last time those players were under Griffin's jurisdiction, and the final requests he made of them were to respect themselves and respect the jersey. No drinking on the bus. No drunks on the podiums as they made their victory tour of the county. 'If one of you becomes an alcoholic as a result of winning this cup,' he said, 'then I want to give it back.'

He reminded them of Nicky Rackard. Full-forward on the GAA's Team of the Century, Rackard had been Wexford hurling's first superstar in the 1950s. Drink, though, had overshadowed his life and threatened to destroy it. He confronted his alcoholism in middle age and became a counsellor to other alcoholics, but he died from cancer at just fifty-three and there was no doubt that his drinking had shortened his life. Rackard was one of Griffin's heroes. With the cup in their hands and thanks to be said, he couldn't forget him. 'I reckoned that without Nicky Rackard there would have been no Wexford hurling. He's one of the great icons of the game, a wonderful man, larger than life. Flawed maybe, a bit human, but that made him all the greater. So I never wanted to forget Rackard, and I didn't want the boys to forget Rackard.

'A week or two after the final myself and Storey brought the cup to Cappagh Hospital to see a child, and we went from there to Rackard's grave. We knelt and prayed, just me and him. We brought the cup back to Rackard and put it on his grave, and I'm very pleased we did that.'

From the past, a bridge had been crossed.

3. Myths and Magic

You may not have heard this story, but you won't require an intimate knowledge of the Offaly hurlers to embrace its veracity. A month before the start of the 2000 championship they went on a weekend trip to Ennis. A challenge match was arranged against Clare on a Saturday evening, and after that the panel was on shore leave. The Offaly manager, Pat Fleury, told the players they were free to 'let their hair down'. In his fourteenth and final year on the Offaly panel, Michael Duignan was a veteran of such trips and wondered about the wisdom of Fleury's general waiver. With Offaly, every overnight trip came with an implicit licence to party. The manager's open invitation to do so simply meant that Ennis could be their Babylon.

'Clare were training for an hour and a half before they played us,' says Duignan, 'and then they bet the shite out of us. We were absolutely hammered. So we went off and went on a fierce session. Didn't go to bed until all hours. I woke up at about half ten the following morning and, Jesus, I was bollixed. Joe Dooley was rooming with me and he was bollixed too. We went downstairs at around eleven o'clock and there was a full session going on in the bar. Johnny Pilkington was singing "Sweet Caroline". The league final was on in Ennis that day between Tipperary and Galway and the crowd were coming in for their lunch, looking at this.'

On their way back to Offaly the players stopped off in Portumna to watch the league final on television, and the session resumed. They trained on Monday night, suffering the horrors of hostile detox. Clare players were astonished at how poorly Offaly had played against them and couldn't see how they could possibly right themselves in time for the championship. Four weeks later, though, Offaly beat Wexford by thirteen points, beginning a summer that would end in the All-Ireland final. Clare were gone from the Munster championship on the second Sunday of June, their summer over.

That was Offaly. Is there anything else you need to know?

In an era when hurling was moved by fundamental change, Offaly met the revolution halfway, on their own terms. They modified the first-time hurling inculcated in them as children, but never abandoned it. They trained harder than any Offaly team before them, but rejected the fashion for commando drills, mountaineering and body-building. On their day they were the most beautiful team of the 1990s because the game they played recognized hurling's essential simplicity. They knew how to get the ball and how to hit it. Fidelity of touch and clarity of striking equated in their minds to strategy. It was no coincidence that in five years out of six between 1995 and 2000 the best game of the year involved them: the Leinster finals of 1995 and 1996; the third Clare match in 1998; the All-Ireland semi-finals of 1999 and 2000. In the making of great matches they were the yeast.

Our picture of them, though, became a caricature. The pat assertion that they trained only half as hard as other leading teams gained currency over the years, and for their own purposes Offaly players tended to issue only half-hearted denials. The reality is that they couldn't have won two All-Irelands and contested two other finals during the most intensely competitive period in hurling's history if they had lacked the basic fitness to survive.

The companion reality is that they didn't need an exaggerated fitness regime for any practical purpose: the hurling they played was based on economical use of the ball, released without delay to spare themselves. They did weights one night a week in Ferbane in 1994, but that was the only body-building programme they did as a group. For the game they played, power was not strictly necessary. On top of that, they didn't need a brutal physical regime as a mental aid. They already knew how to win and were well stocked with self-esteem.

'We didn't do what Clare and Wexford and these teams did because we didn't need to break down any barriers,' says Johnny Pilkington, who spent thirteen years on the Offaly panel. 'We'd done that at minor level [Offaly won three minor All-Irelands in the late 1980s]. Teams like Wexford and Clare didn't believe they had the ability to win All-Irelands. For us, the big thing was skill level. We knew we had to do the donkey work in training because you have to be fit enough to get the ball first. But it's no use getting the ball first if you haven't the skill to use it.'

The caricature wasn't entirely false, though. When Eamon Cregan took over as Offaly manager in the autumn of 1992, Offaly had already fallen a little behind. They had won the previous year's National League by training just once a week over the winter at a time when specialist physical trainers were only starting to come into fashion. Kilkenny appointed one for the first time in 1991 and reached the All-Ireland final; their conquerors that day, Tipperary, already had one. Cregan brought one with him, Derry O'Donovan.

'When Derry came in it was a massive change,' says Duignan. 'I remember the first night we did below in Birr; it was a shambles to see the state of people. A lot of the lads would have struggled initially.'

How bad? Cregan remembers some players being lapped during the warm-up. You couldn't make it up. 'Derry couldn't believe it,' says Cregan. 'There were fellows so far behind that I'd even have lapped them. It was a culture shock for them.'

Martin Hanamy made his debut with the Offaly seniors in 1986 and remained until 1999. In the Offaly panel, Hanamy was held up as an outstanding trainer, a model and an example, but he was familiar with the old culture. 'It was hard for fellas to get out of the rut of "Oh, I've a sore leg, or a sore arm, I can't train." They were getting away with it before, but Cregan was a different kettle of fish.'

Reform, though, took time. 'I remember in 1993,' says Pilkington, 'about eight or ten weeks before the first round of the championship, there were only about ten training one night from a panel of thirty. I remember it clearly. Only about four finished the session.'

But when the running stopped and the ball was thrown in their sessions had an entirely different quality. Behind closed doors in Clare, Ger Loughnane used to bring fiery training matches to a blaze with the petrol of his commentary; in Offaly the intensity was more organic. In training they always hurled like they meant it.

'We used to play a lot of backs-and-forwards matches,' says Cregan, 'and a lot of them were like real championship matches. I'll always remember one incident with Kevin Kinahan and Pat O'Connor. Kinahan was going for a ball in the corner and O'Connor came over and he hit him a root and knocked him flat on his backside. Kinahan said nothing, but five minutes later Pat was coming in with the ball and Kinahan came out and put him up into the air. A word wasn't spoken. I was saying, "Well, Pat got Kevin and Kevin got Pat, let's play on." And that's the way it should be. It was that intense.'

The players knew that Cregan liked that edge. In his days with Limerick Cregan had been a class player with a twist of what his old friend Babs Keating called 'bitterness'. This Offaly team had that mix. 'If you came down to watch us training down the years,' says Pilkington, 'you would have seen Martin Hanamy and Billy Dooley going hell for leather. Myself and Daithi Regan would have had arguments left, right and centre. We'd be marking each other and there'd be strokes pulled all over the place. I remember one ball pucked out between us. Regan was about six foot four, I'm about five foot ten. The ball was coming down and Regan managed to clip me on the ear. We weren't boxing but I fucked him out of it and he fucked me out of it. That was the intensity.

'Prisoners weren't taken. I'm not saying it was dirty, but Hubert Rigney was there and if you put your hand up Hubert pulled. If you do it in training you'll do it in a match, that was the attitude, and that's what went on. John Troy was there. If you clipped Troy, Troy would clip you back. He caught me one day and it was the nicest stroke anybody ever hit me. It was only training but it was straight in front of Cregan. He flicked me with a right slap across the legs. "Play on," said Cregan. He didn't see it.

'Towards the end of our time the Offaly back line leaked goals against Kilkenny, say in '99 and 2000, but before that it was very rare you'd get through the Offaly back line because Kinahan would take you out of it or Hanamy would take you out of it or Hubert Rigney. Brian Whelahan was a nice player. Brian would be able to flick the ball away from you. But Kevin Martin would hit you a shoulder that would take you out of it too.'

The reputation of that Offaly team, though, wasn't founded on the quality of their training matches. The word was that these guys were party animals. That they worked hard and played hard. Some of the stories were true, but what grew from the truth were stories so fantastic that they couldn't be contained. After the 1995 All-Ireland final, for example, it was widely rumoured that Pilkington had drunk three pints on the morning of the match. He was captain of Offaly that day. The story was ludicrous.

What was undeniable, though, was that many of the Offaly panel liked a few pints and didn't like to be lectured about their responsibilities in this matter. When Padraig Horan became manager in the autumn of 1990 he tried to impose restrictions but it exploded in his face. As a deterrent, confrontation didn't work. 'When Padraig took over he stood up at a players' meeting and said that there would be no smoking, no drinking and no going out on Saturday nights,' says Pilkington. 'Two of the lads got up and said straight out that they weren't going to sacrifice their Saturday nights – and those two lads played afterwards.'

Cregan didn't attempt martial law. He trusted the players, mainly because he reckoned that it was the best chance he had of maintaining order. For the most part his trust wasn't abused. 'There'd be no point putting a ban on,' says Duignan. 'You had some tough characters. The likes of Martin Hanamy, the best hurler I ever played with or against. If Hanamy decided during the winter that he was drinking a few pints at the weekend he was drinking them, and nobody was going to stop him. That's the way it would be. The Dooleys and myself and others, we would have a few pints. No point in saying we wouldn't. The couple of lads who were over the top were always over the top.'

Hurling was a huge part of these players' lives and the central plank of their egos, but they weren't prepared to sacrifice everything for the game they played. Weddings came along in mid-season and they didn't think of themselves as elite sportspeople with heightened physical conditions to protect. Duignan remembers Johnny Dooley getting married eight days before the Leinster final in 1994. Joe and Billy Dooley were naturally at the wedding, along with Kinahan, Hanamy and Duignan. They asked themselves the important question but it wasn't a crisis of conscience, as Duignan recalled. 'I remember saying to the lads in the church, "Are we going to have a few jars today, or what are we going to do?" "Of course we are." So, we had a few pints and a load of the lads went to the afters, and Derry [O'Donovan] was there. We trained the next day and Derry kept back any of us who had been at the wedding the day before. He ran the shite out of us for half an hour.'

Hanamy tells one story against himself. It was two weeks before the 1994 All-Ireland final and it was also Vintage Week in Birr, with all of the giddiness that suggested. A pub in town was raising money for relief aid to Rwanda and they asked a few of the Offaly players to cook burgers in the street. Offaly trained that morning and Cregan sensed the danger, but Hanamy, Pilkington and one of the subs, Brian Hennessy, went along anyway. Hanamy was captain of Offaly that year but as the day wore on his sense of duty dissolved in the beer. 'Sure, we got scuttered,' says Hanamy. 'The amount of Guinness we drank. We went down that night to another pub and Pat O'Connor bumped into us. He read us. "Ye bastards, ye might get only one fucking chance at an All-Ireland." Pat was older than us and he was right.' Pilkington remembers it too. 'We had about ten pints in the middle of the street and then went singing in Kelly's pub over the microphone. How that didn't get back [to Cregan] . . . The following year I did something similar and I got ate over it.'

'That's what Johnny used always say to me,' says Hanamy. ' "How is it that yer man can always get away with it?" Sure,

I drank as much as any of them. I never, ever gave up drink for the sake of hurling. I'd have a few pints on the night before a league game but I wouldn't before a championship match. I don't think anyone did. If I heard they did now I'd be disgusted.'

Offaly's loveless relationship with the league was another thing that accentuated their difference. All of the other serious hurling counties showed the league some nodding respect in a bad year and were inclined to see it as a springboard into summer most years. Offaly, however, took a detached view. Coming from Division Two they won the league in 1991 for the only time in their history, but over the remainder of the 1990s they reached just one semi-final.

In large part it was due to their circumstances. In other counties the league is used to blood battalions of fringe players, but Offaly panels don't have sufficient depth for them to put out a shadow team and compete at a respectable level. So most of their league line-ups contain championship players, operating at a seasonally adjusted setting. 'We pretty much knew our championship team in January or February,' says Johnny Dooley, 'so there was no massive incentive to go out and burst yourself in a league match.'

Most of the time they got away with faking it, but occasionally they didn't. In February 1996 they lost to Galway by 1–27 to 1–1. Freakish results are not uncommon in the league, but this one pushed new boundaries. 'Myself and Daithi Regan were subs,' says Duignan, 'and I think it was nineteen points to one coming up to half-time when Cregan put the hand out to myself and Regan to come on. Myself and Regan got out of the dug-out and we were warming up, doing a bit of stretching, and Daithi was shouting at me, "Come on, Mickey, we can turn it around." And a big smile on his face. But I'm facing towards the dug-out and the selectors are looking at me. That's the way it could be with us in the league. Meath beat us when we were All-Ireland champions, a tough game up in Athboy. Antrim beat us over the years. Down beat us one year in Tullamore.'

After Antrim beat Offaly in the 1989 All-Ireland semi-final the northern teams grew fond of playing Offaly, acutely aware of how vulnerable they were over the winter. Offaly knew this too, and cared less. 'Offaly lost to everybody in the league,' says Pilkington. 'At one stage I was hurling Fitzgibbon Cup with UCD, and Conal Bonnar [former Tipperary player] was with UCD as well. We were after getting bet by UCC and we were having a few pints and the lads were a bit down and I said, "Boys, will ye cop on to yerselves. I'm after getting beaten by Antrim and Down and Mickey Mouse teams like that. It's a privilege to be beaten by Cork." That cheered Bonnar up anyway.

'The problem with the northern teams was that you'd have to stay up the night before. You'd stay in the Carrickdale Hotel [in county Armagh] and no matter how often the manager told you "no drinking", you'd still have four or five pints and end up in the nightclub. You'd be saying to yourself, "Sure, it's only a league match. If you lose it, you lose it."'

When he took over in 1997, John McIntyre made the mistake of taking the league too seriously, and though the players liked him he was acting against their natural bio-rhythms. When it came to the championship McIntyre wasn't able to get the best out of them. Cregan, though, copped on quickly. 'They couldn't give tuppence for the league. They hibernate for the winter, and when it comes to April and May they wake up.'

The shallowness of their panel was both a good thing and a bad thing. The county championship in Offaly is decided essentially between six clubs, and it is rare for a player to make the county panel from outside that set. Inter-club tensions were a debilitating virus in Offaly panels in the years before their Leinster championship breakthrough in 1980, but Dermot Healy pioneered a vaccine when he took over as manager in the late 1970s and the condition never returned. Birr and the county board had their rows over the years but that was successfully treated with therapy. When things were going well, the tightness of the panel bred togetherness; when they were going badly, however, it encouraged slackness.

'Between 1995 and 1998 there was a bit of complacency setting in,' says Brian Whelahan. 'There was no new blood coming through, which is one of the reasons why I thought we had no hope of winning the All-Ireland at the start of 1998. We went through a few years where fellas knew at the start of the year that the championship fifteen would be coming from about eighteen players. The beauty of it, though, was that the selectors knew exactly the players they had to work with and they had to make do with that. You chop and switch and change until you get it right.'

The adaptability of those Offaly players was unique. Whelahan was one of the outstanding wing-backs of all time but he served Offaly in seven different positions in the championship. Duignan saw duty in six different positions, and Joe Errity five, including full-back, centre-back, centre-forward and full-forward, right down the spine of the team. As a specialist left corner-back Hanamy was a freak.

Their ease with each other was such that they occasionally made their own changes on the field. In the All-Ireland semi-final replay against Clare in 1998 Whelahan switched himself twice after half-time, from centre-field to centre-forward and then into full-forward. Which meant that two other players, Johnny Dooley and Johnny Pilkington, had to move too. There was scarcely a day when Pilkington didn't catch his breath at corner-forward or wing-forward while one of those lads went out and did a short shift for him at centre-field. On other inter-county teams such behaviour would have been damned as insubordination. Offaly, though, were different.

They knew each other so well, too, because their careers lasted so long. Old players weren't just cast to the scrap heap; they were re-threaded and put back on the road. Eugene Coughlan and Pat Delaney, the great full-back and centre-back on the 1980s team, ended their careers as improvised forwards. The changes that swept hurling from the mid-1990s onwards necessarily meant that inter-county careers became shorter. That was true everywhere else except Offaly. The team that lost the 1999 All-Ireland semi-final to Cork contained seven players that had won minor All-Irelands in the 1980s and two players, Hanamy and Joe Dooley, who were already senior players when those minor titles were won.

But it didn't mean that Offaly could be the same force every year. That just wasn't in them. 'The Kilkenny attitude,' says Duignan, 'is to win everything. That wouldn't be our style. It wouldn't be our psyche. You'd be trying your best. You'd be fierce determined to win whatever you could but you wouldn't be looking to win every All-Ireland, every year.'

The general perception was that they were a difficult group to manage. The Offaly players rejected the substance of the charge, but the statistics spoke up against their denials. When Mike McNamara stepped down after the 2004 championship, Offaly were facing their thirteenth change of manager in seventeen years. The bare statistic becomes more chilling when you add in the context. During that period Offaly won five Leinster championships, two All-Irelands, a National League and contested two other All-Ireland finals. In the first four years of Duignan's inter-county career, 1988 to 1991, Offaly won three Leinster championships and a National League under four different managers. In terms of success there hadn't been a period like it in the history of Offaly hurling, yet managers came and went.

It is not easily explained. Only one manager over that time, John McIntyre, was officially sacked, and he returned seven years later. Babs Keating's position was made untenable after a stray comment ignited player unrest in 1998. Paudge Mulhare's reign in 1990 was always intended as a short-term, stop-gap measure. Michael Bond came and went and came again. Fr Tom Fogarty was invited to re-apply for the job in 2002, after he had spent a year doing it. In everyday life that might have been termed constructive dismissal. Every departure had its own tale. Eamon Cregan's four years in charge stand out as an era of great stability, but at times he wobbled and wondered what he was doing up there.

One difficulty for any Offaly manager was that you couldn't really drop any one of about a dozen players without seriously undermining the team. The manager knew that, the players knew that. Different managers shuffled the deck in their own ways but the picture cards were always the same. The massively talented Roy Mannion was famously cut from the panel in Cregan's time, but that stands out as an exception to the rule.

Mannion's inter-county career, though, perfectly illustrates the challenge any Offaly manager faced. Like holding a bird in your hand, you couldn't squeeze too tightly. Duignan remembers a stand-off during 1990, Mulhare's year in charge. In training Mannion was marking a veteran everyone hated playing against. He pulled early, he pulled late, he was messy. Mannion warned him until eventually he lost his cool. He drew a bad stroke and tempers flared.

'There was uproar,' says Duignan. 'Some of the older lads were going to kill Mannion. Things calmed down anyway. After training the fella that Mannion hit went over and burst Mannion with a box to the mouth. Mannion went away from the panel for a week and Paudge went and spoke to a few of the senior players on the panel saying, you know, these things happen. He got Mannion back training a week later and he had him down the far end of the field and you could see he was reading him the riot act. Paudge came up, called us all in, told us what he had said to Roy. Roy apologized and everything was grand.

'I was talking to Mannion afterwards and I asked him, "What did he say?" He said, "I'm going to pretend I'm eating the shite out of you and when we get up there I'll say I did and you'll say, 'That's right, Paudge.' And the lads will be grand." We won the Leinster championship afterwards and Mannion was outstanding.'

Cregan, though, wasn't able to sustain a working relationship with Mannion. As Duignan remembers it, Mannion's Offaly career ended with a flash of lightning and a clap of thunder. The first incident was at a challenge match against Limerick. Duignan had a broken finger, so he was on the sideline. And so too was Mannion. 'Cregan left him off at the start and put on a fella who wouldn't have a hope of making it. Mannion would take that fierce to heart. Cregan came along with fifteen minutes to go. "Roy." And Roy never budged. Came back down and called him again. No. End of story. That's a hard thing to manage. Like, how do you manage that?

'The turning point came when I was marking Mannion in training in Tullamore. He was a brilliant man under the high ball; it was impossible to get the ball off the fucker. He caught two or three balls over my head and I says to him, "Give us a break there will ya?" Like, we had started school together and lived 20 yards apart. So, next ball that came I caught it and stuck it over the bar. Next thing, Cregan came over and started a big thing about how you should get in under a high ball, and Mannion was brilliant under a high ball. Mannion was looking at him with an expression that said, "I fucking know". One word led to another and Cregan said, "If you don't like it you can go," and that was it. He walked off and never hurled for Offaly again.

'You don't confront a player like him in front of thirty or forty other people. Cregan could have called him aside afterwards if he'd something to say. Cregan wasn't great with people, but he was challenged a good bit too.'

Pilkington wouldn't dispute that. He tells a story of one challenge match that was wilfully sabotaged by the players. The county board were in the habit of arranging a challenge game for the Sunday evening of the June Bank Holiday weekend, which was fine except that there would also be a round of club championship matches fixed for that weekend. One year a couple of the players were sick of it and they put the word around that the game was off. Only a handful of players turned up and Offaly couldn't field a team.

'Eamon walked out on us a couple of times over the commitment of the players,' says Pilkington, 'and he was dead right.'

One evening early in his reign he came close to quitting. He walked into the dressing room to find only five players togging out for training. It wasn't half seven yet but it was close enough and he wasn't hanging around to see who else would show up. He expressed his dissatisfaction to the county board person present, turned on his heels and left. 'I remember,' says Cregan, 'we stopped in Nenagh, myself and Derry, and we bought half a chicken each. We said to ourselves,

"Jesus, we could be up in Tullamore eating a steak after training instead of sitting by the side of the road having chicken." But I didn't want to be wasting my time up there and, okay, they came round afterwards.'

Ultimately, for the relationship to work Derry O'Donovan was a necessity. 'Eamon came in with a certain attitude,' says Duignan, 'and I'd say he had to soften it. I'd say he mellowed when he was with us. He would have come in saying, "This is the way I want it done," and we would have said, "Well, this is the way we do it." There was a change along the way before we were all singing off the same hymn sheet. There were certainly flashpoints and things mightn't have held together without Derry O'Donovan. He was a great middle man. He had the 100 per cent trust of the players. Eamon was a private man but Derry was very close to him. He saw a side of him that we didn't see and he was able to express that side to us.'

Some of the players' behaviour obviously irritated Cregan, but the irritation went both ways. Cregan was highly animated during matches and he had a tendency towards micro-management on the sideline. 'He was a pure perfectionist,' says Duignan. 'If he was on your case during a game he'd never leave you alone. It happened to me during the 1995 All-Ireland final. He never let me alone from the start of the game. Every two minutes he had me over to the sideline to tell me something. Hundreds of people said it to me afterwards: "Why didn't you burst him?"'

But they all respected Cregan's absolute command of the game and his ability to get them into a state of ripeness for summer. Hanamy heard many voices in Offaly dressing rooms over the years but he couldn't think of one more affecting than Cregan's. One speech stands out. It was the Thursday night before the 1995 Leinster final against Kilkenny. Offaly were the defending All-Ireland champions but Kilkenny had beaten them well on the way to winning the league and Cregan had spent all winter telling the Offaly players that nobody had given them credit for winning the previous year's All-Ireland. A young Denis Byrne was Kilkenny's new goal-scoring sensation that spring and early summer, and after a while Cregan came round to that subject.

'He was walking around and talking,' says Hanamy, 'and next thing he hit the table a slap and we jumped. "Denis Byrne is there," he said, "flicking and tipping goals. KILL HIM," he said. "KILL HIM." Now, he didn't mean it like that. But I remember Shane McGuckian was marking him that Sunday and he had him held by the jersey all day long and looking him straight in the eyes. I took that speech from Thursday night right into Sunday. It stayed with me.'

As a rule, the Offaly players preferred their team meetings in moderation. Self-analysis was an awkward topic. In 1997, however, McIntyre liked to have team meetings before every league match. Nothing heavy, just a chat. He sensed that the players weren't comfortable with the idea, but Offaly won their first two league games so the players humoured the new manager. One night McIntyre decided that a bit of variety was needed and he asked a sports psychologist, Betty Cody, to come along. She had worked with other elite GAA teams and the use of sports psychology was becoming more wide-spread. McIntyre didn't tell the players that Cody was coming, he simply told them to show up for training as usual but not to bring their gear.

'She was grand, in fairness,' says Duignan, 'but you're dealing with a certain bunch of lads here. They're fierce solid and fierce straight, but not everything would suit them. At one stage she tried to include John Troy. You'd have to know Troy. If you were talking to him he'd have his head down. He'd look up to talk to you and then he'd put his head down again. He was sitting at the front and she started talking about peripheral vision. Now, of any sportsman in any sport in this country John probably had the best peripheral vision. Unbelievable. Eyes in the back of his head. She picked some picture on the wall and said that an ordinary person looking at that would just see two horses standing in a field. And she said to John, "If you looked at that now, what would you see?" And she probably thought he'd say twenty things. John looks up and says, "Two horses in a field." '

Commando training, early-morning sessions, weights, tackle bags, sports psychology – all of these things worked for other teams. But in the eyes of this Offaly team they were props and costumes. All they wanted was a stage. To be in charge you needed to give them a lot of what they wanted and then they'd reward you with harmony and high perform-ance. You needed to know what buttons to press. Ground hurling, for example. They loved ground-hurling drills and believed that their game would be dysfunctional without that practice in training. During Babs Keating's short reign in 1998 the players challenged him about the lack of ground hurling in his sessions. He relented.

Then Michael Bond came in halfway through the summer of 1998 and he gave them everything they wanted, instantly, instinctively. 'Straight away it was his enthusiasm,' says Duignan. 'The positivity was unbelievable. "Right, lads, I'm Michael Bond, school principal, 550 students" – giving us a bit of background. "I don't believe in losing. Ye're the best hurlers in Ireland. Ye've ten weeks now, ye're going to win the All-Ireland. It's back to basics." Fellas were looking at each other saying to themselves, "Is this lad for real? Which planet did he arrive from?" Next thing it was ball work, ball work, ball work and move the ball. Off we went. It was a breath of fresh air and it was exactly what we needed. If they brought in somebody at that stage that was going to start talking shite we were in trouble. We trained for ten weeks and we got together about fifty-two times.'

In 1998, though, the players were already fit from Johnny Murray's physical training in the first half of the year. For the following season Bond tried to do the physical training himself, and according to Hanamy he was less effective. They stumbled to the 1999 All-Ireland semi-final and lost a classic to Cork.

By the time Pat Fleury took the job in 2000 the team was in the early stages of decay. Appointing Fleury was a deviation from what was accepted best practice. It was ten years since they had plumped for a former Offaly player to manage the team and in the meantime Fleury had sat on county board committees that had invariably approached outsiders to take the job. The players liked Fleury and he guided them to another All-Ireland final, but he couldn't be persuaded to come back for a second term.

A rash of controversies blighted the year. Birr were at war with the county board in the spring and threatened to withdraw their players from the county panel. John Troy quit the panel ten days before the All-Ireland semi-final and couldn't be coaxed back until the following year. Hubert Rigney was up in arms over not being named on the panel for the All-Ireland final, and Aidan Mannion's exclusion from the same panel brought heat on Fleury from his own club. The beast bucked and reared like it often did, and Fleury was saddle-sore by the end of the year.

'Pat would have been the straightest, most decent guy that was ever in the job,' says Duignan. 'But he couldn't stick it. It wasn't worth it. He wouldn't have stayed for all the tea in China. Why would you?'

★

As a group they regarded themselves as self-sufficient, and in the dressing room there was a clear but unspoken hierarchy. Joe Dooley and Martin Hanamy were joint heads of state; Brian Whelahan was the head of government. The cabinet was a fluid group of capable people. Their shared conviction, however, was that there was nothing they couldn't achieve if they put their minds to it. Life could be a cabaret, but hurling was serious.

'The one thing that I think is important to bury,' says John McIntyre, 'is this myth that Offaly were utterly carefree and lackadaisical about their preparation. When they had to, they trained hard. I found them all well intentioned. I would have brought back nine or ten of the panel for extra training [in 1997]. When the squad was training on Tuesday and Friday nights I brought other players back to try to get them up to where I wanted them to be. Brian Whelahan, Johnny Pilkington, John Troy, Daithi Regan, Hubert Rigney – they all came back.'

There was no manager, though, who could lead them if they weren't prepared to be led. They couldn't be bullied, or fooled. You needed their respect, and to move them you needed their consent. 'I suppose it was difficult for a manager,' says Duignan. 'We were a close group and we talked a lot about hurling. We were deep into hurling. We applied ourselves and we trained. We never pointed the finger of blame at any manager when we lost, we pointed it at ourselves. We reckoned if we trained properly, applied ourselves properly, put in the effort, we'd be hard to beat, and that nearly always proved to be the case. When we were properly motivated and training hard we were rarely beaten.

'The type of players we had, we had a lot of strong characters that maybe didn't need a lot of influence or motivation from other players. They did it themselves. You can go right through it. From Kinahan to Hanamy to Kevin Martin to Hubert Rigney, right through Johnny Pilkington, Daithi Regan in his day, the Dooleys, John Troy. They were all, in their own heads, clued in. Serious hurling men. You might need the odd spark here and there along the way but that's all.

'In terms of straight talking Hanamy was probably the most influential. Fucking unbelievable. Whatever Hanamy said fucking went. He was 100 per cent respected and there was no messing and that was that. If Hanamy spoke to the trainer or anybody else about something, it was done. Hanamy would never miss a night's training. If there was a cone over there in the corner of Everest he'd be over and around it. He never went inside a cone doing laps. Every ball he contested in training would be the same as an All-Ireland final. From that point of view Hanamy had ferocious respect as well. A ball dropping out of the sky – bang, he'd take the head off you, it wouldn't matter. He didn't know any other way, and he didn't know any other way to train. There were no short cuts, no messing.'

Hanamy didn't talk very much so his words were loaded with weight. McIntyre remembers one conversation during his year in charge that reflected Hanamy's status within the group. With the championship coming up they had diluted their team for a league game against Limerick which, if they won, would have landed them in the play-off stages of the league scheduled for later in the summer. Hanamy sat down with McIntyre for the meal after training and intimated quietly over tea that he felt management had picked the wrong team. A violent outburst would have wreaked only a fraction of the devastation to McIntyre's peace of mind.

'I drove from Banagher to Galway that night a very troubled individual,' says McIntyre. 'The fact that he had put his head above the parapet to say that to me made me

concerned. What people felt about Hanamy was that if he
had something to say it was important. I didn't have the
courage to ring the other selectors and say, "Lookit, lads,
we've already named the team, but let's change it, let's win
this feckin' match, let's get to the knock-out stages of the
league and take one game at a time." The biggest regret
of my time in Offaly was that Tuesday night and not going
with my gut instinct because Hanamy wasn't saying it for the
sake of it.'

Brian Whelahan's influence was manifestly different. They
mightn't see much of him over the winter because Birr were
often involved in a protracted club campaign, and he suffered
from a chronic hamstring condition for years which limited
his training at different times. The others felt that he used to
be 'ducking and diving' a little bit over the winter, though
they knew he would be ready when the time came. Unlike
Hanamy, Whelahan was a talker. 'You didn't have to ask
Brian to volunteer an opinion,' says McIntyre. 'That's his
nature. I wouldn't be making a criticism of him in that. I'm
not sure if everyone in the squad appreciated his intrusions
but there would have been tremendous respect for him as a
hurler. I would say he was perceived by the players as the
pulse of this Offaly team. In times of crisis they would be
looking to Whelahan to solve it on the field of play.'

Sometimes that crisis would involve a row between Birr
and the county board, and in those situations, according to
Duignan, the Offaly players depended on Whelahan 'to see
the middle ground' and help broker a solution. Match day,
though, was when his impact was greatest. 'The minute Brian
came into the dressing room for a championship match until
the minute we went out on to the field he never shut up,'
says Duignan. 'It was more to jizz himself up I always felt.
Other lads like Hanamy, Kevin Kinahan, Joe Dooley and

myself, we were all very quiet in the dressing room. Totally quiet; wouldn't say a word. You wouldn't necessarily be listening to what Brian was saying but he'd build up the atmosphere. When Brian was hurling well, though, I didn't think we could be beaten. Teams started looking at that and tried to get to him. He could lift the whole team.'

Johnny Pilkington was a different story. The caricature of this Offaly team and the reality it competed against were both expressed in him. He drank, he smoked, he stayed out late and made no attempt to cover his tracks. But he had real class too and a natural athleticism that somehow survived under constant shelling from the good life. When he quit in 2001 he had played for thirteen seasons, appeared in forty-one championship matches and scored a total of 6–57 from play, which made him by a distance the most prolific centre-fielder of the age. And he did it on thirty fags a day. He was talented enough to have played on any of the top inter-county teams, but where else would his excesses have been tolerated? Pilkington knew that he tested the patience of different Offaly managers, but his position was clearly stated and passionately held: he refused to accept that hurling should rule his life and dictate his behaviour. As an amateur he asserted the right to fence off hurling and close the gate behind him when he wished.

There were times, though, when he challenged even the conditions he had set out for himself. On the Friday before they played Wexford in the 2000 championship he went to a wedding, and when the party spilled over into Saturday he kept going until two o'clock on Sunday morning, fewer than fourteen hours before the throw-in at Croke Park. Offaly won handily and Pilkington's performance just about disguised his lost weekend.

'The way our attitude was perceived and the way we came

across as a team had a lot to do with me and a few others,' says Pilkington. 'We came across as, "Ah yeah, it's only a match on Sunday." But when the match came on Sunday it was a different ball game altogether. During the seventy minutes it was a major thing. I crossed the line all right at times but I didn't go too far that I wasn't able to come back.'

He was made captain for the 1995 championship. Hanamy had done the job for two years and it was time for a change. In Offaly the captaincy is not linked to the county champions, but as it happened Birr had won the title with Pilkington as captain and would go on to win the club All-Ireland in March 1995. Outside Offaly Pilkington was a hostage to his reputation, and to distant observers it might have seemed like a perverse appointment. Pilkington, though, would have rejected such prejudice.

'I'm blowing my own trumpet,' says Pilkington, 'but when Martin Hanamy stood down I was the natural one to come into it. That's what I felt myself, and that's what Eamon Cregan felt as well. On the grounds of experience and on the grounds that my performances would have been fairly regular and fairly steady up until the Leinster championship of 1997. It was the natural time. I don't want to put myself on a par with Martin Hanamy – far from it – but we'd have a similar type of game. A workmanlike game. The thing you want is backbone. I was working up and down and getting scores and hitting lads. I just would have been the natural one. Not for my grace or my skill, but for being steady.'

As a character witness, Duignan is happy to take the stand. 'He was a ferocious athlete. Serious. And a serious man to train. Johnny built up this myth about himself. The Offaly myth was nearly built around Johnny Pilkington. Other fellas would do it much quieter but they'd drink more in one session than Johnny would drink in a week. Other fellas we had would put him to sleep in two hours. But he was some man to go to battle with, some man to hurl. Toughness and effort, and he would never let you down.'

His captaincy, though, wasn't a smooth ride. Maybe Cregan hoped that the responsibility would change him, but it didn't. Inevitably, they clashed. A couple of weeks before the first round of the championship Cregan threatened to remove him from the post. Pilkington could understand his distress. Accompanied by another member of the county panel and a couple of Birr players, Pilkington had attended a Friday-night function in Clonmel with the Liam MacCarthy cup and the cup for the club All-Ireland. Offaly were training on the following evening and Pilkington's plan was to be home in good time for that. But the Rugby World Cup was on in South Africa and Ireland were playing France that Saturday. 'One of the lads looks at me and says, "What are you doing?" "Sure, we'll have a look at the match." "Are you going to have a drink?" he says. "Sure, go on, we'll have one." Sure, one thing led to another and for a finish we had to send the Liam MacCarthy cup off in a taxi because it had to be in Limerick for another function that night. We never got to training.'

He survived Cregan's fury and on All-Ireland final day three months later he led Offaly on to the field against Clare. He played well that day too and his second-half goal looked like turning the game in Offaly's favour. But they couldn't finish off Clare when they were wounded and vulnerable. Clare won in a driving finish, and the defeat hurt Pilkington more than he ever thought possible. 'I remember about a year or two afterwards somebody said to me, "Your problem is that you can't let 1995 go." And it does dwell on your mind. It's not 100 per cent on my mind the whole time, it's never stopped me from going to work, it's not life or death, but it is a regret.'

One of Pilkington's closest friends on the team was John Troy. They sat together at the back of the bus; they smoked together in the dressing room toilets before matches, and again at half-time. They drank together too. Pilkington would say that his friend 'burned the candle at both ends', realizing, of course, that he was also intimate with this process and was handy with a match when the candle needed to be lit.

What all the Offaly players say, though, is that Troy was the most gifted amongst them. Others had a higher public profile because Troy was fundamentally shy and didn't do interviews. There were plenty of matches when he achieved less than Brian Whelahan or Johnny Dooley and there were even games when he achieved less than the artisans in their ranks. But his gift for hurling was an ornament on the game. In his best years his genius headlined the beauty of Offaly's hurling. 'If he had pace,' says Cregan, 'he would have been the hurler of the century.'

'He had unbelievable vision,' says Duignan. 'Once he saw it, it was done. There was no split second with him. Once he saw it – done. And great hands. He was the most skilful player I ever played with. A gem.'

His peak in the mid-1990s was short-lived but electric. When Clare beat Offaly in 1995 and Wexford beat them a year later their key strategies were clear: stop Whelahan and stop Troy. But he struggled with fitness, and without Pilkington's natural athleticism the good life took a heavier toll. McIntyre tried everything to get him right for the 1997 championship but in the end he took the field short of championship fitness. When he walked away in 2000 fitness was at the heart of his frustration.

Troy represented the Offaly myth and his experience exploded it. They weren't all like him. They couldn't have been. The way hurling had evolved you couldn't carry a player such as Troy indefinitely and hope the ball would find him. Hurling demanded a base level of fitness just to take your place on the start line.

As a team, Offaly had it. The myth was a great yarn, but it wasn't as interesting as the reality.

From Cregan's first championship as manager in 1993 to this Offaly team's last appearance in an All-Ireland final seven years later, hurling enjoyed the most democratic period in its history. During those years eight different teams contested All-Ireland finals in a game that had been dominated by just three counties for the guts of a century. Clare and Ger Loughnane defined the era; Wexford and Limerick added to the romance; Galway failed and fumbled; Cork, Tipperary and Kilkenny underwent review and reform and came again. But Offaly never left the stage. Their record of four All-Ireland final appearances in that period was matched only by Kilkenny; their tally of two All-Ireland titles was matched only by Clare and Kilkenny.

Nobody exceeded their achievements, yet they felt under-valued. The All-Irelands they won seemed to come with a nagging asterisk. The 1994 final jack-knifed and Limerick were written off in the crash. Offaly scored 2–5 in four minutes and fourteen seconds and from being five points down with fewer than seven minutes to go they ended up winning by six. They were the best team in the country that year but they had underperformed in the final and widespread sympathy for Limerick corroded respect for Offaly's achievement.

The other All-Ireland they won, in 1998, came with more hair-pin bends than any other campaign in GAA history. They changed managers halfway through the season, cheated certain death when the referee blew up early in the All-Ireland semi-final replay against Clare, and became only the second team – after Cork in 1941 – to win the hurling All-Ireland without winning their provincial title first.

How they were perceived and how they were ranked didn't bother them while they were playing – or at least they weren't about to offend their image by protesting in public. But it does concern them. Hanamy bristles at the memory of a newspaper poll which he claims ranked them as the worst All-Ireland champions of the 1990s. Pilkington seems to remember another poll that expressed similar disdain. 'I saw some paper did a ranking on all the All-Ireland winning teams. The Offaly team of the 1990s was nowhere. The Galway team that won two in a row [1987 and 1988] was way ahead of us. I reckon we'd have beaten the shite out of that team. I think even the Offaly team of the 1980s was put ahead of us. Ridiculous. The '90s team had much more hurling. You had the hardness in it, you had the skill.'

It's funny what the memory preserves and what it discards. The conclusion of the 1994 All-Ireland final was the most dramatic imaginable but, talking to Offaly players now, the 1995 final against Clare is a more potent memory. Subconsciously, winning that final would have cleared whatever debt was outstanding from the 1994 final, but more than that it would have consummated their peak as a team. They had played the best hurling of any team that summer. They had played better hurling than Clare were capable of at that stage in their development. They were odds-on favourites for the final and they lost. 'When you talk to people in Offaly about hurling,' says Pilkington, 'they'll talk about '94 for about two minutes, they'll talk about '98 for about five minutes, and they'll talk about '95 for the rest of the hour.

'I think we lost the All-Ireland after the Leinster final against Kilkenny. We beat Kilkenny and we played the best hurling of those four years under Cregan – and now, Kilkenny played very well as well. I just noticed that in training after that fellas just weren't putting in that extra step. About two weeks before the All-Ireland we had a team meeting and I stood up as team captain and I said, "Lads, I don't think we're going to win this All-Ireland because I don't think lads are pushing themselves to the absolute limit." I got criticized for it, but I think that's what beat us. We weren't prepared to step another little bit.'

That defeat has exercised Duignan's mind too, and the regret is no less acute. 'They talk about Clare's legendary fitness, but it wasn't Clare's fitness that beat us in the final, we just played shite. At the time Clare were the people's champions and we always needed an edge and we just couldn't find one for that match. It was an unusual position for us and I don't think we handled it very well mentally. I don't think we discussed it. We just thought it was a game of hurling and you go out and you play. That's the way we always played and we didn't get too wound up about who we were playing against, tactically or anything like that. We had our own style of hurling. We moved the ball fast and we didn't really bother about anybody else.

'Looking back now I often think about that day. Even when we went out on to the field. We were pucking around and the Clare team came out. I played hurling for a long time before that and after and I never noticed the crowd – ever. But when the Clare team came out that day I nearly fucking went weak at the knees with the roar that went up. And the atmosphere. There was fierce hype and noise and the bodhráns and the racket, and I think it even got to experienced players. When I played I couldn't tell you whether there was one person or 50,000 at the match. I was just oblivious to it. But that day was different, and I don't think we were ready for it.

'That was our best team by a mile. The hurling we did that year – all year – even in training was way ahead of anything we did before or after, but we didn't win the All-Ireland.'

To come back three years later and beat Kilkenny in the 1998 All-Ireland final, having lost to them in a dire Leinster final two months earlier, wouldn't have surprised those Offaly players. Their capacity to beat Kilkenny on any given day was one of the things that defined their status and underpinned their collective ego. 'I reckon that the Kilkenny team in '98 wasn't good enough,' says Pilkington, 'and I'd no fear of losing to them. I watched the video about a year ago and, yeah, there was only about three points in it with five or ten minutes to go, but I remember D. J. Carey getting the penalty and saying to myself, "There's no panic here, we're going to win this game." And it went over the bar.'

But when Offaly caught the slope of decline it was Kilkenny who dictated the gradient. Kilkenny beat them by ten points in the 1999 Leinster final and by eleven points a year later. Offaly clawed their way back to the 2000 All-Ireland final with a sweaty win over Derry and a brilliant victory over Cork; Kilkenny were waiting for them. At their peak Offaly would have delighted in the conditions of combat for that day. Kilkenny had lost two All-Ireland finals in a row, and whatever fear they carried of losing three ought to have been doubled by the sight of Offaly marching on to the battlefield.

But the great Offaly team had passed away and only its ghost showed up in Croke Park that September.

'Beating Cork in the semi-final had been a massive thing,' says Duignan. 'Offaly had never beaten Cork [in the championship] and there was a fierce over-reaction to that. There was a kind of feeling, "Whatever happens now, we've beaten Cork." There was fierce celebrating for a couple of days. In terms of the reaction of the players and the public it was way over the top.

'We were over all that before the final but we were getting on a bit and we'd made a big effort against Cork. I was injured all the time. It was game, treatment, more treatment, a game. No real training, just the odd bit here and there. Whelahan was the same, and there were other lads. It was getting near the end. Johnny Dooley's knees were at him big-time, Joe Dooley was getting on, and Hanamy was gone.

'Our plan was if we can be there with Kilkenny with twenty minutes to go the pressure will get to them. Hurl away, hurl away, stick with them, even if they get four or five points up. Keep at it, keep at it. We felt if we were within three or four points of them with twenty minutes to go we'd beat them. We felt we'd finish stronger and the fear of losing three in a row would choke them.'

The plan, though, was still-born. By half-time the game was over. At the end thirteen points separated the sides. The final annihilation.

On the way back to the banquet in the team hotel that night the players had no idea how they would be received by their supporters, but they would have feared the worst. Over the years the players knew what a tough audience their supporters could be and they had just suffered their third hiding against their greatest rivals in fourteen months. They braced themselves. 'I often felt that lads would have a hero status in other counties,' says Duignan, 'but there was none of that in Offaly. It was what you were expected to do. You're from Banagher or Birr, you hurled for your club and you hurled for the county. And the lads wouldn't be long telling you that you were fucking useless. Players would be going around like big men in other counties, but you didn't get that in Offaly.'

That night in Jury's Hotel, though, the team was wrapped up in a huge embrace. When Offaly lost the 1995 All-Ireland final some of those with tickets shunned the post-match banquet in the team hotel; after the 2000 final the room was packed. As the players entered each one received a standing ovation. 'There was disappointment,' says Duignan, 'but there was no great depression or resentment or bitterness. It was very strange. There were people I knew who would be giving out even when Offaly won, but there wasn't a word out of them. Going around the county in the week afterwards there were people coming up to me saying, "Ye were great ambassadors, ye've had a great run." It felt like a celebration of the team.'

They had been a celebration of hurling, and hurling had rejoiced in them.

By the way, a year after he quit inter-county hurling, Johnny Pilkington quit smoking. Where else would you get it?

4. Love in a Cold Climate

I

By 1997, early-morning training sessions were a popular accessory for any hurling team with ambition. It was the fashionable way to say you cared. In general Kerry's hurlers were comfortable with their place outside the mainstream, but just this once management wanted to dress them up like everybody else. They had drawn Clare in the first round of the Munster championship and they knew that some of Clare's training sessions would be illuminated by the day's first light. So the Kerry management called an early training session one Saturday morning for Banna Strand. Not at dawn, mind you, but at the civil hour of eight o'clock.

Two showed up.

John Meyler was the Kerry manager and Eddie Murphy was his assistant. Murphy had been stuck in Kerry hurling for ten years, as a player first and then as a coach, and he would have been prepared for anything. He turned to his friend with a consoling thought. 'Don't worry, John,' he said. 'When Roger Casement landed here there was nobody to meet him. At least we had two.'

After five years on a hard road that Kerry team was running on empty. They had reformed to make themselves competitive, but then hurling suddenly changed at a rate that their metabolism couldn't accommodate. The revolution had promoted counties from the fringe of hurling's elite, but it had condemned those counties beyond the fringe to an even more marginalized existence. By 1997 Kerry hurling was gasping, lapped at the back of the field, unable to go with the pace.

'Early-morning stuff?' says Murphy. 'We were lucky to get them at night.'

In 1891, twelve years before Kerry won their first football All-Ireland, they won their only hurling title. The names of those Ballyduff players are honoured in a plaque on the perimeter wall at Austin Stack Park in Tralee, a little head-stone to an achievement long since buried. A team photograph exists for every All-Ireland winning hurling team except for Ballyduff. Not even that much was left for posterity.

Kerry became a football county with a hurling neighbourhood. Nine parishes in the north of the county faithfully turned out nine senior hurling teams. Pockets of hurling blossomed elsewhere from time to time, but those flowers were growing wild and sometimes the soil turned against them. The hurling area of North Kerry was the walled garden.

After a couple of bad beatings in the Munster championship in the late 1970s Kerry ran for the cover of the B championship and stayed there until 1987. By then Murphy had left his native Cork and thrown his lot in with Kerry. He was a hurling blueblood by birth. His father, Willie 'Long Puck' Murphy, had won five All-Irelands with Cork and, true to his breeding, Eddie had worn the red jersey as an under-age player.

The Kerry team he joined were makeweights in the Munster championship. They gave Limerick a fright in 1989 and rattled Waterford three years later, but in other years they took a hiding and one year they slipped into Division Three of the league. Murphy, though, was a fanatic and an optimist.

'There was latent talent there,' he says. 'If Kerry players really took it seriously, if they had the ambition to make the grade at county level, to be known outside their parish – that was the key thing. A lot of the Kerry players were happy to be known within the confines of their own parish. How many Kerry players had the ambition to be known at Munster level, at All-Ireland level? They had seen Kerry teams for years being subservient to the major counties. They probably had no wish to get out of that.'

Without achievable goals, though, where could ambition come from? Life as a Kerry hurler came with a certain fatalism as standard. Mike Casey was blooded as a seventeen-year-old, before he'd even played senior for his club Ardfert. He quickly learned the rhythms. 'Fellas got sick of it, of course they did. Going out and getting beat and getting beat and getting beat. But at the start of the year you went away out again. You kind of said, "There's few enough that's playing and if we're not playing there's nobody playing." Things usually started off fine. Fellas trained away for the league and maybe we'd win one or two matches, but then somebody would give you a big beating. The Christmas break would come and then it was hard to get fellas back out in the New Year. That's when you knew you were a weak county.'

But behind it all lurked a loose conviction that they could be more than they were allowing themselves to be. Con Roche, a former Cork hurler and All-Ireland winner, was imported from across the county bounds to coach the team in the mid-1980s, and when he finished another Cork man, Tom Nott, took his place. In the idiom of the GAA, outside appointments are the recognized shorthand for ambition. But something was missing. Roche and Nott brought their technical expertise but it wasn't enough just to improve the Kerry players as hurlers. The challenge was greater than that.

Meyler was different. There was nothing glamorous about his appointment. He wasn't famous or sought-after, but he had hurled for his native Wexford and was sub for Cork when they won the All-Ireland in 1986. He was a winner. He won eight senior championships with St Finbarr's in Cork and captained their footballers to win an All-Ireland. Before he went to UCC he had scarcely played any soccer, but before he left he scored a hat-trick in the final of the Collingwood Cup, the inter-varsity tournament. Before long he tried his luck with Cork Alberts in the League of Ireland. That was the kind of guy he was – undaunted. He had confidence and drive and an earthy way with people. As Mike Casey once put it, 'He'd talk to Our Lord himself.' Casey meant it as a compliment. Meyler's manner didn't wash with the Cork hurlers in 2002 when he was a selector in the year of the strike, but it worked in Kerry.

Murphy knew Meyler from UCC, and when Meyler got the Kerry job he had no hesitation hitching his wagon to the train. 'Meyler would have a natural arrogance within himself that comes from success,' says Murphy. 'Every successful man has it – an inner arrogance, an inner confidence. You have to have supreme confidence.'

Five turned up to Meyler's first training session, but he didn't take it personally and he refused to be deterred. Soon the players came and management got to work. In the worst of the winter months they went to an indoor equestrian centre near Tralee. Meyler vowed to make them fit. Then he set to work on their heads. As a player Meyler had been aggressive, committed and unbending, and as a coach this was his template. He expected the players to have his attitude and his cussedness, but that took learning.

One day in his first season Kerry had surrendered badly to Wexford at the opening of a new club pitch. Meyler was furious. He shut the dressing room door and opened fire. When he finished he noticed that a gallery had gathered outside. The new dressing room had a door but no glass in the windows. 'Meyler delivers verbal tirade as hurlers routed' was the headline in the *Kerryman* newspaper a week later. The law had been laid down.

In Meyler's first winter they reached the quarter-final of the league for the first time ever. Tipperary came to Killarney on a wet Easter Sunday and were made to hustle for their nine-point win. Nobody took any notice. Nobody suggested that Kerry were coming. The match was a footnote. They were a footnote. Out of our sight, though, Meyler had closed the gap between dreaming and believing. By the time they travelled to play Waterford on the last Sunday of May 1993, Kerry had trained 120 times. For the Kerry hurlers it was an all-time record.

Kerry hadn't won a match in the Munster championship for sixty-seven years, but they knew Waterford were vulnerable and they knew they were ready. 'A week and a half before the game I went down to watch Waterford play Kilkenny in a tournament,' says Murphy. 'I took notes, copious notes — about ten pages of A4 pad. We were training the following night in Austin Stack Park and I said to the players, "We'll beat Waterford." And that's not being wise after the event. I felt we'd beat them. They weren't going well and I felt they were there for the taking.

'Meyler is very good in the dressing room. He has good presence in the dressing room. The players were fired up for it. Basically, for the first time ever a Kerry team didn't afford the opposition any respect. That was the big difference. They went at Waterford from the start. Waterford got a goal in the first minute. People might have said, "Same old story." But we had Waterford sussed. The key was putting Mike Shea on Noel Crowley. He was the fulcrum of their team but he was actually one-sided. We told Mike Shea to take him to his weaker side the whole time. Crowley was a great war-horse for Waterford and he was a good player, but Mike Shea would upset a parish. He was tough, and by Jesus he led by example that day. We had our homework done. We had a good team, good solid players who were fit for once. And we had got inside their heads. You've got to give these guys ambition. If you get Kerry hurlers on your side they can move mountains for you.'

Mentally, they were bolshie enough to tough it out. Waterford pulled five points clear after half-time but Kerry held on tight. A great goal from Christy Walsh brought them back into the match and a lucky goal from a long-range free by D. J. Leahy gave them impetus. By the finish they were three points clear, 4–13 to 3–13.

'When the final whistle went it was the most incredible feeling that I'd ever felt,' says Murphy. 'It was like utopia. We were nobodies who had come from nowhere. It was the greatest feeling of our hurling life. We felt we had achieved something out of the ordinary, something that would compare to any sporting event that year.'

There were no television cameras there to capture the sensation. No footage exists, not even on a home movie tape. Who would have bothered? Only a couple of hundred Kerry people had travelled to support the team, but after the final whistle they turned into a mob and colonized the pitch. Soon they stormed the dressing room. Order was called for Liam Cotter, vice-chairman of the hurling board, to sing 'The Rose of Tralee'. He sang the same verse twice. Nobody cared. Then disorder reigned again. Murphy did a radio interview in the showers. Meyler cried. 'There were herds of people in the dressing room,' Murphy continues. 'The heat was like a sauna. It was harder in there than out on the field. Going home we were hanging out of cars and everything. It was unbelievable.' The party continued in Murphy's house that night. One of the neighbours complained about the noise, and at about three o'clock in the morning Gardai called to the door. 'When they saw me they recognized who I was and the first thing they said was, "Congratulations." They came in and had a cup of coffee.'

The feeling lasted a couple of weeks. On the morning of the semi-final against Tipperary they went for a puck-around in a field in the Golden Vale near the hotel where they had stayed the previous night, and Murphy remembers the local kids looking for autographs. 'It made our players feel important for the first time in their lives. They felt like stars. The same day Tipperary brought us back to terra firma. They beat us by 4–21 to 2–9. The defeat to Tipperary put us back. There was a chasm in standards that day. The difference in pace was frightening. Deep down we were hoping for a respectable performance, but the game was over at half-time. It was a lousy feeling.'

That was the oppressive reality. In hurling, the gaps grew wider the further you travelled from the elite. Football had different conditions. Acquired strength and athleticism and the applied wisdom of sports science brought a levelling of standards. You could still tell the gifted players from the competent ones, but a team of well-trained, well-motivated, ambitious players could bring their artisan's competence to the highest level and compete. That was the nature of the game. Over the last few years Limerick, Fermanagh and Westmeath had started off from a place in football's pecking order that Kerry's hurlers would have been intimate with and made themselves major players in the championship.

Realistically, that dream wasn't available to Kerry's hurlers. Their player-base was too small, the skills deficit was too big. They had half a dozen players who would make it on to any county panel but no more than that. 'If the All-Ireland was run on a divisional basis North Kerry would have a good whack off it,' says Murphy. 'That's the way I'd put it to you. You're dealing with a few clubs in a five-mile radius. My old club in Cork city, Bishopstown, would have a bigger pick than Kerry, numbers-wise.'

Waterford were a shambles in 1993 and Kerry were prepared more professionally than at any time in their history. Kerry could not have won under any other circumstances. After Clare in the mid-1990s, though, none of the elite teams was ever that badly prepared again. Limerick were undermined by disharmony in 2003 and Kerry put the heart across them in the qualifiers, but they had waited ten long years for that chance.

Under Meyler, though, they kept reaching up. Secretly, they fancied themselves against Clare in the 1994 Munster semi-final but froze on the day and took a beating. They picked themselves up for the league and won promotion that winter to Division One. The next time they met Clare, in October 1995, they were hosting the All-Ireland champions in Tralee. A presentation was made to Ger Loughnane and Anthony Daly before the match and local school children formed a guard of honour to greet them on to the field. And then Kerry beat them.

'That was our first ever match in Division One,' says Murphy, 'and there was great euphoria afterwards. We got a standing ovation coming off the field. Obviously Clare were on the tear and they probably weren't focused, but they didn't want to lose either. They didn't want to lose to Kerry anyway. I remember Ger Loughnane's speech to us after the game. He was talking about playing the big counties and he said, "Keep the fuckers down – keep them down."'

Over the winter Kerry took up arms against the big

counties. They walked away with a few ribs of Offaly's hair and some of Waterford's but there were no more scalps. They led Tipp by four points at half-time and lost to Kilkenny by just four points; Murphy says that the Kilkenny manager Nicky Brennan 'jumped for joy' at the final whistle. But they couldn't save themselves from relegation and after that the team lost its stomach for the hard climbs.

'The last two years, 1996 and 1997, were a bit of a downer for us,' says Murphy. 'There was a bit of dissension in the background. A bit of hassle as such. Meyler didn't leave under the terms he would have liked to have left. He gave five great years to Kerry, but it didn't end up great that time. We left of our own accord but I suppose the majority felt that we'd brought the team as far as we could.'

Numbers at training were small before the 1997 championship match against Clare in Ennis. The consequences were unavoidable. 'I remember in the Queen's in Ennis that day – in the backyard of a pub – Meyler made an impassioned speech before the game. There was pride at stake. There was no such thing as victory, just pride. And we lost by twenty-four points. I remember going up to Ger Loughnane after the game and apologizing for it, and Ger said, "Ah, it was a game anyway."

'Meyler and myself would be two proud bastards. We'd eat steel before we'd lose a game like that. We knew our time was up. The Clare game couldn't come and go quick enough.'

Murphy never lost his fanaticism or his optimism. Over the years he has coached every Kerry team from U-14 to senior. For three years in a row he served the U-14s, U-21s and seniors all at once. A few years after Meyler left he answered the call to work with the seniors again.

He knew what glory was because he had tasted it once. But it wasn't for the glory.

II

Sean McGuinness closes his eyes like a seanchai, to give his mind's eye a better view. Stories pass his lips like the next breath, each once presented as a little piece of theatre, his voice lifting and fading to light the set. 'Wait'll I tell ya,' he announces, and the curtain goes up.

'The first night I went down Hugh Dorian said to me, "McGuinness, have you any sense?" He put his hand out and he said, "Look, there's County Down." He had his thumb out to the side and he said, "That's the Ards peninsula. And you see that nail on the thumb? That's where the hurling is. That's all you have. You're not right in the head coming down here." '

And a great barking laugh rolls up from McGuinness's chest as if he was hearing the punch line for the first time.

His story and their story never lost its romance. Hurling has changed so much that it may never happen again, but it happened once. Before the great revolution Down rose up, a bonfire of insurgency many miles from hurling's great pasturelands. From three clubs they produced a team that contested two All-Ireland semi-finals and survived for three years in Division One of the National League. Before Clare arrived this was the height of sensation.

When McGuinness took over in the autumn of 1989 his native Antrim had just contested the All-Ireland hurling final; Down had escaped from Division Three of the league and were without an Ulster title since 1941. Whatever way you measured the distance between them it amounted to a gulf. Down had escaped Division Three before but were invariably recaptured; three spells in Division Two had yielded a total of one point. They had decent players but they didn't have harmony, and without harmony they couldn't have a team.

Before McGuinness arrived the only thing that the three Ards clubs could agree on was their contempt for the county board and the certainty that nobody on the peninsula could unite the county team. Club rivalry was circular and bitter. It used to be said that when Ballygalget and Ballycran players went to the pictures in Portaferry they bought their popcorn in different shops on either side of the cinema. When McGuinness walked into the Down dressing room the divisions were mapped out in simple geography: players from each club sat along a different wall.

Yet the community was so small that bloodlines crisscrossed the clubs. The Down full-forward Martin Bailie from Ballygalget had cousins in the other two clubs; the Down selector John Mallon had nephews in all three. When Granny Coulter died in the summer of 1992 training had to be cancelled because it was a family bereavement for fourteen of the panel. If McGuinness could reach deep enough, the fundamental basis for reconciliation was there.

But first he had to knock their heads together. 'There's an old Belfast saying,' he says. '"There's no point in buying a dog and barking yourself."' Players can't remember what McGuinness said on his first night at training, but they can hum the tune: 'Right, lads, I'm not taking any mucking about here.'

Before he could lay the foundation he had to move the earth. On the week of his first home league match the Portaferry selector arrived at training and informed McGuinness that his club's players wouldn't be available because of their upcoming game in the Ulster club championship. McGuinness sacked him as a selector on the spot. Portaferry held an emergency meeting the following night and the selector contacted McGuinness to tell him that the club had reversed their position. The new manager said fine, but the team was now picked and all the Portaferry players would be subs.

'At two o'clock one Portaferry player was in the dressing room,' says McGuinness, 'and at about ten to three the rest of them walked in – this was for a three o'clock match. So I ran the three of them out and I said, "If you're not all here on Tuesday night for training I'll get you suspended by the board." I had no authority to say that, but I said it anyway. Everybody from Portaferry was watching because they've seen these boys come in late and then they've seen them walk out again. They had to walk across the pitch in order to get out. We were beating Meath by eight points that day with a few minutes to go and they got three goals to beat us. I felt like throwing myself in Strangford Lough. But it was the best thing that ever happened. They could see that this fella wasn't going to take any shit.'

Their first away trip was another window into the prevailing culture. They stayed overnight and McGuinness gave them permission to walk downtown and have a pint, providing it was only one pint and on condition that they were all back in the hotel by eleven o'clock. By the time McGuinness went to bed at a quarter to three only five of the panel had returned. Looking back, he had been forewarned. He'd been round to one player's house to ask why he wasn't travelling and his wife had said that he hadn't come home from the last away match until Tuesday. He was grounded. 'The next day I hardly said a word before the match. Afterwards I never said a word. The following Tuesday night we put in a good hour and a half and I brought them into a semi-circle. Let me tell you, I gave them my tongue. And if any of them dropped the head I said, "You're not even man enough to look me in the eye." Then I took them in and before we got into the showers I gave them another tongue-lashing. There wasn't any more bother.'

The Down players knew enough about McGuinness to understand that he wouldn't bend. What they didn't necessarily know would only have confirmed their first impression. He grew up on Divis Street, off the Lower Falls in west Belfast. It was a tight community of about fifty houses on the only Catholic street on that side of the Falls. The Sarsfields GAA clubhouse was at the corner of the road but there were no green fields nearby so they learned their hurling on the street. The club had a reputation for fielding hard teams and they were comfortable with that.

Sarsfields did better at football than at hurling, and in general Belfast was a football city. McGuinness, though, was a hurling man. Injury ruined his playing career, but in 1983 he was elected as a senior selector with the Antrim hurlers and before he knew it he was manager. The other two selectors were from rival clubs in north Antrim and this elevated McGuinness to the status of compromise candidate.

Three years later fewer than 300 people were in Croke Park to witness Antrim losing by just five points to Cork in the 1986 All-Ireland semi-final. It was Antrim's best championship performance in over forty years. An *Irish Press* journalist, who had written in his preview that Antrim had no right to be there, was hunted from the Antrim dressing room afterwards by the sharp stick of McGuinness's righteousness. 'I was always known as a straight fella,' he says. 'I said what I thought.'

The Down hurlers knew this too.

There were things, though, that McGuinness had to learn about the psyche of the hurling community in the Ards. What turned the clubs in on themselves was their sense of isolation. Travelling south to play any of the mainstream hurling counties was, to use McGuinness's atlas, 'a two-day camel ride'. None of the routes into the Ards peninsula was a main road; they were narrow and twisting. McGuinness remembers driving out of Greyabbey on one bad winter's night, travelling along a road that was flanked by Strangford Lough on one side and a lake on the other when a wave somersaulted from the Lough and over his car. 'It scared the living daylights out of me. I went down there and told them what had happened and they all started laughing. They said that happens all the time. "It doesn't fucking happen in Andersonstown," I said.' When Ards people said they were going 'across the water' they didn't mean travelling to England, they meant taking the ferry across the Lough to Downpatrick. This sense of separation was mirrored in the attitude of the county board: they felt unloved and disregarded, utterly dependent on themselves.

'The hurlers always complained about being the poor relations,' says McGuinness, 'and they were. When I went down first the jerseys they had were five years old. I rang Donal McCormack [county board chairman] and told him. He said they never asked for new jerseys. "Well," I said, "I need jerseys. I need everybody to get two pairs of togs and two pairs of socks." "No problem," he said. Those boys never got tracksuits in their lives. So I said to the boys, "See, if you stay up in Division Two I'll have new tracksuits for you and new bags." They couldn't believe it. I said, "I'm telling you." I said to Donal, "See, if we stay in Division Two I want you to arrive with the stuff, open the boot of your car and you'll be like Santa Claus. It'll break that whole feeling that was there between the hurling clubs and the county board." He arrived down the following week with Puma King boots, which were the best boots you could get

at the time – £94 a pair they were. The boys couldn't
believe it. There was a kind of us-and-them thing between
the hurling people and the board and I thought we broke
that whole thing down.'

The hurling people in the Ards had other things to contend
with, too. The Troubles didn't intrude directly on their daily
lives but occasionally they had to cope with terror and devastation. The Ballycran clubhouse was burned to the ground
by Loyalists in 1974, only five years after it was completed.
They won the Ulster club championship that year and
restored their clubhouse with volunteer labour and wilful
defiance. Both achievements ranked side by side.

Over the years the arsonists kept returning. Ballycran
suffered more than the other clubs, but no club was spared.
The 1980s were relatively quiet, but at the beginning of the
1990s the Ballycran clubhouse was burned down twice and
Ballygalget suffered the same fate. According to Des Fahy, in
his book *How the GAA Survived the Troubles*, the paint wasn't
even dry on the 1991 restoration of the Ballycran clubhouse
when it was razed again fewer than twelve months later.

The proximity of the clubs to the Loyalist town of New-
townards made them vulnerable. Nobody was ever injured
in any of the attacks, all of which took place in the middle of
the night when the clubs were deserted. But after the 1992
attacks Loyalists issued a general threat against anyone working on GAA halls or buildings. Some Ballycran members
couldn't live with the risk and walked away. And still, the
clubhouse was rebuilt.

McGuinness's parents were burned out of their house on
Divis Street in 1969. There were some things about life in
the Ards that he didn't need to learn.

The clubhouse attacks, though, were at odds with the
general mood of relations between the two communities in

the hurling areas. Mostly, people got along. A Protestant, Norman Thompson, once played in goal for the Down hurlers, and a Protestant landowner sold Ballygalget their field when some Catholic farmers wouldn't part with their land. He only asked that they wouldn't fly the tricolour while he was alive and for a year after he died. He was still expelled from the Orange Order but the club respected his wishes, and when he passed away hurlers carried his remains on one leg of their final journey.

When Down won the Ulster title in 1992, the significance of the victory crossed cultural divisions. 'I remember we got a letter from the Lord Provost of county Down [the Queen's representative],' says McGuinness. 'And a wee bit at the end: "I really admire Noel Sands [the Down captain]. I remember having to chase him out of my pheasant garden when he was chasing pheasants with a catapult."' You can imagine the laugh when McGuinness read that yarn in the dressing room.

All these years later the fun they shared is more vivid in McGuinness's memory now than the matches and the triumphs. The nicknames were like something out of children's books: Blob, Hog, Twah Sheets, Kirby, Noddy, The Hunter. 'I used to ring up the lads and the wife would answer and you'd say, "Is Noddy there?" And she says, "Noddy? Who's Noddy?" I couldn't remember their real names half the time.'

The long bus trips were a pantomime. Joe McCrickard, hurling chairman in McGuinness's time, used to be leaned upon to tell his ghost stories. And then the singing would begin. In school they had all learned songs from the musicals and some of the lads were typecast for life. John McCarthy had played Colonel Von Trapp in the school production of *The Sound of Music*, and when the jukebox was revved up on the bus McCarthy wasn't allowed to play any other part. 'The

Hog, big Danny Hughes, was a desperate case. Danny used to do "Oklahoma". "The farmer and the cowpoke should be friends . . ." Hugh Gilmore [Twah Sheets] used never to shut up. He sang Wolfe Tones numbers from when he got on the bus to when he got off. Then Gary Savage [Gazza] would start up: "Do you wanna be in my gang?" He thinks he's Gary Glitter. He could be asleep on the bus and somebody only had to start singing and he'd jump up.'

The team wasn't young when McGuinness took over but age was no barrier to longevity. It was all about thrift. Every penny was minded. Old pennies, new pennies. Some players attempted retirement and failed. The group dynamic that McGuinness had created was so powerful that it was easier to stay.

After the 1992 season Gerard McCoulter, the full-back, tried to make a bolt for it. He was thirty-two and weary of the grind. When Ballygalget won the Ulster club championship in 1975 he was a fifteen-year-old sub, and on it went from there. McGuinness rang the house to try to coax him back. 'His wife answered the phone. "I'm looking for Gerard," I says. "Sure, you'll see him at training," she says. "Nah, nah, he says he's finished." "What?" she says. "I couldn't listen to him in the house. He'll be sitting here saying, I wish I was around at that training. I'll make sure he's there," she says.' Three years later Coulter won his second Ulster championship and captained Ulster in the Railway Cup.

The triumphs were precious. When they beat Antrim in the 1992 Ulster final it was their first victory over them for twenty-one years in any senior competition. There had been signs of a breakthrough the previous year but nobody believed it could happen until it did. 'I'll always remember sitting in Sands' pub [in Portaferry] – this was before the championship – and I said to wee Noel, "You'll lift the Cup this year and you and me will dance on Nana [Sands'] bar that night." So I'm sitting at the bar after the Ulster final, and I don't drink. But every time I turned around my glass was full of whiskey. Mrs Sands kept filling it up and myself and Sandsie did a tap dance on top of the bar.'

Cork beat them by three goals in the All-Ireland semi-final but Down stayed with them for the guts of an hour and there was no disgrace in defeat. Down hurling had always been on the map, but among the hurling states it was like Alaska – distant and remote. That day they were at the centre.

'There were hurling officials on the team bus going to Croke Park who had been hurling officials ever since there had been a hurl held in Down, and they were crying on the bus with emotion. I had to say to them, "Get away out of the road, you're going to upset these players." We stopped on the way home in the Carrickdale Hotel and there were 600 people at a reception. Down had won the football All-Ireland the year before and all them lads were there, but nearly to a man the Down team that won the football All-Irelands in 1960 and '61 were there. Sean O'Neill was dressed head to toe in his Down tracksuit and you'd want to see the flag he had.'

The other great days were in the depths of winter. In McGuinness's time the league started in October and Down were always ready. When the big teams were dozing before Christmas, Down picked their pockets. They survived in Division Two in McGuinness's first year and won promotion to Division One for the first time ever the following year. For three years they held tight.

They had victories over Dublin and Laois at a time when both of those counties were competitive in the Leinster championship. They beat Offaly three times too, once early in 1995 when they were the reigning All-Ireland champions. Two of those wins were in Offaly, one in Tullamore, one in

Birr. McGuinness felt they were brought to Birr to show them who made the world. 'And we did them by more that day. I said to one of the Offaly boys coming off the field, "That big pitch really suited us today."'

Beating Kilkenny in Nowlan Park in March 1993 trumped all their achievements in the league, though. The way the league had panned out the winners of that match would qualify for the quarter-finals and the losers would be relegated. Kilkenny fielded their strongest team of that campaign, naming twelve of the players who had won the All-Ireland final six months earlier and another, P. J. Delaney, who would be a star of the 1993 final six months later. Yet Down prevailed. With three minutes to go they were three points down. From the bottom of their hearts they dredged four points without reply and at the final whistle it was 1−12 to 1−11.

McGuinness was snatched from the celebrations and brought up to the RTE radio commentary position for a live interview on *Sunday Sport*. 'I'm at the top of the stand,' he said, 'but I can't feel my feet. I'm walking on air.'

On the way home they stopped in a hotel outside Portlaoise where they often ate on their journeys down south. They had stayed there the night before, and by the time they walked into the lobby for their evening meal the hotel manager had assimilated the significance of what had taken place in Nowlan Park. 'He walked in with a bottle of champagne and he said, "Right, lads, it's an open bar for the Down panel."'

They lost their place in Division One the following winter and failed in a play-off to get it back in the spring of 1995. That summer they regained their Ulster title, but McGuinness had already decided that his sixth year would be his last. His team were on their last lap. A year after he left they were relegated to Division Three, and the following year they couldn't get out of it. 'We stayed three years in Division One and I think trying to stay up burned us out.'

They had never burned so brightly, though. All these years later you can still see the light of those days.

5. '98

At 7.15 p.m. on the evening of Friday 7 August an advance party of Clare supporters arrived in the lobby of the Limerick Inn. Eight of them, two wearing county jerseys. By the middle of the evening their number had swollen to a hundred or more, from a babe in arms to a man in his eighties and all life in between. A fax from a listener read out on Clare FM during the week had urged supporters to congregate at the hotel, where the Munster Council was meeting to decide Colin Lynch's fate. The replayed Munster final had been consumed by a blaze of bad temper and Lynch had been seen striking a match. Clare screamed that it was a stitch-up. The fax reflected the mood of embattlement and solidarity.

Shortly after 8 p.m. Ger Loughnane arrived, accompanied by the Clare county board chairman Robert Frost and county secretary Pat Fitzgerald. Loughnane paused outside the door of the hotel to explain to waiting journalists that Lynch's grandmother had been taken off a life-support machine that afternoon and in the circumstances Lynch wouldn't be attending his personal hearing. The removal of Lynch's grand-mother from a life-support machine could have been either good news or grave news, but this clarification was neither sought nor given. Grave news was assumed.

To a rapture of cheers Loughnane walked through the lobby and into an area adjoining the boardroom where the Munster Council was sitting. Two Gardaí, one in plain clothes, sat inside the door of the waiting room. Gerald McCarthy, the Waterford manager, arrived shortly afterwards to answer charges of abusing an umpire. He decided not to join the Clare delegation. The battle lines had been drawn in another sphere of combat but they were clearly portable and effective elsewhere.

The Munster Council secretary, Donie Nealon, was one of the officials sitting in judgement that night. In his report to the Munster Council convention seven months earlier he had rejoiced that hurling was in 'a golden age'. That night nothing could have been further from his mind. The most poisonous summer in the modern history of the GAA was unfolding in his jurisdiction. That week, during an incendiary broadcast by Loughnane on Clare FM, the Munster Council had been publicly accused of malpractice, prejudice and vindictiveness.

Once again, Loughnane was taking hurling to places it had never been before.

What you must remember is that this volcano had been rumbling since the summer before. It started with Anthony Daly's acceptance speech after Clare's Munster final victory over Tipperary when he said that Clare were no longer 'the whipping boys' of Munster. Beating Tipp in a Munster final was a hugely significant milestone for Clare, and Daly's assertion wasn't designed to cause offence to the vanquished. However, it struck a chord with the Tipp PRO Liz Howard and she took issue with it in an article she wrote for an U-21 match programme a couple of weeks later. She used the phrase 'conduct unbecoming to hurling', and when Loughnane eventually discovered the contents of Howard's article he decided to retaliate in print.

Daly has no doubt that Loughnane's intervention was cal-culated to deflect the heat away from him, and Loughnane went to great lengths to achieve his objective. In an open letter published by the *Clare Champion* newspaper Loughnane criticized Howard and went on to detail his experience of Tipp's arrogance. He accused the former Tipperary manager Babs Keating of ignoring accepted protocol by failing to visit the Clare dressing room after Clare beat them in the 1994 championship; Keating, who resigned immediately after that match, claims that he couldn't gain entry past the throng of well-wishers. Loughnane also said that before the 1994 match the then Clare manager, Len Gaynor, had told the Clare players how little Tipperary thought of them. '[He] drummed it into the Clare players, inch by inch, leading up to the 1994 Munster championship,' wrote Loughnane. 'Session after session: "Tipp think nothing of Clare. 'It's only Clare,' they say."'

Loughnane met Howard at a match in Thurles, after her article was published and before his response was conceived. They had known each other as children in Feakle and Loughnane used to go hunting with Howard's father, Garrett. All of this, as well as a flavour of their meeting in Thurles, was conveyed in the *Clare Champion*. 'When you started your "We're not arrogant in Tipp" refrain,' wrote Loughnane, 'I wanted to tear strips off you.' He didn't, though. He sharpened his pen instead.

Gaynor was a former Tipperary player who was now the Tipperary manager, and Loughnane's remarks appeared only weeks before Clare were due to meet Tipp in the 1997 All-Ireland final. Gaynor didn't deny the accuracy of the comments attributed to him by Loughnane, but they had clearly been intended to motivate the Clare players and were never intended for public consumption. Loughnane had broken that confidence and had wilfully raised the ante from Howard's article.

Worse was to follow, however, during *The Sunday Game* broadcast on the night of the All-Ireland final. Eamon Cregan, the former Limerick player and Offaly manager, was a regular analyst on the programme that summer and he gave his appraisal of the match in the studio while Ger Canning stood by to interview Loughnane in the Clare team hotel. All-Ireland finals are often disappointing, but for the only time in the 1990s the 1997 All-Ireland final had been the game of the year, and Loughnane had been gushing in his praise in all of his post-match interviews. Cregan was more circumspect, however, and when the coverage switched to the team hotel Loughnane opened fire on Cregan. At one stage he accused Cregan of 'looking after his job in Tipperary', where Cregan was a building society branch manager at the time. It was a stunning and withering outburst.

In an interview over the following winter Loughnane conceded that he shouldn't have mentioned Cregan's work or personal life. However, that tone of contrition had evaporated by the time Loughnane wrote his book. 'If I have a regret it's that I didn't go further,' he wrote. 'I think it was totally small-minded of him. What he said didn't seem to me to be a fair judgement of the game.'

In the space of a month at the end of that summer Loughnane had revealed elements of his personality that only his players would have recognized. They knew how cutting he could be and what excesses he might indulge to express an opinion. He had broadcast and written the kind of things that any of us might say behind someone's back. Somehow, though, such openness didn't seem like a good thing.

In the case of Howard it was certainly strategic; with Cregan it was something different. There wasn't a diplomatic response which could satisfy his desire to knock Cregan back and make him see that he was wrong. He couldn't just argue with Cregan's viewpoint, he had to shove it down Cregan's throat.

At the end of his open letter to Howard, Loughnane wrote something that, twelve months later, we could clearly see wasn't just the posturing of an idle threat. 'Do not ever again,' he wrote, 'attack a Clare hurler and expect to get away with it.'

By the summer of 1998 Howard was out of the firing line. Others had taken her place.

The replay of the 1998 Munster final had a clear lineage. How far back do you want to go? In the draw for the Munster championship made at the end of 1997, Clare were paired with the winners of Cork and Limerick. By the following February Loughnane was searching for a peg to hang the year on. He speculated about another crack at Limerick and the electricity it would generate, given that Cregan was the Limerick manager now. 'I know it's criminal to say,' said Loughnane, 'but if it's Clare and Cork I think we'll be in a bit of trouble.' It wasn't that he feared Cork as a coming force, he just worried about Clare's ability to get themselves worked up for Cork. They hadn't lost to Cork in the championship for ten years, and Ger O'Loughlin was the only one of the existing panel to have experienced that loss.

They met Cork in the league semi-final and a young Cork team beat the All-Ireland champions by eleven points. Everybody smelt a rat. The general perception was that Clare had taken a dive and hadn't even bothered to disguise it. That they had trained on the day before the match; that they had trained for two hours on the morning of the match. Anthony Daly's wife Eilish had to field calls from cranks ringing the house to complain. Already, four months before Loughnane's Clare FM broadcast and the night in the Limerick Inn, there was a feeling that Clare were capable of doing anything.

The stories weren't true. They had trained on the Thursday

night as usual and they had gone to Templemore for a pre-match puck-around on the morning of the game in Thurles. They certainly weren't wound up for the match, though, and when that Clare team weren't wound up they were liable to be flat. And so they were – flat as glass.

'I remember looking over at Loughnane during the match,' says Daly, 'and the look of disgust on his face. Sometimes he could do that. If training was going very bad he might put on an attitude of not wanting anything to do with us. "Look at the state of ye," kind of thing. "I don't train ye." He was just disgusted with us. It was one of those things we were saying ourselves afterwards – Loughnane didn't even want to leave a roar off him. After the match, though, he was like a lunatic.'

The following day was a Bank Holiday Monday. They did a light training session in the morning and Daly asked Loughnane for money from the holiday fund. He planned to hire a mini-bus and take the players drinking in west Clare that night. One last blow-out before they entered the dark tunnel that would lead them to the Munster semi-final.

'I made them all vow before we got off the bus in Doolin that we'd have one good night and that would be it. I said, "Lads, we'll drink it out here for as long as they'll let us." There was five weeks to the match and I said, "We'll train like we never trained before." We kind of made up our minds that night. We were all oiled up and tongues were loosened and everyone was talking, and I remember saying, "We'll give it everything," and we did now. We trained like lunatics, and maybe that would express itself in the way we played against Cork afterwards.'

It was Cork and not Limerick in the Munster semi-final, but after the beating Cork had given them in the league and the training they'd done since then Loughnane had no difficulty getting his players to the optimum state of agitation. Daly remembers leaving the dressing room with smoke blowing out of his arse. Cork were already on the field, pucking into the goal at the Town End. The Cork manage-ment, though, had chosen to occupy the dug-out towards the Killinan End, and as the Clare players stormed down the tunnel a steward roared at Daly to go left.

'The Cork mentors were standing there,' says Daly. 'JBM [Jimmy Barry-Murphy] and Con [Murphy, Cork doctor] were there together and [Tom] Cashman was standing in front of my eye line. I let a roar at him, "Get out of my way!" and we went clean out over the rope that was there at the end of the tunnel – you were supposed to go around it. We were wired. Con told me years later that JBM turned to him and said, "We're in trouble here, Con." There's no doubt we were up for it and that's when we were at our best. We had to have a bit of cause. There was a bit of a schemozzle early on. It was more body language than anything. It was only "Fuck you," with faces on us.'

The clear impression, though, was that Clare had bullied Cork that day. Cork players felt it and weren't ashamed to admit it years later. Denying it would have been ridiculous anyway. That Cork team wasn't set up for combat, and eventually Clare pulled away.

Waterford had a different constitution and a different style of management. The feeling had grown from 1997 that one day a team would meet Clare head-on and it wouldn't be pretty. Somebody would go toe-to-toe with them at the limit of legitimate aggression and step outside the limit if that's where the battle took them. That team turned out to be Waterford.

'We [the Waterford management] went to the Cork–Clare match and we were in the Old Stand in Thurles, maybe ten seats up from the Clare dug-out,' says Shane Aherne, the Waterford trainer. 'We watched everything – now we really watched everything. We saw their antics along the sideline and we saw their antics on the field, and we basically said to the players, "Don't allow them to intimidate you – don't come back from anything. Whatever you get, give it back, and we'll do the same on the sideline."'

The Clare management were used to having the run of the sideline, to prowl and patrol. Loughnane's presence radiated so much energy that it had become an integral part of Clare's performances. The players fed off him. As manager of the U-21s in 1992 he was a picture of calm detachment, but during the senior semi-final against Cork in 1995 'he threw off the shackles', as James O'Connor put it. 'Loughnane was suddenly everywhere. He was on the pitch waving a fist in your face. That's what he should always have been doing.'

Waterford recognized the significance of Clare's sideline to the mood and tempo of their performances on the pitch and they resolved to match them. On the field Waterford were in Clare's face, and on the sideline they were too. The Clare selectors were marked and shadowed. Once in the second half the Waterford selector Greg Fives stood alongside the three Clare selectors as they contemplated a move. For a moment his audacity went unnoticed.

The Waterford manager, Gerald McCarthy, had been animated and verbose during the semi-final against Tipperary, but for the drawn Munster final against Clare he was a ball of fire. He was told by the linesman Pat O'Connor not to encroach on to the field, but after Loughnane had made a couple of incursions McCarthy made his feelings plain to O'Connor, walking in pursuit of him as he back-pedalled up the line. Late in the game, with Waterford chasing down a draw, one of the umpires mistakenly waved a Waterford shot wide and was overruled by the referee. Shane Aherne, who happened to be in the neighbourhood, was the first person on the umpire's case, but McCarthy quickly arrived and he had more to say after the white flag was finally raised.

Willie Barrett was the referee, just as he had been for the Cork–Clare semi-final. He hadn't been firm that day and his permissiveness suited Clare more than it suited Cork. Dickie Murphy, the leading hurling referee at the time, had perfected the art of allowing aggression to breathe without choking the match, but it was a fine art and Barrett wasn't a master of it. He allowed the drawn Munster final to bowl along in much the same way as the semi-final. In the belly of the match an ulcer was growing. A week later the ulcer burst.

When the Clare players reflect on the drawn match an incident of sledging frames their memory of it more potently than anything else. 'Still beating up the wife, are you?' one of the Waterford players shouted at Daly. The Clare captain and his wife Eilish had been hounded by this scurrilous and groundless rumour since their marriage ten months earlier. Daly wasn't alone in his fury. On the way home that night the Clare team stopped in Killaloe and Daly informed those players who hadn't heard the comment for themselves.

'He said it in front of seven or eight players,' says Daly. 'Fellas were violent about it. It was nasty now. We wanted to put them back in their box. That came more from the players now than Loughnane that week. He said that in his book, that he didn't need to say too much to us. I told them, I said, "Look, whatever you think of me, whether you like me or not, that's the next thing to being called a child molester."

'Now, he [Loughnane] did have a go at [Colin] Lynch "for being destroyed", and he had a go at [Ollie] Baker for running away. "You never ran away in your life," he said to him, "but you fucking ran away" – that sort of thing. He played on fellas' heads that when Waterford put it up to us physically and dirty we didn't want to know about it.'

Apart from the sledging incident, the tone of Waterford's performance in the drawn match wouldn't have troubled Clare if they had been prepared for it. In terms of physical aggression it was no different from countless performances that Clare had given. Off-the-ball stuff went on, but Clare were never squeamish about that: off-the-ball stuff went on in their training matches behind closed doors in Cusack Park. No big deal. Hadn't Loughnane prepared them for whatever the Munster championship could throw at them? Wasn't that his boast?

The problem was that Clare hadn't been psyched up for a battle, and a blow is always worse when you're not braced for it. They'd had no beef with Waterford, nothing to get mad about. After the draw, however, that deficiency was addressed. The thought of being pushed around cut to the core of their reformed identity. It smacked of the old days. For the replay Clare were braced for everything and armed to the teeth with attitude and motive.

'I do admit it was a war-like atmosphere against Waterford,' wrote Loughnane. 'It was the same on both sides. Clare went into the game like never before. It was a day to kill or be killed. The players weren't thinking about winning an All-Ireland. It was about putting Waterford down.'

Waterford players refuse to accept that they were the aggressors in the drawn match. The Waterford captain Stephen Frampton regards Loughnane's version of events as retrospective justification for Clare's approach in the replay. 'I would say Loughnane said that as a bit of psychology in that they needed a reason to go and thump us around, and so he talked them into it,' says Frampton. 'These guys are after thumping you around the first day; go out and give it back to them. I can say, hand on heart, that I don't remember being more pumped up [for the drawn Munster final] than we would normally be for a championship match. He just needed to use some kind of trick to get his guys prepared.'

Frampton was a good hurler and a tough player. Waterford had been through their share of battles in the nine championships that Frampton had played, so he wasn't a virgin soldier. But he says he wasn't prepared for Clare's response in the replay. 'We were taken completely aback by the second match. Really couldn't believe what was happening. Before the ball was thrown in I got smacked by a young greenhorn that was only starting out with Clare. He came over and gave me a good jolt with the hurley. I just looked at him and I said, "I can't believe you did that." The young greenhorn was Alan Markham, starting in just his third championship match. In his book, Loughnane says that Markham was one of the players he singled out for a galvanizing word between the draw and the replay. 'Players . . . had allowed themselves to be pushed around in the drawn game, and that was never, ever going to happen again.'

It takes two to make a war, though, and Waterford didn't stand back. Before the ball was thrown in James O'Connor broke his hurley off Brian Greene under provocation and it set the tone for their afternoon. 'I stuck out my hand to shake hands,' says O'Connor, 'and he didn't take it. Next thing I got a dunt in the back. I turned then and went to shove him away and broke my hurley off his shoulder. In fairness to Greene, I'd given him a roasting the first day. His pride was stung and he was going to try to stop me hurling. I was waving my hands at the linesman at one stage and he did nothing about it. I spent most of the game wondering should I turn around and fucking deck him.

'Fuck it, we weren't going to let them do that to us again

the second day, and it was a case of "Well, if Willie [Barrett] isn't going to blow for stuff and look after us, we're going to look after ourselves." But, look it, I'd say all over the field their backs were belting the shit out of our forwards and our backs were doing exactly the same thing.'

Barrett had lost control before a ball was even pucked. After the drawn match the Munster Council had issued strict directives restricting the movement of both management teams. Everyone was supposed to be in the dug-out, but Waterford refused to comply when they saw Clare selectors standing outside the designated area. While Barrett was trying to sort this out the four centre-fielders were lined up for the throw-in.

'The most important part of the replay was the throw-in,' says Frampton. 'You had two fellas in the throw-in for Water-ford the complete opposite of each other. You had Peter Queally, who is an aggressive and physical type of player, and you had Tony Browne, who would stay away from it. He would hurl the ears off anybody but is not interested in the physical aspect of it at all. Unfortunately he got bet around the place at the throw-in. Colin Lynch was like a raging bull, and if Peter Queally had been with him at least they'd have kicked the shit out of each other and got on with it whereas Tony didn't know what to do.'

Queally, though, wasn't the target. Browne was the player who had scored three points in the drawn match and had ruled centre-field.

Lynch's pulling at the throw-in was clearly over the ball and reckless. 'Lynch let fly three or four times but the only person he actually hit was [Ollie] Baker,' wrote Loughnane. The most cursory viewing of the video refutes that version of events. Lynch made contact with each of the other three players at the throw-in, including his centre-field partner

Baker. He didn't come close to hitting the ball. Barrett awarded a free to Waterford and took no further action. At that moment Barrett needed to assert his authority. Instead his inaction immediately undermined his authority.

'Lynch should probably – definitely – have been booked,' says O'Connor. 'When that was let go there was stuff going on all over the pitch.'

If the law was strictly applied Lynch should have been sent off for striking with the hurley, but in reality nobody is ever dismissed at the throw-in. On top of that, when a player was sent off for striking with the hurley it was often described in referees' reports as 'rough play', which carried a lesser suspension. That was a wider disciplinary issue, but it framed the context for Lynch's actions. There was so much looseness in the enforcement of discipline that he knew he could be wild at the throw-in and not be sent off.

Fewer than five minutes later the Clare full-back Brian Lohan and Waterford corner-forward Michael White became entangled in a brawl and were sent off. White caught Lohan on top of the shoulder with his hurley; Lohan swung with his hurley and missed. For what was arguably a lesser offence than Lynch's both players were dismissed.

While the Lohan–White brawl was developing into a mêlée Lynch and Browne paused for a moment on their way to the scene. In front of our eyes, about 55 yards from the Town End, Lynch and Browne struck each other across the upper body with their hurleys. It was seen by the linesman Pat O'Connor and eventually he attracted Barrett's attention. Both Lynch and Browne were booked on O'Connor's testimony. Later, in his referee's report, Barrett described the offence as 'rough play'. But it wasn't, it was striking with the hurley. If the law was properly applied both players should have been sent off.

Ultimately, Lynch was suspended for three months and no action was taken against Browne. Over the following couple of weeks it was often forgotten that there was substance to Clare's argument. Justice had been selectively applied. The fierce campaign to highlight the injustice, however, marginalized the power of rational argument.

The mayhem began with the RTE Radio phone-in programme *Sportscall* on Monday night. Listeners called to express their disgust at the scenes witnessed in Thurles the day before and laid the blame squarely on Clare's shoulders. Opinion writers on the sports pages of the newspapers quickly followed up over the following days. The President of the GAA, Joe McDonagh, privately expressed the view to the Munster Council chairman, Sean Kelly, that action would have to be taken, and a disciplinary process was put in train.

The Munster Council met nine days after the match to discuss the referee's report and a letter was sent to Lynch outlining the case being brought against him. 'You are hereby charged with repeated striking with the hurley,' read the letter. The Munster Council, however, was in a tricky procedural position, and Loughnane recognized this. The referee's report enjoys an elevated and ring-fenced status in the GAA's disciplinary process, and in his report Barrett couldn't undo the errors of his performance. The scenes at the throw-in had been appalling and Lynch had clearly been the primary aggressor. But Barrett hadn't taken the appropriate action and the incident didn't appear in his report.

What happened between Lynch and Browne five minutes later was off the ball and off camera. Barrett responded by booking both players and in the normal course of GAA disciplinary affairs higher authorities usually baulk at taking further action once some action has been taken by the referee.

Much later on, when Lynch brought an appeal to the Games Administration Committee, the Munster Council produced an eye-witness to confirm that Lynch had struck Browne with the hurley. But why wasn't the same eye-witness used to prosecute Browne?

There was a general acceptance, outside Clare at least, that Lynch had stepped way over the line of tolerable behaviour and should be punished. Nobody could deny that he was guilty of 'repeated striking with the hurley'. The manner of his prosecution, however, was full of holes and it was handled in a way which invited Clare to scream that their man had been victimized and scapegoated.

What further incensed Clare and fed their paranoia was that unsavoury incidents in the Waterford–Tipperary semi-final and the Cork–Limerick first-round match should have resulted in sendings-off and didn't. The Limerick goalkeeper, Joe Quaid, was clearly seen kicking an opponent on the ground and got away with it. In those matches the referee's report was allowed to stand and the Munster Council didn't see fit to act on video evidence.

So, Loughnane loaded his bazooka and took aim.

'I remember him saying to us, "Trust me, I've never let ye down,"' says Fergie Tuohy. 'In fairness, he hadn't let us down. And we did [trust him]. "What you read in the papers, what you're hearing, what you're seeing, I've taken care of it, trust me, trust me." After the Munster final all you did was trust the man. I didn't have any doubts at the time because you had to believe. There were people around the county had doubts but you couldn't have doubts because if you had doubts then you didn't believe in the group you were in. Even if it was all wrong, we were all going to do it together and it was going to be the right thing for us at the time. That is what we had. It was unique, what we had. He asked us to do that [trust him] and we did that. In hindsight, the whole thing was fucking crazy.'

It was normal practice for Loughnane to grant an interview to Clare FM on the week of a match, but what Loughnane had planned this time was something altogether different. The interview was scheduled for the Wednesday before the All-Ireland semi-final and two days before the Munster Council were convening to pass judgement on Lynch's case. Loughnane first mooted it with Clare FM on the previous Friday and indicated in advance the inflammatory nature of what he planned to say; they asked him to take legal advice. On the eve of the interview the national newspapers were informed of the upcoming event, and just before the broadcast Clare FM phoned GAA reporters based in Dublin so that they could eavesdrop on the interview. Though he was appearing on a local station, Loughnane wished to address the nation.

The flow of the 70-minute interview was clearly choreographed and at different times he read from a prepared script. Its content was dynamite. After legal advice two national newspapers were unable to reproduce parts of it on Thursday morning. Earlier in the week the *Clare Champion* was forced to prune a separate Loughnane interview, also on legal advice. He borrowed some of his tone and idiom from Amnesty International, some from a bar-room slagging match, and the cocktail had a mule's kick.

Clare, he said, had been treated like 'absolute criminals'. The Colin Lynch affair was 'an absolute scandal'. Lynch, he claimed, had been denied 'basic human rights'. He accused the Munster Council of hypocrisy, of improper conduct and of privately passing sentence on Lynch before his case had even been heard. He described the media, variously, as 'spivs' and a 'mob' who were leading the campaign against him and Clare. He referred to 'Gestapo' forces in the stands at Thurles, feeding the case against Lynch, and a 'Don Corleone' figure looming in the background influencing the Munster Council's business.

Most extraordinarily of all, he told a story of Robert Frost, the Clare county board chairman, overhearing three priests discussing Lynch's case in the VIP section of Croke Park on the day of the All-Ireland hurling quarter-finals. 'It went on the lines that the Clare team were tinkers,' he said, 'Loughnane was a tramp and the Clare team must be on drugs. That was the general tenor of their conversation. One of the priests . . . said that the Munster Council was going to get Loughnane up into the stand the next day and that Colin Lynch would be suspended for three months. Now, remember that this event took place three days before the Munster Council met to discuss the referee's report.'

Loughnane's legal adviser had evidently stressed the importance of not naming people in his attacks on the Munster Council. At different times in the interview Loughnane injected the phrase 'I will not name him' into his submission, evidently believing that this was an effective vaccine against litigation. However, he would then go on to identify his targets by the position they held in the Munster Council, which amounted to naming them. In the event, nobody sued.

'I remember listening to the radio thing at home and laughing my head off,' says Daly. 'We were training that night and we were all saying it. "Did you hear the radio? Oh Jesus." I remember Fingers [P. J. O'Connell] saying to me, "Did you ever hear the bate of it in your life?" and he was from the same club as [Robert] Frost.

'He [Loughnane] has to cringe when he hears that interview again. In fairness, he has to cringe. I know what he was trying to do. He was trying to back up Lynch and give a swipe back at the same time. Lynch was never anyone's saint now, don't get me wrong, but in fairness Our Lord was treated better than him.'

Whatever the players thought privately of the tactics, they were all agreed that it was a just war. If carpet bombing was the only way to liberate Lynch they weren't going to protest.

Two nights later Loughnane arrived at the Limerick Inn, striding towards a Munster Council meeting that he had no permission to attend, hoping to influence people whose integrity he had attacked on the airwaves. Nobody else could have conceived such a strategy.

A little more than half an hour after he arrived, shortly after 8.30 p.m., the evening took its most terrible twist. The RTE reporter Marty Morrissey received what he believed was clarification that Lynch's grandmother had died and reported it in a live link with the GAA magazine programme *Sideline View*. Minutes after the broadcast, members of the Lynch family called RTE to say that this was untrue. Distraught by his error, Morrissey drove to Ennis Hospital and made his apologies to the Lynch family. They accepted them graciously and Morrissey stayed for an hour in the company of Colin Lynch and three other members of the family.

Meanwhile, in the hotel, word of the affair reached the Clare delegation and Loughnane burst out through the double doors of the waiting room. 'Where's Morrissey?' he said a couple of times as he marched along the corridor and into the lobby, followed by an RTE camera and a gathering knot of supporters. In the car park his search ended with an RTE producer. 'It was an absolute disgrace that your station would put out a statement like that,' he said. 'The family are devastated, absolutely devastated. They've been phoning us from all over the place. Hasn't this family suffered enough? You have a lot to answer for putting the family through a trauma like this. Nobody here said she was dead. You must have no respect for Clare. Most of all you must have no respect for the Lynch family.' And as he retreated another crescendo of cheers rose up.

The Clare delegation had submitted a letter to the meeting stating that Lynch would not be attending but not outlining why. It said that Lynch wished to be represented by James Nash, a solicitor from east Clare. At 9.10 p.m. the Munster Council chairman Sean Kelly met Frost privately, but in their seven-minute meeting Frost would not tell Kelly the circumstances of Lynch's absence. Frost said that they would tell the meeting themselves but only if Loughnane could be present with them. They were using the information as a bartering chip. The Munster Council had no mind for trading. They rejected Frost's request and wouldn't allow Lynch to be represented by Nash. Under GAA rules a player must represent himself at a personal hearing.

At 10.20 the Clare secretary, Pat Fitzgerald, grabbed a few words outside the meeting with Jimmy Hartigan, a Munster Council delegate from Limerick. He said in a hushed voice that 'there were more important things than hurling going on tonight', but still would not reveal the reason for Lynch's absence. The whole world knew except the people who needed to know most.

At 11.50, almost four hours after the meeting began, Frost and Fitzgerald were called in and told that Lynch had been given a three-month suspension. Minutes later Loughnane walked though the crowded corridor and out the front door of the hotel, bathed again in the spotlight of a hand-held camera and questioned as he walked by an RTE reporter. He looked straight ahead as he spoke. He said that Lynch's three-month suspension had fulfilled his prophecy and on the fourth question ended the interview. As he walked into the darkness of the car park the crowd cheered him for the third time.

Offaly awaited them in Croke Park two days later. Now, that was a different story.

At the beginning of the year Michael 'Babs' Keating succeeded John McIntyre as Offaly's manager. He took over a panel whose reputation for beautiful hurling competed with their name for insubordination. When he sat before the county board interview panel Keating says '90 per cent' of their questions concerned discipline. How he proposed to establish it; how he might possibly maintain it.

Keating had walked into far worse situations in his time. It was only four years since Offaly had won an All-Ireland; when he took over Tipperary in late 1986 they hadn't won either a Munster championship or an All-Ireland since 1971. The following eight years turned out to be Tipp's most successful period since the 1960s. He finished with Tipperary in 1994 and took over Laois two years later, committing himself for two seasons. He improved them without transforming them and then walked away. Offaly, though, was a different challenge. Here was a team that had won an All-Ireland and could win another. The players knew that. They just had to get round to it. It was on their list of things to do. *Mañana.*

Keating brought Johnny Murray with him as his trainer, an army man who had ridden shotgun with him in Laois. Keating also brought with him his unique talent for raising money and making players feel enhanced by material tokens of esteem. Everything was fine at first. And then they flew into turbulence.

On the evening of the first Sunday of May, Tipperary had arranged a challenge match against Offaly in Clonmel.

Proceeds from the game were being given to the Tipperary player John Leahy, who owed a substantial five-figure sum in damages arising out of an incident in a Manchester nightclub. Given its sensitive nature, the purpose of the match wasn't openly advertised, but it was well known and it was a cause close to Keating's heart. He had given Leahy his breakthrough with Tipp in the late 1980s and over time Leahy had become a family friend.

Only half of the Offaly panel turned up. Literally. The match was delayed by thirty minutes but the numbers didn't improve and eventually Offaly borrowed some of Tipp's subs to fake a match.

There were reasons and excuses. The league semi-finals were played in Thurles that afternoon and there was an unusually large crowd of 35,000 in Semple Stadium. Roads clotted with match traffic stood between the Offaly players and Clonmel and some of them turned back when they saw the congestion. On top of that, matches from the group stages of the Offaly club championship had been fixed for that weekend – some for that afternoon. A few players were tired and sore and just couldn't be bothered with another match that evening.

'What the game was for didn't come into the equation,' says Johnny Pilkington, the Offaly centre-fielder. 'It was more an attitude: "I'm fucked if I'm going to Clonmel to play Tipperary in a challenge match and I'm only after playing against Banagher in the championship." That very Sunday John Troy was playing for Lusmagh and got hammered by about twenty points and was expected to go off then and play a challenge match.'

Naturally, Keating was furious. 'It was the most embarrassing night I ever suffered,' he says. 'Even if it was in Cork or Limerick, but it was my own town [Clonmel]. There were about 3,000 people there. I suffered on the road home that night.'

Although it wasn't reported at the time he resigned that night and it took a couple of days of intensive diplomacy to bring him back later in the week. He unloaded his anger on the players, and they patched things up. Under the surface, though, there were other fault-lines. Keating sensed that his two selectors, Pat McLoughney and Paudge Mulhare, 'didn't agree with my style of training'. The players were grumbling too. Murray's stamina training had spilled over from the winter and spring into early summer. At the end of the championship they would eulogize the work that Murray had done with them, but back in May they were grumpy. As a group they were set in their ways. They liked to be coached and trained in a certain fashion and they were used to managers coming round to their requirements.

In the middle of June they stumbled over a depleted Wexford team with a last-minute goal from Johnny Dooley, but in the week of the Leinster final against Kilkenny the fault-lines shifted. The earthquake was coming. 'I went down to play in the supporters golf classic in Birr on the Thursday before the match,' says Keating, 'and as I was going away Tony Murphy [hurling board secretary] said to me, "I'll see you at the meeting later." Now, a team meeting had never been discussed with me at training on Tuesday night. There was a coup going on behind my back, have no doubt in the world about that. I bit my tongue and went along to the meeting.'

Offaly lost a dire Leinster final by five points to Kilkenny. Throughout his managerial career and in his highly successful *Sunday Times* column Keating had a reputation for being frank and direct in his commentary, and he was no different that day in his remarks to the media after the defeat. Among other things he described the Offaly players as being 'sheep in a heap', and that phrase echoed for days. Keating assumed they'd be able to take the belt and get up. They didn't. They looked for attention.

Keating made a short speech in the dressing room after-wards, and then Brian Whelahan approached him. '"Are you aware that fellas were out drinking?" he said to me. I said, "No, Brian. I'm not living in Offaly, but you obviously are." I called for order and I said that Brian Whelahan had something to say. He lifted them out of it. He tore into the fellas who were drinking. I just said to them, "It's your team, it's not my team. I'm only passing through."'

Keating repeated his criticisms in a radio interview. Pilkington and a couple of others heard it in the car going home that evening. On the following morning Pilkington was called by Liam Horan of the *Irish Independent* for his reaction to Keating's remarks, and Pilkington didn't hold back. The players were meeting in Whelahan's pub for their post-match Monday session and the Dooley brothers, Joe and Johnny, were already there when Pilkington walked in. 'We were talking about the training set-up and we were saying we were going to have to sit down and have a meeting over this,' says Pilkington. 'We were talking about his comments on the radio and I just remember saying to the lads, "Wait till you see tomorrow's paper." And the lads said to me, "What are you after saying now?"'

Keating met his selectors and some county board officers in the Spa Hotel in Lucan that night. They discussed the match and his comments. They sketched out a team for the All-Ireland quarter-final, made plans for a couple of challenge matches and decided that a couple of players needed to be tackled about their behaviour. Pilkington was one of them.

'The meeting lasted three hours and I came out of it thinking that it had been very positive and constructive,' wrote Keating in his *Sunday Times* column the following weekend. 'Then I opened Tuesday morning's *Irish Independent* and there was Johnny [Pilkington] condemning me. I was prepared to confront Johnny and I was fully prepared to continue as Offaly manager, but around lunchtime I got a phone call from Brendan Ward [Offaly county board chairman]. I knew from his tone that it wasn't the Brendan Ward I had spoken to on Monday night. He said the mood in Offaly wasn't good.'

Keating told him to watch the evening news that night and he'd have what he wanted. He rang the RTE newsroom and dictated a statement of resignation to the sports reporter Colm Murray. The first that the Offaly players knew about it was when Pilkington took a call from Brian Carthy of RTE radio looking for his reaction. Pilkington refused to comment.

'On Tuesday evening four or five players met to discuss what way we were going to approach this,' says Pilkington. 'We met in Sid's house [Brian Whelahan]. Sid was there and Hubert [Rigney, team captain], myself, Johnny Dooley and I can't remember who else. What we said was we're all going to have to be seen as one here. We decided to make a statement fully supporting my comments.

'At this stage the county board's position was that they had sorted out the problems with Babs Keating on the Monday, according to them. Then there was a clip on the television that night of Brendan Ward saying that in the light of the way Babs had treated our players he's not acceptable. Yet, on the Monday they were keeping him on. So, in a way, it was player power.'

The poisonous Munster final replay was still twelve days away. The summer of '98 was simmering to the boil.

★

Fourteen years after his last stint as an inter-county manager with Galway Michael Bond was approached to answer Offaly's emergency. A school principal on his summer holidays, Bond was flattered by the invitation and the dubious honour of becoming Offaly's third manager in fewer than twelve months. He breezed into training and started sweeping up the mess.

'He was over in the corner of the dressing room in Tullamore togging out,' says Michael Duignan. 'Hadn't a clue who he was. I called over Joe Dooley and I says, "Who's yer man?" And he said, "That's John Connolly, the fella that trains Queensland in rugby." And Joe would be a serious fella. "You're not serious are ya?" He says, "They're after bringing him in to do a bit of training with us." None of the lads had ever seen him before so you don't think he's a GAA man. Who would you be expecting? Someone that you knew, some ex-player. We didn't know who he was until we went out on to the field.'

First impressions were bracing. 'Bond was a funny geezer,' says Martin Hanamy. 'He walked in like an army man – you know, all this really fucking sharp talking. I never heard of him in my life and nobody else did either. But he was very good. I was late that night and he made me do twenty press-ups, which I actually admired him for. He was laying down the law straight away.'

They had eleven sessions during his first fourteen days in charge and everyone pledged their hearts to the cause. The sessions were all ball work, which was just the way the Offaly players liked. They were humming. Then they played Kilkenny in a challenge match in Nowlan Park.

'They absolutely annihilated us,' says Bond. 'At that stage, if I could have turned the clock back I'd have run. It was desperate.'

He didn't change the plan, though, and by the time they met Clare in the All-Ireland semi-final they had a confidence that nobody outside the panel would have shared. Clare arrived in Croke Park distracted and diminished from a week of megaphone diplomacy. Lynch was suspended, and so too was Brian Lohan; Clare had no quarrel with Lohan's punishment, although they decided to 'retire' his number three jersey for the term of his suspension. They said it was a mark of respect to Lohan, but it was widely perceived as more insolent back-chat to the authorities.

Loughnane was suspended from the sideline too, banished to a seat in the stand. Under the letter of the law he wasn't allowed on to the field for the pre-match puck-around either, but Loughnane refused to concede that ground. The Croke Park authorities were informed that they wouldn't be given the correct Clare team to announce over the public address if Loughnane wasn't allowed to mingle with his players during the warm-up. Eventually the authorities blinked.

'I remember he came out on to the field,' says Tuohy. 'There were cameras flashing. Did he look at them? He just stared. He strutted. People were saying he wasn't allowed on the field. The next thing he walked out on the field.' It was an entrance in step with the week.

Clare led by four points entering the last ten minutes but ended up needing a last-minute free from James O'Connor to draw the match. At the time it seemed like a compelling climax. It was nothing. The replay thirteen days later reduced it to a footnote.

In that match, with two minutes of normal time and about another three minutes of stoppage time remaining, referee Jimmy Cooney blew for full time. Clare were three points up and on the attack with Barry Murphy in possession on the 21-yard line, out wide towards the sideline under the Hogan

Stand. They weren't in a comfortable position, though. Clare had led by ten points four minutes into the second half but Offaly had conjured two goals in one five-minute spell, and having scored two points in a row before Cooney's premature whistle they were the team with momentum.

In Jim O'Sullivan's book *Men in Black*, Cooney explained his mistake. At some point in the final quarter he booked a player from both teams and before play resumed his attention was drawn to an off-the-ball incident. He had stopped his watch but in his anxiety to get the ball rolling again he had neglected to restart it. After a while he noticed what had happened and started using a second watch, making an informed guess that three minutes of stoppage time would be sufficient. The problem, though, was that his back-up watch had been programmed for a thirty-minute half.

The Offaly players immediately sensed that something was wrong. Brian Whelahan had just asked the linesman, Aodhan MacSuibhne, how much time was left and had been told that there were four or five minutes to go. So he was the first to confront Cooney, and others followed. Cooney looked over at one of his linesmen, and he put up five fingers. Before Bond arrived brandishing his meticulously managed stop-watch, hanging on a string around his neck, like a miraculous medal, Cooney had realized his cock-up.

The possibility of restarting the match, however, was quickly lost in the ensuing chaos. Security men were already by Cooney's side, directed to usher him off the field, and Croke Park officials arrived in convoy to fast-track the process. Kerry and Kildare were due to play in the All-Ireland U-21 B hurling final directly afterwards, and before Cooney even reached the tunnel the Kerry players had swept on to the field.

A few minutes later Offaly supporters started to climb over the fence at the Hill 16 end of the ground to begin the sort of demonstration that had never been witnessed at a GAA match before. When the invasion finished there were about 2,000 Offaly supporters on the pitch. They resisted every entreaty over the public address until the Offaly chairman Brendan Ward addressed them from the podium of the Hogan Stand, three-quarters of an hour after their protest began. He said that the Offaly county board would do everything in its power to secure a replay, and with that assurance the crowd slowly dispersed. At 6.30 p.m., more than ninety minutes after the final whistle, the last dregs of the protesters moved away.

Offaly and Clare players mingled in the Croke Park bar afterwards, most of them convinced that the outcome would be allowed to stand. Clare immediately took the line that the referee's decision was final, a position they had practised at length throughout the Colin Lynch affair. In his post-match quotes Michael Duignan quickly borrowed some of Loughnane's idiom, asserting that a rematch was the only way that the 'human rights' so close to the Clare manager's heart could be protected in this case.

Over the next twenty-four hours turmoil visited both camps. Offaly went from Croke Park to their base in the Spa Hotel in Lucan, and Bond called a team meeting. He emphasized the possibility of another match the following weekend and proposed a training session for Sunday after-noon. At this point Duignan exploded.

'We had a few pints [in Croke Park],' says Duignan, 'and we went back to the hotel for a bit of grub. It was probably one of the most heated meetings that ever took place in the Offaly team. I was fairly centrally involved. I had a fair lash at the players – this, that and the other. Everyone got a lash. The county board weren't spared either. There was serious talking.

'It all revolved around going training the following day. I was making the point, "We're gone out of the fucking championship. It's a bit late to be worrying about training now. Ye're all getting excited about the thing – why weren't ye half as excited a couple of hours ago?" Something along those lines, except the language was a bit more flowery. It was heavy going. Johnny P [Pilkington] was in the middle of it, Billy Dooley was in it.'

'That meeting was a disaster,' recalls Pilkington. 'There's an unwritten rule about meetings: there should never be alcohol in anybody. I said, "I'm not going training tomorrow, I'm going to wait until the decision." And Joe Dooley said, "No, we have to get back into this." And Duignan got all hot and bothered. The meeting broke up after about twenty minutes.'

That evening Marty Morrissey tipped off Loughnane that RTE had been put on stand-by for a rematch the following Saturday in Thurles. The Clare players had been drinking for a while at this stage but Loughnane sought out Daly in the hotel bar and the drinking was supposed to continue at a more moderate pace. On the following morning Loughnane went with Fitzgerald to a Games Administration Committee meeting in Croke Park; both counties made their submissions and, as expected, a rematch was ordered. Loughnane had instructed Mike McNamara to take the players for a run in Belfield while the meeting was being held. Loughnane didn't want him to go too hard on the players, but McNamara had other ideas.

'It was about half ten or eleven o'clock in the morning,' says Michael O'Halloran, 'and, you know yourself, fellas were dying, and fellas would have been drained anyway from a hard game in Croke Park and the whole build-up and the tension. Now you've got to get up with drink inside you and go around Belfield – and he [McNamara] was in foul humour. He ran the shite out of us. We went back to the hotel for a shower and then faced a bus journey to Ennis – three or four hours. The mood on the bus was shite. I remember I got off in Limerick with Sandra [his wife] and she said to me, "You barely said goodbye." Everyone was down. It was going to be very hard to lift it.'

One hope they clung to was that Lynch would have his suspension reduced, making him available for the third match against Offaly, as a kind of quid pro quo for Clare's gracious acceptance of a rematch. On the following Wednesday the Management Committee heard Lynch's appeal in Croke Park but nothing was changed. His suspension stood.

An incident involving Duignan and David Forde in the second match only heightened Clare's continuing sense of grievance. Duignan had clearly struck Forde with the hurley and should have been sent off. The offence came at a time in the match when Offaly were three goals down and seemingly beaten. In *Men in Black* Cooney concedes that he allowed the circumstances of the match to cloud his judgement. 'My first instinct when I saw it was, "Send him off,"' said Cooney. 'But as I came over to him – and this is the truth – I looked at the score and I said, "Oh God, there are nine points between them and if I do this I'm only making trouble for myself. It will be gone out of Offaly's reach at so early a stage and they'll only get negative in their hurling." That's the way I read it and I decided to leave him on. But it was probably a wrong decision. It was. He should have gone. I saw the incident clearly. If David Forde had stayed down I would have had no hesitation in putting him off, but David jumped up and ran off.'

In Thurles the following Saturday Loughnane pinned a photograph of Duignan to the wall of the Clare dressing room. Years later they often shared an RTE studio as *Sunday Game* analysts, but on that afternoon Duignan was the fan for Clare's fire. The flames rose and fell again. Clare were spent.

Duignan was prepared in any case. 'Michael Bond called me aside before the game and he said, "You can expect a very hostile reception out there. The crowd could get on to you." I said, "Michael, are you fucking serious? That doesn't happen at a hurling match." For the first twenty or twenty-five minutes there was fierce booing every time I went near the ball. It didn't matter then because I was ready for it.'

All of the momentum was with Offaly now. Their public had embraced the team again after the despair of mid-summer. Duignan remembers crowds of 1,500 or more showing up at training during the Clare trilogy when normally fewer than a hundred would come to watch. For the third match in Thurles the Offaly following was enormous. 'From about half eight in the morning to half ten or eleven there was a constant stream of traffic going to Thurles through Birr,' recalls Pilkington. 'Constant horn blowing, flags out the window. We went down a bit later and arrived in the square in Thurles and there was Offaly people all over the place. The day itself was fantastic. It was the first day that I understood all the talk about Munster final day in Thurles. You had Clare and Offaly people in the square and it was just a big party.'

The match was a classic. Offaly produced their best performance since the 1995 Leinster final and on the day it was too much for Clare. They lost by three points having led for just one minute of the seventy. To have put up such resistance, though, was another assertion of the qualities that had made them champions. They were unbending. That's what made them. They were overthrown, but they hadn't surrendered.

Had they regrets? Of course. They still regarded themselves and were seen by many as the best team in the country that year, but they hadn't won the All-Ireland. 'It's the one that got away, there's no question about it,' says James O'Connor. 'Coming off the field after losing the third game to Offaly was probably one of the all-time lows.

'The whole year was a bit of a circus. I remember at the end of it thinking that it was nice to go back to leading a semi-normal life in the sense that it just seemed to be one controversy after another. I would feel that we didn't get a fair crack of the whip in the media . . . I think the players deserved better than they got in the media. I think we suffered from some stuff that Ger did – the whole radio thing and all that. Maybe the perception of the team suffered as a result, and I think it pissed off some of the players that we were portrayed as a dirty team. We were a hard, physical team, we were aggressive, but we needed to be that way and if we weren't playing that way we wouldn't have achieved anything like we did achieve . . . Maybe if Loughnane was doing it again he'd have done things differently that year.'

In interviews later and in his book, Loughnane repeatedly said that he wouldn't change anything. O'Halloran wonders, though. 'It wasn't good that year; you could never say it was. I know to this day if you met the likes of Ger [Loughnane] and Tony [Considine] they would say that '98 was the greatest year and we had to do what we did and they wouldn't regret a thing. Deep down I think they would. A slight problem in Clare at that stage was that Loughnane was too powerful and you'd nobody really strong enough on the county board or anywhere else to say anything, to just rein him in and say, "Leave it." It didn't happen, and maybe it should have happened.'

The Lynch affair kept rumbling on in the corner of the public eye. The club championships in Clare were stalled until Lynch's suspension expired so that he wouldn't miss any matches, and the Munster Council brought a complaint about Loughnane's interview on Clare FM to the GAC.

Three days before Christmas the GAC delivered their verdict, which was critical both of Clare's tactics and the Munster Council's procedures. Loughnane, however, highlighted one line in the verdict as vindication for his campaign: 'We acknowledge that there have been some inconsistencies in the manner in which some disciplinary matters have been dealt with by the Munster Council and that Clare may have perceived grievances.'

Offaly won the All-Ireland, avenging their Leinster final defeat to Kilkenny. At board level during the summer Offaly continued to express their opposition to the back-door system where the beaten provincial finalists returned to the championship in the quarter-finals; and then, in just the second year of the new system, they became the first back-door champions.

The smoke and fumes cleared. Talk of a Golden Age went quiet.

6. DJ & BW

At the end of 1990 *Gaelsport GAA* annual carried a couple of photographs from the Leinster hurling semi-final between Offaly and Kilkenny. An action shot covers nine-tenths of the page, but the image that screams for attention is shoe-horned into a strip at the top. It shows the electronic scoreboard overhanging the old Nally Stand, which reads: Cill Chainnigh 0–1 Uíbh Fhailí 3–7. The match hadn't even reached half-time. Kilkenny's lonesome point was D. J. Carey's first score in the senior championship. From a free.

It wasn't enough to spare him, though. After half an hour he was replaced. Before the match one of the Kilkenny selectors had warned Carey that if he didn't 'get stuck in' they wouldn't be slow to take him off. It was reported that Carey had carried a groin injury into the game and afterwards that was cited as the reason for his substitution, but all these years later he says plainly that he got 'a bit of a roasting that day'. Carey was five months short of his twentieth birthday, skinny and coltish, his strength scrambling to catch up with the late spurt in his growth. He was passing through that difficult phase between nascent star and star. There were still people who forced themselves to question what their eyes insisted to be true.

Carey's marker for most of the half-hour was Brian Whelahan, nineteen years old and making his first start in the championship too. The ball followed Whelahan like a lap dog that day, as it often would for the next fifteen summers.

Offaly won by sixteen points and Whelahan hasn't forgotten how well they played, but apart from that what he remembers most is the feeling of exhaustion. After Carey went off he was out on his feet. Martin Hanamy quit his easy chair in the corner and allowed Whelahan to take a breather for five minutes; in the second half Whelahan asked him to do it again. The days when the game was played at his pace would come later.

That match was staged at the edge of the nation's sporting consciousness. Ireland and Egypt shared a goalless draw in the 1990 World Cup that afternoon and only 17,436 could resist the pull of that spectacle to be in Croke Park. Kilkenny and Offaly were meeting for the ninth time in ten years. What was there to miss?

The two greatest hurlers of their generation started out together as a footnote. A premiere without a red carpet.

On the Monday night after Offaly won their first All-Ireland title, in 1981, Pad Joe Whelahan was in the County Arms Hotel in Birr for the homecoming. He had been an Offaly player for thirteen seasons but early that year they had let him go. Surrounded by the rapture of the evening, Pad Joe felt a little sorry for himself and got talking to Damien Martin, the Offaly goalkeeper and a friend since childhood.

'I won't win any All-Irelands now,' Pad Joe said to Martin, 'but Brian will win everything in the game.'

The object of his father's hubris was just eleven years old. He was small and light but his gift wasn't just in Pad Joe's eyes: it was plain for the world to see.

Pad Joe's prophecy has been fulfilled. In the spring of 1999 teachers from Crinkle, a village outside Birr, asked Whelahan if he would mind putting his trophies on display to help raise funds for the school. Whelahan agreed, and on the day of a

National League match in Birr a back room in the County Arms was cleared for the exhibition. They charged £2 for adults, 50p for children, and his subjects streamed in to view the crown jewels, leaving £2,000 in their wake. Everything in the game, like Pad Joe said.

Providence is part of the story. Brother Vincent Costin arrived in Birr just a few weeks before Whelahan was born in 1971. The Pilkingtons, the Erritys, the Hennessys and the Cahills were already walking the earth, though their legs wouldn't have been steady yet. The most gifted generation of hurlers ever born in the town would grow up listening to a man who would cherish their talents like gold. Birr won a senior county championship in 1971 and didn't win another for twenty years, when all of those infants were young men and Whelahan was captain. That year Brother Vincent was transferred back to Cork, his teaching and his influence deposited like minerals in the soil.

Maybe Whelahan wouldn't have turned out any differently. Maybe he didn't need the gentle wisdom of Brother Vincent. Maybe what was in him would have burst out anyway.

The Presentation Brothers used to live on Moorepark Street in the town, near Whelahan's house. They had a shed with a huge wall that faced on to the road and that was the companion for Whelahan's practice. He remembers coming home from training and going straight out to the wall. That was just what he did. For teenagers growing up in Birr the counter-culture was taking a flagon of cider to the Mill Island, a park in town. Whelahan let that pass.

His early life, though, wasn't without its complications. He was only seventeen when his son Aaron was born and suddenly life had thrust the ultimate responsibility on him. 'It was a huge thing at the time. It's something that you never legislate for. Mary [now his wife], obviously, was the person most affected at the time. We were lucky enough that we clicked and hit it off. At the end of the day, whether we got married or not, Aaron would have been a major part of my life, one way or the other.'

When he first started playing for Offaly, Pad Joe was always around, which didn't make it hard and didn't make it easy. Brian was still under sixteen when he made the minor panel in 1987; his father was manager of the team heading for two All-Irelands in a row. For the first round of the championship Brian expected to play against Wexford but they picked one of his clubmates instead. Another lad would have brushed it off and consoled himself with the certainty that time was on his side, but it wasn't in his nature to tolerate second best. Eighteen years later so many other experiences have shaped his career but still that one survives every audit, stored and quoted. 'I was gutted. I made up my mind after that game that I was never again having the feeling of being a sub on a team. It wasn't going to be my fault that I wasn't picked. I was going to do everything I could, and that's why every time I went out on the field I was very hard on myself.'

Two years later his father was manager of the seniors when Brian was sent on late in a doomed All-Ireland semi-final against Antrim. Still a minor, they pitched him into the half-forward line to fight a blaze that was already out of control. People said he was only there because his father was the trainer, but when the switch was made Pad Joe was at the other end of the field. The other selectors made the substitution.

The fact was that Whelahan didn't need anybody's patronage. His status came directly from his talent and the values that governed it. He was captain of Birr by the age of twenty simply because he was already the dominant influence in the

dressing room. Precocity had wiped away the usual conditions.

With the county it took a little longer, but not too long.
On the Offaly team of the 1990s Martin Hanamy and
Joe Dooley and a couple of others sat at the top table, but
Whelahan was always in the chair. On match days he never
stopped talking from the moment they stepped into the dress-
ing room to the moment they left it. 'You wouldn't neces-
sarily be listening to what he was saying,' says Michael
Duignan, 'but he'd build up the atmosphere.'

Every Offaly manager expected the benefit of his opinion,
and there was nothing to be gained from setting down limits
to the dialogue. When Eamon Cregan was looking for a
centre-back in 1994 it was Whelahan who convinced him of
Hubert Rigney's worth. Others may have thought it, but it
was Whelahan who made it happen.

That Offaly team developed a reputation for hard living
which has survived despite evidence that it was only strictly
true about a handful of players. Whelahan bristled at some of
the stuff his teammates did. Other players would just quietly
look after themselves, but that wasn't his way. He was the
conscience for the group.

'Down the years I was the one that it would never be said
to until after a match that something had happened because
I would go totally spare. I wouldn't care who he'd be. If I
found out that somebody had acted the shite before a match
I couldn't handle it, no way. I wouldn't do it. My attitude
was that the night of the match and the following day were
yours. I enjoyed myself them couple of days. But not before
a match.

'There were a couple of incidents that I didn't hear about
for about a year and a half afterwards. Nobody would say
because they'd know my reaction. I would have challenged

lads on different issues but only in the context of the good of the team. Having said that, the group of players we had were the players that we were going to have success with. Whatever was going on in-house I would have tried my best to make sure whoever was involved was still back in training. We all knew what we could achieve when we were right and that's why maybe more stuff was tolerated than in other counties.'

As a player, Whelahan bestrode the 1990s: the second half of the 1994 All-Ireland final; all of the 1995 Leinster final; the third Clare match in 1998; the second half of the All-Ireland final that year; the All-Ireland semi-final a year later; a league quarter-final against Cork in Thurles ten years ago when Whelahan and Brian Corcoran traded pucks, up and down, as if it was a clay court rally at Roland Garros.

Offaly players will tell you that John Troy was the most gifted ball player on their panel, but on the field Troy couldn't give the team what Whelahan did. 'When he was hurling well,' says Duignan, 'I didn't think we could be beaten.' By 2001 Troy was gone, with six or seven uneven years at the top behind him. Whelahan ploughed on.

Because he was so good, people looked for holes. Centre-back was his position for Birr, but he was never really comfortable there with Offaly and that was held over him like an asterisk. 'Offaly always had a strong physical presence at centre-back,' says Whelahan. 'People like Pat Delaney and Hubert Rigney. I wouldn't have anywhere near the physical presence of those fellas. Nothing was coming through the centre while Hubert was there. I wasn't that type of player.

'But I went in centre-back during the All-Ireland final in '94 and that worked out and I've always regretted not going in centre-back in '95 [against Clare]. Hubert was injured going into the game and for the last ten minutes he was in agony – though Hubert would never tell you. Fergie Tuohy got a few points, and if Offaly had rejigged it a bit I maintain that wouldn't have happened.'

Clare had a plan for Whelahan in that All-Ireland final, just as Wexford had a plan for him in the Leinster final a year later. The Clare manager Ger Loughnane believed that if Clare could hold Whelahan and Troy they would win the match. Whelahan had experienced this before. In the 1992 All-Ireland U-21 final against Waterford he was imperious in the drawn match. With Offaly a couple of points down he was sent forward in the last few minutes in an attempt to rescue the game. He pointed a 65, caught the puck-out and drove it over the bar to force a draw. For the replay Waterford programmed one of their wing-forwards to spoil Whelahan and relieved him of all other duties. The 1995 All-Ireland final, though, was the first time that such pressure had been applied to him in his senior career.

'That was something I found very amusing. I usually watch very little to do with the '95 All-Ireland; I remember the game obviously from my own memory. I remember walking into someone's house one evening and seeing a video that Clare brought out and one of the Clare players was talking about what they were going to have to do to stop me from hurling. And I was thinking, "Why in the name of God would they have to be making plans like that for? I'm a back." Then I saw after the Wexford game in '96 that Clare had helped Wexford with a plan for me.

'I copped on very quickly what they were doing in '96. They pucked balls straight down on top of me. I was marking Larry Murphy. Three or four balls came down and Larry was just basically making sure that the ball went in and the man that was picking it up was Larry O'Gorman. When the ball was in mid-air he was gone in behind me. He ended up getting a point or two – or maybe a free or two from those puck-outs. I was on to the midfielders at the time to come back. It was a game plan that worked very well for them.'

Those game plans were the greatest compliment Offaly's opponents could have paid him. He wasn't short of awards either, though it wasn't long before his status had no more to gain from gongs of recognition. He finished up with four All Stars to DJ's nine by the end of 2004, but the difference didn't mean anything. The irony was that nothing clarified his status more emphatically than the controversy caused by his omission from the All Star selection in 1994. He was the Texaco Hurler of the Year and the Players' Player of the Year, yet in a tangle of bureaucracy and ignorance he was left off the All Stars team. The integrity of the scheme was so mortally wounded that the scheme itself was immediately reformed.

Ultimately he didn't need the awards as much as the awards needed him.

Hurling changed before their eyes. Carey remembers showing up for his first National League game in the autumn of 1988, straight from the minor panel. He was sitting in the dressing room in Nowlan Park an hour before the game, the first man there. Half an hour later Christy Heffernan was the second player to arrive. 'And then,' says Carey, 'fellas started sauntering in.'

There was no question of a pre-match puck-around somewhere else or a structured warm-up on the field. The value of stretching was only barely acknowledged. Dermot Healy was the Kilkenny coach when Carey started and he was a forward-looking and enlightened fellow. He knew a bit about stretching, but the older players knew nothing. 'I remember doing a calf stretch,' says Carey. 'In them days you held another guy on the shoulder and you didn't push but your back leg was flat on the ground. I knew how to do it but I was doing it with Ger Henderson, and Ger had me three-quarters of the way across the field before anyone told him you're not supposed to push.'

The rules of engagement changed though the fierceness of the combat remained the same. Because of his talent Carey was always a target for assassins and bullies. For all he has been through he is remarkably intact. He fans out his hands and miraculously all of his fingers are in a position to respond, defiantly straight after all the belts. Every finger on his left hand was broken at least once and the hurling glove he wears in matches on his right hand protects the thumb and finger that will forever be held together by pins.

There was never a time when he was just another player and never a time when he didn't face the threat of blackguarding. In a match for St Kieran's College once he had his nose broken in an off-the-ball incident: three players surrounded him and one pulled on his face. He got over that, but another assault more than ten years later forced him to add a face guard to his helmet. 'It was a dirty belt actually. It was in a club game and a guy was rising the ball just in front of me. I was behind him, ready to shield him, and he came up with the top of the hurl and straight into my face. I got the belt around the jaw and it pushed up the bone and I lost my sight in one eye for three weeks. I was lucky. If it was an inch more . . .'

The game got faster and backs became more sophisticated – which didn't mean that they laid down their arms. Carey and his breed had to find a new way to survive in the jungle. 'When I started off as a forward you'd get room to run out and pick up a ball because the fella would stay a couple of yards behind you and hope to block you down. Nowadays the back wants to get out ahead of you and win the ball, and they're skilful enough to actually take that ball in full stride and drive it the length of the field. But in the old days – I'm talking about the late '80s and into the '90s – there was very little holding and dragging and pulling. That's a big part of the game now. It's gone very similar to football that you give the lad a little tug to hold him back.

'Your role changed too. Kilkenny needed me to be scoring in the '90s, they needed Billy Fitzpatrick in the '80s, they needed Eddie Keher in the '70s. I'm only picking out those players: Cork and Tipp needed their guys as well. And everyone else worked for them. Now, everyone must be capable of creating and taking scores. Now, you must win your own ball. If you looked at earlier times you had the Mick Crottys and the Pat Delaneys and the Billy Purcells and these guys creating scores and Eddie Keher finished them – which he would do every time. Nowadays it's different.'

Nothing altered, though, as much as the quality of fame. Guinness arrived with their sponsorship and their smart billboard campaigns and it coincided with Clare's breakthrough, the explosion in attendances and the expansion of television coverage. The championship suddenly had romance and variety, and hurling became sexy in a way that it never had been before. For players with status and the spirit of enterprise there had never been more opportunities to exploit their fame.

When he was in school Whelahan had no career path in mind, just a vague sense that hurling might stand to him in the outside world. And so it did. After his Leaving Cert he took a job with Tullamore Frozen Foods as a helper on the lorries. As his celebrity grew they promoted him to a sales rep. That was the kind of job good GAA players had been offered for generations, but it was also the limit of what GAA celebrity could do for you if you weren't prepared to take a risk.

So Whelahan did. In 1994 he acquired a pub in Birr. That September Offaly won the All-Ireland for the first time in nine years and for the rest of the decade Offaly and Birr were never far from centre stage. As a safety net he kept his job as a rep for a few more years, but the pub continued to prosper and in the autumn of 2003 he broadened his interests, taking over a newsagent's in the middle of town.

At first Carey followed a similar path. From the factory floor at Cadbury's he moved to a job on the road with Three Rivers Oil until he decided to take the big leap. At twenty-three, the same age that Whelahan had been when he became a pub landlord, Carey set up his own business: D. J. Carey Enterprises.

In the beginning there were teething problems. At one time he had fifteen people working for him, but the operation had grown out of proportion to its prosperity and he was forced to pull back and restructure. Now he employs nine people selling nearly 500 cleaning and detergent products, and business is booming.

Carey knew that his fame offered him opportunities beyond his business. His popularity was huge. Kids loved him. He played with a charisma and a personality that other players didn't have. He scored goals, he went on daring solo runs, he filled the stands with a buzz. In Ger Loughnane's description he was a 'wizard'. He was the GAA's first superstar.

As a GAA player, though, his name was virtually worthless as a commodity. He was asked to give coaching clinics and present medals, and under the GAA's rules he wasn't entitled to ask for a bob and he wasn't entitled to receive a bob. 'The odd day,' he says, 'you'd get petrol money or diesel money, and then more often than not you'd get a trophy that's probably worth a hundred quid or more – which is big money. But you'd prefer to have got the money's worth because you're after going there. I don't care, unless you're born into money a few bob for everyone comes in really handy.'

When Kevin Moran's sports agency Proactive organized an Irish launch in 1997, Carey was one of the GAA players to make an appearance. At the time GAA players weren't at liberty to accept payment for endorsements, but his presence was a clear statement of Carey's attitude. 'Someone has to pioneer the thing,' he said at the time. 'Someone has to be first. We'll do it.' A couple of years later, when the Gaelic Players Association got off the ground with an aggressive players' welfare agenda, Carey became involved and went on to be president. Where he stood on these issues was abundantly clear.

When the GAA finally relaxed its rules nobody was in a better position to benefit than Carey. By the end of 2002 he had hired the services of Barbara Galavan, whom he describes now as his manager. She had worked with U2 for seventeen years and had handled such diverse celebrities as Bill Whelan and Ronan O'Gara. When Carey brought out a video of his life in the summer of 2003, she produced it for him. When a company wants Carey for a golf day or a personal appearance, they contact Galvin. She quotes the price and handles the negotiation.

From an early stage Carey knew that there were downsides to his high visibility. If he continually said no to demands on his time the word would soon have spread and the massive goodwill towards him would have soured. But saying yes wasn't sure-fire protection for his reputation either. Carey was taking GAA celebrity to places it hadn't been before, and small minds struggled to process it.

'I can always remember I was asked to do an opening in

Kilkenny six months in advance, and as it turned out it was the Friday night after the All-Ireland final. We won the All-Ireland final – I think it was '92 or '93 – and Pat O'Neill [Kilkenny and Young Irelands teammate] had the cup on the Friday night. Now, I'd been asked six months previous to do this opening, but the commenting was, "Oh, he's gone for the money" – and I didn't get one penny for it. Now, I had won the All-Ireland as well as Pat but, you know, that was the comment – "He's gone for the money."'

Carey grew up with O'Neill and Charlie Carter. They were born within two months of one another, attended the same class in school, played on the same teams all the way up through the age categories, and in 1998 all three of them finally started an All-Ireland senior final together. But by then they weren't especially close. The circumstances of Carey's life removed him a little from everyday life in Gowran, where he had grown up and lived until a couple of years ago. In every GAA community in the country there are GAA heroes, but Carey wasn't an ordinary hero, and one price for his extraordinariness was a degree of separation.

'No doubt about it. You know, I would have many, many, many, many friends, but in terms of close friends there wouldn't be that many. I would always like to think that I'm courteous to everyone but I've always felt that there's a certain distance you have to keep because you don't want to be quoted. You know, because you'll always be asked, "Well, what do you think of yer man?" And if you make a comment on him it will be relayed back, truthfully or not.

'You make sacrifices. I wanted to be the best I could possibly be so I've made decisions to not drink, not smoke, not go to pubs – that sort of thing. So yes, there would be a certain distance: there would have to be from my point of view a certain distance. I would know of top players in different sports and they would keep a lot of stuff to themselves as well because they don't want to be quoted or misquoted.

'Some people would be seen around the place far more than others. Like, next Sunday night, win or lose the [2004 Kilkenny] county final, I'll be back in Dublin that night because the two kids will need to be got out to school the following morning. Whereas the rest of the lads in Gowran will be celebrating or commiserating.'

The first glimpse we got of Carey's double-edged relationship with his public came in early 1998 when he announced what turned out to be a six-week 'retirement'. Those close to him could see it building up. In the dressing room after Kilkenny lost the 1997 All-Ireland semi-final to Clare, people heard him say that he was finished. When his club Young Ireland's lost the county final a couple of months later he uttered the same thought in public, and people dismissed it as a knee-jerk reaction to crushing disappointment. In November, though, he rang the county board chairman John Healy to say that he was going, telling him to expect a letter confirming his decision and asking him to make the announcement. Healy requested a meeting and after four hours of talks persuaded him to take more time. At the end of the following January Healy received the phone call he was dreading, and within two weeks Carey's retirement was the sensation of the GAA world.

What emerged were circumstances we could never have envisaged and a picture of Carey we had never seen before. Everything we knew about him was superficial. The Carey we saw on the field was confident and unflappable and assured; the Carey we met under the media's soft light was quietly spoken and uncontroversial. But retirement bared him – the insecurity, the sensitivity, the need to be wanted.

People had got in on him. Rumour-mongers. Gossips. Knockers. What was worse was that these people were known to him. Not neighbours, but close enough to home. Eventually he rationalized it to himself as jealousy. 'Money,' he said, 'seems to be the root of a lot of things.' At the time, though, he couldn't see that. He reached that understanding of the situation much later.

'I done it because I was playing a game I loved and constantly being knocked,' he said five years later. 'People were spreading stories. I was supposed to be fighting with this lad, that lad and the other lad. I was continually being knocked for something I wasn't being paid to do and putting in such a huge effort . . . But then you kind of learn. You learn that it comes down to a few . . . They'd never say anything to my face. They would always try to be as lick-arse to my face as they could be. Once or twice I confronted one or two. It was a waste of time, purely and simply because you're giving in to them.'

He returned to the team before the end of the 1998 league, persuaded by trusted friends that he was crazy to quit in his prime. But his comeback didn't stop the rumours. All kinds of fictional stories circulated about what kind of 'deal' Carey had done with the Kilkenny Supporters Club to smooth his return. They didn't have any slush fund for such a purpose. There was no deal. Like he said, it all came back to money.

Carey's antennae were sensitive to all kinds of things. On the morning of the Kilkenny press night before the 1998 All-Ireland final one tabloid ran a news story quoting an unnamed county board official running Carey down. Another guy might have shrugged it off, but there was a gap in Carey's defences which allowed this stuff to hurt him. He was incensed and confronted all of the leading board officers, all of whom denied it. That evening at the press night Carey rubbished the story, describing the source as a 'phantom county board officer'. Days later a letter arrived from the reporter providing detail which verified the story. What was he to think?

Carey's relationship with his public was more complex than any of us had imagined. The adoration was the sound we heard in Croke Park and it was the sight of kids swarming him after matches, but it wasn't the only response to his status and his talent.

In the spring of 2002 he quit again under the weight of injuries, and in mid-summer he returned under the weight of pressure. When he rejoined the Kilkenny panel not everyone rejoiced. Radio Kilkenny invited their listeners to text their comments and as far as Carey was concerned it was a signal to attack. 'It wasn't nice what went on,' he said a year later. ' "D. J. Carey should be sitting in the stand with all the other oldies." D. J. Carey is this, D. J. Carey is that. Blah, blah, blah and blah, blah blah before we played Tipperary. And yet, after the All-Ireland, it was, "Jay, doesn't he have to put up with an awful lot." I was a great fella then, you see. "Wow, doesn't he have to put up with an awful lot? Isn't he a great fella to be able to put up with it all and get on? Look at the amount of pressure he was under in an All-Ireland semi-final taking a 65." I've been taking 65s all my life. There's no pressure in that. That's not the pressure in my life.'

More rumours surrounded him than any other GAA player. A couple of years ago a story swept the southern half of the country that he was dying of cancer. He knows how it started. Suffering from stomach pains, he was sent to hospital in Waterford for tests. The tests took place in the same area of the hospital that housed the oncology facilities. Somebody saw him there and his cancer was born.

It was often rumoured that his marriage was over, and

eventually those rumours became true. This began a new and sinister phase in Carey's fame – tabloid intrusion. With a couple of fleeting exceptions the Irish tabloids hadn't applied the same news values to the lives of GAA players as their British stablemates did to professional footballers and showbiz celebrities. A Meath footballer was once reported in the *News of the World* to be a 'love rat', but the reaction to the story was so hostile that the newspaper didn't return to the private lives of GAA players. The *Sunday World* plastered a Dublin footballer's drink-driving conviction on their front page, but they too were knocked back by the sense of fury in GAA society, which was a huge audience for them.

In Carey's case, though, the tabloids wouldn't be deterred. He knew before the 2003 All-Ireland semi-final against Tipperary that a couple of papers were on his tail with a view to going to press on the morning of the game. The Kilkenny manager Brian Cody was aware of it too, and on the week of the match he approached Carey. 'He said to me, "I presume you've heard what's going on?" He said that I had the full support of the players, and I just said, "Well, if you think there's anything that's going to bring down the team, I'll pull out. There's no problem, absolutely none."'

The story didn't appear anywhere that Sunday, but it wouldn't go away. On the Thursday before the All-Ireland final against Cork the *Mirror* declared that his marriage was over. He was about to captain Kilkenny in an All-Ireland final but his peace of mind was violated by trespassers. 'We hired security guards for the week of the All-Ireland, myself and Sarah [Newman, his new partner]. We had security guards with us the whole time that week because the threat was we were being followed and we were being photographed and all sorts of stuff was going on.'

There was all manner of lurid speculation about how the

Sunday papers might follow up Thursday's revelation in the *Mirror*. On his Friday-night chat show on TV3, Eamon Dunphy prefaced an item on hurling with Liam Griffin and Ger Loughnane by pleading with the Sunday papers for restraint and decency. 'It's not too late to row back,' he said. Inadvertently he had thrown coal on the fire. Far beyond Dublin's little media village people wondered what Dunphy could be referring to and the story kept building.

'At the end of the day my marriage had broken up. Whatever they were going to write other than that was libel, and that would be proven down the road.' In the event nothing else broke in the papers on the morning of the All-Ireland final. Carey had a quiet game, but Kilkenny won and he lifted the cup. He got on with his new life and accepted the same kind of public engagements that he always did. He and Sarah appeared on an RTE travel programme and were interviewed for a cover story in the *RTE Guide* to promote the show. It was mainstream and harmless. In the months after the All-Ireland final, however, Sarah's wealth from her successful business career provided the next pretext for the media's intrusion.

'They put my partner Sarah in a very vulnerable position by quoting the worth of her business that was way off the mark. The angle they're trying to get at is, "Well, the reason he left [his wife] is because she had so much money." The consequence they actually don't care about. Like, we've had a number of break-ins at the house. Not here, where we were before. They had photographs of the house we have in Mount Juliet [golf course] published in the paper and all that. Unfortunately the law doesn't protect the individual; these people can do what they like. So they'll print the house, and that's a target. They'll print when we are in Mount Juliet, or where we were on one of those occasions our house was broken into – and there was €30,000 worth of stuff taken out of it.

'And then the amount of nasty letters that would come about God wouldn't do this for profit. God is this and God is that and God is your only judge. The amount of those sick letters that you'd actually get because of what people print.'

Life was a lot simpler for Carey when the greatest challenge to his reputation was his record in All-Ireland finals. Whenever his admirers tried to fast-track him into the pantheon of all-time greats the doubters pointed to his record in All-Ireland finals and sought an injunction. That was the battle ground.

The cold facts are these. Including 2004, he has played in nine finals and failed to score from play in four of them; in two of the other finals his tally was one point from play. Before the 2000 final only one of his twenty-eight championship goals had come in an All-Ireland final, and that was from a penalty. Four years later that tally in finals had risen to three.

The statistics irritated Carey because he felt people couldn't look beyond them – or chose not to. He always regarded himself as a team player and thought that people didn't notice those performances when he made more scores than he took. He didn't feel he had the public's permission to play like that.

And maybe the statistics just irritate him anyway. He made his reputation as a finisher. That was where his status came from. His circumstances changed, the game changed, but the old conditions remained the same. People looked for the totals in brackets after his name and found the basis for their judgements there.

Of course the statistics were blind to many things. In the 1993 final – when his only score from play came ten seconds into injury time with the game already decided in Kilkenny's favour – he landed a free from 60 yards out, ten minutes from the end, when the sides were level, and followed it three minutes later with another tough free from under the Hogan Stand, when the sides were level again. He had shot four wides in the first half of that match but his head didn't drop and his nerve didn't fail. Maybe his record in finals didn't play on his mind, but he couldn't claim that he didn't think about it. Before the 2003 championship he detailed the case for his defence.

'I don't know what we scored in the 1991 final – thirteen or fourteen points, something like that [0–15]. I got eight points in that final. Okay, let it be said I got seven frees. Fine, grand. But if I was hitting the frees in the 1999 final – and I'm glad Henry [Shefflin] was hitting them – I might have got seven or eight. I was held scoreless. Fine. It was a bad day for Kilkenny; we didn't play well. Yeah, I laid on a point or two but, okay, didn't play well. Yes, stand up and be counted. But I had played very well up to it in pressure games.

'They say that on the big occasion I didn't play well. We had an All-Ireland quarter-final against Galway in 1997 and we were nine points down at half-time. I scored 2–7 or 2–8 in that game and we won by four or five points. If you're nine points down in a game, that's as big as you can possibly produce. In the 1992 All-Ireland final I think I scored a goal and four points in the game. Whatever way 'twas got, 'twas got. Kilkenny, against the gale in the first half, scored a goal and two points. It was I got the goal and two.

'In 1998 I think I might have ended up at centre-forward or was playing there for a lot of the game. I kept an awful lot of ball going through, and I'm not blaming anybody inside that the ball was coming back out. In the 1993 final a lot of stuff happened around me. I know that myself, John Power and Eamon Morrissey, we mightn't have gone fantastically well that day, but we took serious watching. We mightn't have been doing the scoring, but [Adrian] Ronan was able to sneak in and P. J. Delaney was able to sneak in and they done the business. And a lot of that was because yer man took serious watching. I know I took a couple of bad slaps in the first few minutes of the 1993 final but I wouldn't have taken that unless I was being watched. I wouldn't have been taking it for the whole game unless I was being watched. Again, I've no problem with that sort of criticism. If that's the standard I've set then it's a compliment to myself that it can be written up that yer man has failed in All-Ireland finals.'

In the 2000 final he scored 1–4 in the drubbing of Offaly, was named Man of the Match and sealed his selection as Hurler of the Year for the second time. He struck early that day, and it changed the whole landscape of the game. Michael Duignan played his last game for Offaly that day and he will never forget the impact of Carey's goal. 'The first ball that went up the field the ball dropped out of Claff's hand [Niall Claffey] straight to DJ. Goal. That lifted every one of them. To see the change in the Kilkenny players. They were nearly coming out of their skin. The whole thing was lifted. DJ got the goal – of all people.'

In the 2002 final he hit Clare with another early goal on the way to 1–3 from play, 1–6 in total. Those were the kind of All-Ireland final performances that had always been expected of him. That pressure had always sat on his shoulders from his very first All-Ireland final in 1991.

There was a telling moment five minutes into that match. Christy Heffernan broke behind the Tipperary half-back line and headed for goal. Space beckoned, and soon the target was only 30 yards away, dead straight ahead. The situation demanded that he shoot for a point, but he didn't. From the corner of his eye Heffernan spotted Carey running in parallel, 15 yards to his right. Heffernan was captain of the team, playing in his fourth All-Ireland final, but overriding the imperative to take responsibility and shoot was the instinct to feed Carey. The hand-pass was over-hit, the chance was lost. At just twenty years of age, Carey had already been anointed as a match winner. The go-to guy, as they say in American sport. Against Wexford and Antrim that year he had revived Kilkenny as they prepared to draw their last breath. Heffernan was making the percentage play.

That was the other thing. His form leading into finals was often so good that expectation levels were wild. Before the 1999 final he had scored 5–9 in the championship, most of it from play because Shefflin was hitting the close-in frees. His form in 1993 had been so good that a subdued performance in the final still couldn't deny him his first Hurler of the Year award. For his detractors, though, All-Ireland finals were handier to remember.

Brian Whelahan's experience of All-Ireland finals was altogether different. He played in four, won two, and on both winning days he was named Man of the Match. Birr ended up winning four All-Ireland club finals and he was Man of the Match in the first two of them. It was a bullet-proof record.

Not that it went to his head. In the Whelahan household vanity stood no chance. Brian was the last man to arrive back in the Offaly dressing room after the 1994 All-Ireland final, detained by idolaters and interviewers. Pad Joe was already there, waiting with a pin for his balloon. 'I put my hand on his shoulder,' said Pad Joe, 'and told him that the most impor-tant thing now was to keep his feet on the ground.'

Before the All-Ireland final a year later the Offaly bus left the team hotel without him and nobody noticed his absence until it was too late to turn back. He followed in a taxi. He made a smoother journey to Croke Park for the 1998 final, but in a sense the match started without him. He was flattened with a flu bug and wasted before a ball was pucked.

'I remember arriving in Birr that morning,' says Michael Bond, the Offaly manager. 'Mary Whelahan [Brian's mother] met me and said, "Brian is in an awful way." He looked like something the cat had brought in. Your heart sank, but you had to keep smiling. He shouldn't have been on the field at all.'

Brian McEvoy plundered three points off him in the first half an hour before Whelahan was given sanctuary in the forwards. From there he exploded in Kilkenny's face – 1–3 from play and a handful of assists. He recounts it like a story against himself. 'I was delighted to get out of wing-back at the time. I knew myself I wasn't hurling well. Our back line was under pressure and the ball was coming through me a lot more than it should have been. Confidence wasn't good. I felt under tremendous pressure going up into the forward line. I was saying to myself, "I could be taken off here." That was in the back of my mind. It was a relief to be out of the situation where I was going to be the cause of any more scores. It gave me time to get involved in the game, and after five or ten minutes I got a bit of confidence . . .' And the story tapers off without any mention of the flu or the fireworks.

He didn't have any impact on the 2000 final but by then he had been selected as the only active player on the Hurling Team of the Millennium. The selection was an honour, naturally, but the garland wasn't weightless around his neck. 'The following year, 2001, I started to think about it a little more and I said to myself, "You're going to have to pull your socks up."'

'I remember coming off the field after the 2000 All-Ireland final and a supporter from Kilkenny lambasting me over being picked on the team. I was bad enough after being beaten by

Kilkenny by whatever it was [thirteen points], but to be met by this coming down the steps to the dressing room, I was fit to hit him. He was probably hinting at the fact that DJ wasn't on the team.'

Carey's omission caused a fuss. Picking a Team of the Millennium was an impossible conceit in the first place, and if Carey had been picked somebody else's cause would have ignited a campaign. From the Team of the Century chosen sixteen years earlier Nicky Rackard was replaced at full-forward by Ray Cummins, even though neither man had struck a ball in the meantime. Yet Carey's omission became an issue.

'It would have been very nice to have been on it,' says Carey. 'It would have been a great honour to have been on it. I wasn't on it. There's not much I can do. I think one of the excuses given at the time was that I had only two All-Ireland medals – I think that was one of the excuses. But I think there was a lot more players only had one. My own grand-uncle Paddy Phelan, for example, who was supposed to be a magnificent man. It's great that there was so much controversy that people thought I should have been on it, but again it's only someone's opinion.'

The 2000 All-Ireland was the end of that great Offaly team. In the most competitive period in the history of the game they were contenders every year for a decade. With the exception of one year, between 1992 and 2000 they either won the All-Ireland or were beaten by the team who did. At the time Whelahan would have wanted more, but in time he was grateful for what they got.

'Maybe we could have got one more All-Ireland. Having said that, the standard in that period from 1990 to 2001 was unbelievable. I think the standard at the moment is way below it. Maybe the physical strength of teams has gone up. The actual hurling standard of teams has gone down. With the amount of good teams that were around we probably got as much as we were going to get out of it.

'We got two, and we would nearly have had to be professionals to win any more because you lose that bit every time you win an All-Ireland. You definitely lose an edge. When you're playing against teams of your own standard the whole time someone is going to catch you. It got hard after a while and we probably went off the boil a bit. We were starting to lose players too. At the end of '99 we lost Martin Hanamy, the best corner-back I've ever seen. Kevin Kinahan will tell you that hurling beside him was like having an extra pair of legs. We lost big players after '99 and 2000. You're trying to fill gaps then, and in a county like Offaly you just don't have the numbers.'

Whelahan stayed, though, and confronted the inevitability of decline. In the summer of 2002 he thought the dance was finally over. He could still hear the music but his feet didn't move to it like before. In the Leinster semi-final Kilkenny beat Offaly by three goals at their ease and Henry Shefflin filled his pockets against Whelahan – seven points from play. Whelahan tried to hold the centre and read the breaks; Shefflin paid him no heed and everywhere he wandered the ball followed him. During Whelahan's career there had been days when teams targeted him as a point of strength and bowed to his pre-eminence with a strategy of containment; that day, however, it was as if Whelahan had been identified as an exploitable point of weakness, a point of access. And though he fumed, there was nothing he could do to upset their plan. Somehow, and in a way he'd never been before, he was defenceless.

'At one stage there was a sideline ball and Henry [Shefflin] starts calling for it,' says Whelahan. 'I'm standing there and he's calling for this thing. I said to myself, "Fucking hell, anyway I'm going to win this ball." I was still beside him when he got the ball, pucked it over his shoulder and over the bar. It was like, no matter what, the ball was going to come into his hand. I just said, "Well, that's it." He's confident enough to call for this ball while I was standing next to him. It was just a sign of the times, that there were new men on the block.

'My confidence was shattered. I made a switch myself with about ten minutes to go. I said to Joe Brady, "You go in centre-back." I don't think he knew that it was me making the switch and not the sideline, but it didn't matter. I wasn't staying there any longer.

'A player might never tell you, but the same belief in yourself goes. It does go. You start to take more on board. When you're nineteen, twenty, twenty-one, what real cares do you have? At the end of the day I'm going out to mark someone. I'm not questioning whether I'm good enough, I'm not questioning whether I have the ability, I'm just going out and I'm going to hurl him. Suddenly you're there five, six, seven years later and you're there saying to yourself, "I'm marking so and so. Is he fast?"'

He could have left then, but he stayed. Of the Offaly players who won minor All-Irelands in the 1980s Whelahan and Joe Errity were the only ones left on the senior panel in 2003, and for 2004 Errity didn't come back.

For Whelahan there was nothing left to be done that he hadn't already achieved. There was nothing left to prove. His presence wasn't going to be the difference between Offaly winning an All-Ireland and losing it. In the championship's great casino they weren't sitting with the high rollers any longer. His presence alone wasn't going to protect these young Offaly players from a hiding if a hiding was coming.

Offaly reached the 2004 Leinster final against Wexford and that day in Croke Park Whelahan marshalled the defence from centre-back, revisiting in flashes the majesty of his prime. Halfway through the second half, though, his hamstring went and he couldn't continue. Offaly lost and went into the qualifiers against Clare, but Whelahan wasn't fit to take his place and they were well beaten.

In April 2005 he retired. Sort of. Less than two months later he was back.

Carey didn't even contemplate retirement. Seventeen years after he joined the Kilkenny panel as a sub goalie for the 1988/89 league, he started the 2005 league as an experimental centre-back. Extraordinary.

They gave us everything, and there's no sign of us settling our debt.

7. The Power, the Glory, the End

There is a photograph of James O'Connor, taken under the Hogan Stand minutes after the 1997 All-Ireland final. His fist is clenched so tight that the veins in his forearm are standing up and his white teeth are gritted hard, stretching the spare flesh on his cheek. The fringe of his sandy hair is grafted on to his forehead with sweat and, as he stares straight ahead, past the camera's lens, his blue eyes are fiery and faintly chilling.

The image was married to the moment. The hurling championship had ended with the Hurler of the Year deciding the All-Ireland final with the last score of a convulsive match. The best match of the year. The best All-Ireland final in twenty years. As O'Connor's winner dropped over the Tipperary crossbar at the Hill 16 end of Croke Park, Ger Loughnane was standing behind the goal, his arm raised in triumph.

The Clare team didn't know it then, but they had reached their summit as a group. Over the next couple of seasons there were days when they would match and even exceed the performances of 1997 but they never again put such a sequence of performances together. To win that All-Ireland they had to be better than they had been in 1995. They had to change, evolve, challenge themselves and go again. They did.

Less than an hour after the match O'Connor stood in tracksuit bottoms and polo shirt in the winner's dressing room summarizing the match with extraordinary clarity, the game-face from the photograph packed away with his boots, the self-possession that made the winning point restored to his demeanour.

'I just remember after we won,' says O'Connor, 'there was an awful sense of satisfaction. The goal was laid down at the start of the year. We had to win the All-Ireland. At this stage we weren't talking about winning the Munster champion-ship. We had to win the All-Ireland, otherwise '95 would have been seen as a flash in the pan, a once-off. I just remem-ber there was a desperate sense of satisfaction. At the time I think journalists remarked how cool we were afterwards. Like, '95 was mad and euphoric, but in '97 we were in the dressing room taking it all in and thinking that it was just an inner satisfaction. We laid out what we wanted to do and we'd proven ourselves. To me it was more fulfilling than maybe winning it in '95.'

Winning the 1995 All-Ireland had taken more out of them than they would have wished. The celebrations had lingered in their system, like damp in their bones. In the final three weeks before the first round of the 1996 championship they attacked the deficit in their physical preparation and crammed in too many heavy sessions. On a day of blistering heat in the Gaelic Grounds they should have beaten Limerick but they missed too many chances, and when Limerick came with one surging run at the end Clare were caught at the post. They had landed at another crossroads.

'I remember after that match in Limerick,' says Michael O'Halloran, 'Clare people saying to us, with good heart, "Forget about it. You've given us the year of our lives and all that." But like, as serious sportsmen, people who dedicated nearly their entire life to training, it just didn't tally with what the Clare team were thinking at the time. We were young, we were as good [as] if not better than what was around at the time, and we saw ourselves maybe dominating [hurling] in the way that Meath dominated football for four or five years while they were at the top. You're not going to do it for ten years but you could certainly do it for three, four or five years when you're at that age.'

They reconvened shortly after the 1996 All-Ireland final and committed themselves to an intensive gym programme from October to January. Players had dabbled in weights before but this was collective and structured. The game they played was built on aggression and stamina, and in the gym that winter they added power. Block upon block. 'I remember living in the gym that winter,' says O'Connor. 'By the following summer I was in incredible shape physically. We had a huge stamina base and we felt strong. There were games where we got scores in the last ten minutes because of the work we'd done, and we were still in great shape later on in the year.'

At times during that summer of 1997 the power of their hurling was breathtaking. At one stage in the first half of the Munster final against Tipperary they were leading by 0–10 to 0–2, without any breeze to distort the figures. Colm Bonnar was the Tipp centre-back that day and all he remembers is the Clare centre-field coming at him 'in a swarm'. At one stage of the All-Ireland semi-final against Kilkenny they were ten points up; in the All-Ireland final they went from being four points down at half-time to being five points up with ten minutes to go without even scoring a goal to accelerate the process. They had that capacity to produce bursts of scorching power, and in those periods no team could live with them.

It was unsustainable over seventy minutes though, and it couldn't mask the weaknesses in their make-up. They scored twenty points in that All-Ireland final against Tipperary and committed seventeen wides; their performances were always liable to have such a bipolar personality. They didn't have as many scoring forwards as other counties, they didn't score enough goals, they didn't have a high cruising speed. They weren't able to kill teams softly. They had to hurl at full pelt, close to fury. Their opponents knew that if they could survive the flurry of punches they would have a chance to counter. After the Kerry match in 1997 they didn't win any game by more than four points, even though they were at least four points superior to every team they played that summer. In the Munster final John Leahy had a chance to level the match in the last minute, and in the All-Ireland final he had a chance to win it at the death. The power and the vulnerability existed side by side as a defining paradox.

Unlike in 1995, though, nobody disputed their status as the best team in the country. In Niall Gilligan and Colin Lynch they had produced the two best newcomers to championship hurling; their defence ranked alongside Offaly's as the standard for every other team; James O'Connor was the best forward in the country; their centre-field of Ollie Baker and Lynch was peerless, and between them that pair articulated the essence of the team: the dynamism, the drive, the growling, the snarling, the understated class.

And in a sense they had won the perfect All-Ireland. They had beaten Cork, Kilkenny and Tipperary – Tipperary twice. All the fat cats of the old oligarchy, sacked in their castles.

So, where could they go from here? Between 1995 and 1997 it seemed that every question of honour had been satisfied, every hoarded resentment expended, every account settled. What was left to drive them?

Loughnane considered quitting, and for a few months at the end of 1997 the possibility hung over the panel. The league final between Galway and Limerick was held in Ennis that October. Not all of the GAA reporters could be accommodated in the press box so an overflow was organized in the stand. The Clare trainer Mike McNamara sat behind us, and at half-time he leaned forward with the news of Loughnane's possible departure. The media enjoyed a good relationship with Clare in those days but it still wasn't their practice to conduct private business in public. We could only speculate about McNamara's motive and not a word of the speculation appeared in print. The rumour went unreported.

The players weren't prepared to be so passive. Anthony Daly, Brian Lohan, Sean McMahon and James O'Connor went to Loughnane's house in Shannon three times before Christmas and petitioned him to stay. They were met with resistance and failed to receive a commitment. 'We felt, "Look, you can't go now. There's a lot more in the team,"' says O'Connor. 'Mike was a fantastic physical trainer but, like, Loughnane was . . . you know, as long as Loughnane was available we certainly wanted to have him. Mike and Ger were two fierce strong personalities and when they were pulling together and working together they were a powerful combination. I suppose we might have been aware of Mike's desire to get the job at some stage but Ger and Mike were certainly a more effective proposition than Mike alone would have been.'

Whatever the players felt about Loughnane they all recognized his raw charisma and they appreciated his central importance to the group dynamic. Their feelings about him were complex in many unspoken ways and simple in one compelling way: he was the boss. Loughnane wasn't interested in their affection and he didn't moderate his approach to win their hearts; he was only concerned about their response to him. If he couldn't affect them, Clare were sunk.

The instrument of his power was his oratory – direct and elemental. 'Post the '95 All-Ireland and post '97 you attended all these functions and different things,' says O'Connor, 'and there'd be 101 speakers. I don't think I ever heard Ger make the same speech twice and he just had the ability to hold an audience in the palm of his hand.' In the dressing room on match days it was a captive audience. 'The best person inside a dressing room before games was Ger Loughnane,' says Fergie Tuohy. 'If you're going to compare everyone to Ger Loughnane, everyone is useless. We broke so many hurleys before a ball was ever thrown in. If you saw Ger Loughnane with your hurley you'd be just hoping it was your fourth or fifth one. He mightn't break it but it was going to be hit off the counter or the table and it could come back to you in two. Instead of listening to him you'd be saying to yourself, "Jesus Christ, what's going to happen to this one?" He often might have a Clare jersey and he'd leave it up to your puss and let you sniff it and tell you what it was all about.'

Once or twice he took a different tack. O'Halloran remembers the All-Ireland semi-final against Galway in 1995 when he played to their emotions more gently. 'He genuinely said, "Listen, everyone is very proud of you, your families are very proud of you, you've won the Munster championship, go out there and make them proud again." But he wouldn't be into that touchy-feely kind of thing.'

Generally, Loughnane's dressing room performances followed a familiar script and, like a Bond movie, the special effects were the key. His voice and his eyes filled the silver screen. Loughnane was dealing with a group of discerning, hard-headed, ambitious young men but somehow his words carried his flock with him, like a preacher from the Bible Belt.

'He always had an angle on something,' says Daly. ''95 was

okay, we won, but then '96 it was like "Tom Ryan [Limerick manager] has insulted the Clare jersey." I remember being in the dressing room that day wearing my Clare jersey, and I'll tell you, we got it up for that match. We lost, so the following year it was "Good teams win one All-Ireland, great teams win two." Then we'd never beaten Tipp in a Munster final so that was the be-all and end-all. Then it was Kilkenny. "We'll get these bastards; they're laughing at us!" And then when we had Tipp again in the All-Ireland final – sure there was no need to say anything about that. In 1998 the big thing was putting Munster titles back to back. And sure after 1998 he had an angle on everything. He never said something where you came to the conclusion, "That's ridiculous." He had a way of saying it, whatever he was saying. "Donie Fucking Nealon! [Munster Council secretary]" and the mad eyes on him staring at us.'

He kept his biggest set-pieces for match days, but on training nights during the summer he might give them a quick nip of the hard stuff. 'He'd gather us in, pick the team for a training match,' says O'Halloran, 'and just give it a twenty-second blast of what we were going to do to them – whoever we were playing. And he had great conviction. You'd actually believe it.'

The players regarded him as a psychologist and they recognized the training matches as his clinics. Closing your mind to him was pointless because if he wanted your mind he would have it by burglary. You could say that his technique was tough love, except with Loughnane every common practice was magnified. With a player such as Baker, Loughnane's technique was vicious love. 'When I think of him [Baker] I think of constantly nagging, threatening and verbally abusing him,' wrote Loughnane in his book.

Before the 1997 All-Ireland final the Clare management

smothered Baker in vicious love. He hadn't been good in the semi-final against Kilkenny and they took him off when they thought the game was safe. In terms of importance to the team Loughnane rated Baker in the 'top three', so they set about priming him for the final. One night in training Loughnane, McNamara and Tony Considine abused him high up and low down.

'He wanted me to play well in the final,' says Baker, 'and that was his way of working my mind. It worked. He played me right every time. I'd know what his motives were behind it. He always played me and it always worked, even though you'd say to yourself, "No, he's not going to do it to me this time." Next thing it would work again. He'd always get into your head and get the best out of you – even though there's only a certain lifespan in that.

'That was the way he treated me, and I suppose you either take it or you don't. There would be no question of snapping back at him. He'd ate ya. You'd be gone then and he'd still be there. I wouldn't have been the only one. There were others on the panel that got it as well. When he got into these training matches and he got into the mode of the whole thing, anything at all could come out [of his mouth]. You might think, "He can't really say that," but none of us ever really stood up for each other because you could be next.'

Though they were grown men and strong individuals, they deferred to Loughnane without question. The relationship was based on respect, but it was more than that. 'There was definitely a fear factor there,' says O'Connor. 'You know, he's a stern character. If Loughnane was on the field blowing for training fellas would be running out of the dressing room door, they wouldn't be walking. He had that hold on us.'

If any of the players had a problem they didn't deal directly with the management; they spoke to Daly and, like an ombudsman, he pursued their complaint. Daly always got a hearing. At different times other senior players might make suggestions to Loughnane too, but there was no recognized forum for such an exchange.

'I got on well with him I'd say,' says Daly, 'but you never really got too close to him. The kind of fella he was you didn't really know what was going through his mind. But he'd listen to you if you had something constructive to say and it would go into the brain – or the computer, as I used to call it. He definitely had a savage brain.'

'Johnny Callinan went to school with Loughnane,' says Tuohy, 'and he says he was a straight-A student. He says he could have been anything – a solicitor, a doctor, a judge.'

There was a certain amount of slagging and banter, but the players wouldn't have been close to Loughnane socially. He wasn't really a drinker, for one thing. 'Sure he wouldn't be able to hold it,' says Tuohy. 'He'd be drunk after three or four pints.' In that arena they had a better relationship with McNamara. 'I suppose Mike had a pub in Scariff and at times there would have been late nights in Mike's place,' says O'Connor. 'You could probably talk to Mike on a level that you couldn't with Ger. Maybe Mike was a straighter man to talk to. Ger was Ger; he was this larger-than-life figure. You felt you could maybe talk to Mike more on a human level. Mike had a drollness about him and a light touch at times that was maybe different to Ger.'

When it came to slagging Loughnane, Fergal Hegarty had a unique talent. A gifted mimic, he had Loughnane's voice and idiom off pat. When it came to hurling, Hegarty and Loughnane had a difficult enough relationship. Hegarty didn't build on his impressive seasons in 1995 and 1996 and before long he was one of those players Loughnane was liable to replace before half-time, or bring on and take off, as happened to Hegarty in the 1997 All-Ireland final. But when it came to cabaret, Hegarty had the upper hand. 'Hego was a gas man and good craic, and he'd be having a go at Loughnane constantly,' says Daly. 'Hego could take him off perfect. Loughnane would laugh but he'd hate it at the back of it all. He couldn't cope with it at all. He'd no sense of humour in that sort of way. He couldn't laugh at himself at all.'

In evidence, players tell a story from the team holiday at the end of 1997. On their way to Hawaii they stopped off for five days in San Diego. Wives, partners and girlfriends were flying in for the Hawaiian leg of the trip but in San Diego it was just the panel, their immediate entourage and golf. On the third day they decided to have a competition. It was $20 to enter – to be paid up front – and partners were drawn out of a hat. Loughnane and Considine, however, decided to play together, as they often did.

The scorecards came in and it transpired that Loughnane and Considine had the best score. Loughnane and Considine, however, hadn't paid their $20 up front and they hadn't been drawn out of the hat. They paid their money in the clubhouse afterwards and their case was heard. Johnny Callinan was the organizer and he sought clarification on golf society rules from James O'Connor, who was accepted by everyone as an honest broker; they both agreed that Loughnane and Considine's score couldn't be admitted. Fergie Tuohy and Barry Murphy were declared the winners. Later that evening they assembled for the presentation.

'I remember that night in the bar,' says O'Halloran. 'Word got back to the boys that they weren't after winning and they were snotty. The bar was designed like *Cheers* with the counter in the centre, and we all sat together and the two boys came in later on and sat at the opposite end of the bar. So we were drinking and started taking the piss, and Johnny

Callinan, who was part of the holiday fund committee, he was wearing a blazer so we borrowed that and we had this presentation, like the Masters and the green jacket. I pretended to be an American golf TV guy and I did an interview with Tuts [Fergie Tuohy] for the craic and the boys were bursting laughing. At the end then Tuts says, "All I can say is, the winner takes it all."

'The next morning we were catching our flights to Hawaii. We were up early and Loughnane wouldn't talk to anyone. I'll never forget going in for breakfast at about five o'clock in the morning, and he walked right past me. I said, "Good morning, Ger." No response.'

Tuohy takes up the story. 'We got a bus from San Diego to Los Angeles airport and I was in the jacks in the airport and I met Jamesie [O'Connor] in there washing his hands. "How are they now?" I says to him. "Ah Jesus," he said, "I got on the bus this morning and they wouldn't even salute me." When they wouldn't salute Jamesie there was something drastically wrong. "Fuck him," I says. "Any time you see him give him a big salute." The next thing one of the cubicle doors swings open and out comes Considine.

'My lady was arriving to join us along with Sparrow's lady and Dalyo's lady. We had all been checked in as a group, and I was sitting down talking to her in the airport and the next thing two airline tickets fell at me. No conversation. And this is my future wife here. "What's wrong there?" she says. I told her the story, and she was nervous enough now about coming in the first place. "I've come halfway around the world," she says, "and ye aren't even talking."'

A couple of days later in Hawaii another golf outing was organized and every name was in the hat. The first name out was F. Tuohy; the second was G. Loughnane. Partners. Murder.

'It was the only time ever in my life I topped my drive on the first tee,' says Tuohy. 'It went about two yards. That kind of broke the ice for the whole group. We were driving around in the buggy and there was nothing much being said except maybe, "Do you want a drop of water?" The next thing on the tenth green I shanked my putt and hit his ball, and after that it was obvious we weren't going to be competing for any prizes. Next thing he says to me, "Well, are you enjoying the holiday?" "I am, Ger," says I. "Well," he says, "is Tracey enjoying the holiday?" "She is," I says, "bar the two days that you fucked up." He got a big fit of laughing and then we started talking about hurling. "Do you think I should go?" I remember him saying to me inside in the buggy. "No, you should stay," I said. "Who's the next fella that's going to come in and motivate us like you?"'

That was at the heart of it. Whatever he said, whatever he did, whatever they thought of him, they still wanted him. Needed him. He was indivisible from their success and their ambition and their drive. All both parties required was a sustainable working relationship, and as long as the players accepted Loughnane's conditions they had that.

When it all finished years later, Baker put it into perspective. 'We wouldn't see much of him. He leads his own life now. I have the height of respect for the man and for what he did, but I don't think he ever wanted any of us to be his friends afterwards. There'd be mutual respect I'd hope. I would hope he would have the same respect for me as I would have for him, but I don't think he would ever yearn for my friendship. He was our manager, our teacher, our leader, so he didn't need our friendship. It was never going to happen.'

Another year dawned. Loughnane stayed.

★

The group had a dynamic wider than its relationship with the manager, and Daly was critical to that. He was middle management. His outlook and his attitude were symbiotic with Loughnane's but he had a gift for interacting with people, a quick wit and a winning manner. He had an extra-ordinary talent for captaincy but he carried himself like one of the privates. He took a pint and loved the craic, owned greyhounds and liked a flutter. His status didn't generate distance. The other players respected him and were fond of him in equal measure. Even in a dressing room dominated by Loughnane and McNamara, Daly could project his own personality. In his presence the craic was different and the seriousness was different.

He was just twenty-two when Len Gaynor made him captain in 1992. It was as good a time as any. The qualities he possessed, the aspects of mind, the layers of his character, were not derived from age or experience; they were innate. 'He was a real leader you know,' says Gaynor. 'He was an up-front guy and he wasn't afraid of anyone or anything. Nothing daunted him. Nothing put him off. Heavy defeats didn't bother him either. It bothered him to lose, but it didn't shake his confidence or his morale. There were older guys on the panel and we asked one of them would he be inter-ested, hoping he wouldn't – and he wasn't. Daly took the job and we were delighted.'

The captaincy wasn't a burden for Daly because it was a natural extension of his personality. In the broad spectrum of the panel he was a median point. 'It didn't matter whether you were a nuclear physicist or a block-layer,' says O'Connor, 'Daly had the ability to relate to you on your level. The guys who were savagely intense could relate to the drive in Daly. And he could empathize with the guys who were slaughtered by the training, too, because he never enjoyed the slog.

'As captain he was just himself. When things got tough in Crusheen, or on the hill in Shannon, he could say something that would make people laugh. He could always say the right thing at the right time, and he said what he thought. You know, he's a confident guy. He's not afraid to stick out his chest. He has a charisma that only certain people have.'

'A lot of people said that Clare's success would never have happened without Loughnane,' says O'Halloran, 'but I think an equally valid observation is it wouldn't have happened without Dalyo either. Maybe that's over-exaggerating it because at the end of the day he's a player like the rest of us, but he was excellent. Captaining Clare – you could say it was what he was born to do.'

Daly's captaincy overshadowed his hurling in the public eye, but he was a formidable hurler. When Clare needed a full-back in 1993 he took it on his shoulders; when they needed to create a strong half-back line in 1995 he accepted the move from his best position at corner-back to a new challenge on the wing. There was always a perception that he would be cleaned out for pace, but it rarely happened. In the long Clare summers between 1995 and 1999 there was one day each year when he was taken for three or four points, but that was the height of it and he ended each of those championships in credit. He had the stuff to survive, and at the core of it all was an elemental instinct to compete.

Daly was comfortable with the guerrilla warfare of the championship. When, in their transformation from losers to winners, the Clare defence pushed physical force to the limit of the law and beyond, Daly took up arms like the rest. 'I had a bit of a bad reputation for getting involved with fellas – mouthing a bit,' he once said. 'I stick to my guns to this day, though, that I never started a mouthing match. But I often said, "If they want to start it, they'd better be prepared to listen." Like Dan Shanahan turned around to me in the drawn Munster final [1998] after scoring his third point. "You're not on Seanie McGrath now, boy," he said to me. And I said, "You're definitely bigger and a good bit uglier." He was going well; why didn't he leave it at that?'

Was he ruthless? He would have said so. 'Maybe when I was a bit younger and I was sick of Clare being beaten I was more psyched to do anything to win,' he said a few weeks before his final championship appearance in 2000. 'I was ruthless, I thought. I would have been willing to do anything. Over the years maybe I've mellowed a bit, although I'd still like to think that I'd be determined to do anything.'

The All-Irelands changed all of their lives, but his more profoundly than most. The Trustee Savings Bank decided that Daly was a wasted asset serving behind their branch counter. They gave him a job on the road and fitted him with a company car. His first car. Imagine.

Before the following year's championship he had taken leave of absence to open a sports shop in Ennis. There were gains to be made from Clare's success if you had the guts to take a risk. For Daly it worked. Business was good and he was emboldened to spread his wings further. Before the end of 1999 he opened a pub in west Clare, becoming the third publican from Clare's All-Ireland winning teams.

But fame took a toll as well. Clare was a county not used to success in elite sport – any sport. They had produced GAA stars, but not All-Ireland winners and not superstars. Not everybody in the community could find the correct response, and Daly had to find another layer for his skin. 'After 1995 I would have been too self-conscious for a while. Conscious of what people thought of me. You know, a fella would come up to me and say, "Did you hear the latest joke about yourself? What's the difference between God and Anthony

Daly? God doesn't think he's Anthony Daly." That sort of shite. I usen't to find it at all funny at the time, but if a fella said it to me now it would be like water off a duck's back. There's people that count and people that don't matter a damn. You grow out of it. If Stephen Sheedy told me to cop on to myself I'd take notice, you know. But, I suppose, maybe people see the business going well, you appear to have a decent lifestyle, and they just want to drag you back down.'

A week after the 1997 All-Ireland final he married Eilish, and for a few months the price of fame was unacceptably high. Scurrilous and groundless rumours about their marriage began to spread almost instantly. They were barely a week into their honeymoon in Mexico when Fergal Hegarty shared a taxi with a girl who claimed that the marriage was already in trouble. 'According to yer one I'd Eilish killed outside in Mexico,' says Daly, 'and she was coming home early. And that multiplied. It went ga-ga.'

The stories got worse. It was said that he had also broken up with a former girlfriend because of physical abuse. An acquaintance of his ex-girlfriend said it to a friend of Daly's in an Ennis nightclub one evening and the friend reported it back to Daly immediately, before it got out of hand. Daly was still on good terms with his ex-girlfriend and her family and he made them aware of the situation. They were appalled, and reeled off a solicitor's letter to the source of the allegation. She stood her ground at first, denying everything, but Daly's friend agreed to be a sworn witness and she finally came clean. 'She wrote a letter to me retracting everything,' says Daly, 'and saying that she had no foundation for anything she'd said, and she wrote a letter to my ex-girlfriend's family saying that she was very sorry for any upset caused.

'But I'll tell you, it was a bad few months now. We went up to meet Eilish's parents one night just to say, "Look, you might hear these stories going round. It's not true. We're getting on great." I just told my mother myself. The badness there was unreal.'

Anthony and Eilish have three children now. The pub is booming and the shop is flying. He quit inter-county hurling at the beginning of 2002 and became manager of Clare eighteen months later.

At thirty-three he was young, but it was as good a time as any.

The Clare team of the late 1990s took their identity from many things – their fitness, their bite, Loughnane. But in a sense they were defined as a team by their relationship with Tipperary. Tipperary broke them and Tipperary made them.

To Clare, Tipp represented hurling's establishment; they were the face of the oppressor. Clare's championship history with Kilkenny was ancient and for some reason they didn't feel any bitterness towards Cork, despite the heart-breaking Munster final defeats of 1977 and 1978. In the 1998 Munster semi-final they beat Cork in the championship for the fourth time in six years and on the Clare panel that day Ger O'Loughlin was the only player to have experienced a championship defeat to Cork, ten years earlier. Tipp, though, were different. Historically, Tipp were the county that every other serious county tested their machismo against. Those conditions suited Clare fine.

After 1994 Clare and Tipp didn't meet in the championship again for three years, but in the meantime a couple of league matches generated enough heat to keep the pot boiling. The ultimate irony, though, was that by 1998 Clare had challenged Tipp's hereditary position as the team that neutrals felt compelled to hate.

Their feelings for each other matched any feelings projected on to them from outside. At a function in Carlow a few weeks before Clare and Tipperary met in the 2000 Munster championship Ger Loughnane told a story against himself which captured the prevailing mood. He was in the company of Tony Considine when a van with a south Tipperary registration pulled up and a man stuck his head out the window. 'I thought to myself, "There's going to be trouble here." "Ger," he says to me, "any chance of an autograph for the wife?" I thought it was most unusual for a Tipperary supporter to be looking for an autograph – it's usually my head they're looking for. So I gave it to him. "Christ," he said, "she'll get some surprise when I give her this. You've no idea how much she hates ya!"'

It was a story of its time, and there were others like it. On the night of the 1999 league final, when Tipperary beat Galway in Ennis, some Tipp supporters revealed a T-shirt from their summer collection. Its central motif was a map of Ireland from which Clare had been lanced, and underneath ran the caption. 'A Perfect Island'.

And so it went, pawing and scratching. The hurling public loved it. For a while hurling was in the thrall of Clare and Tipp. It wasn't just the movie, it was the soundtrack too, and the razzmatazz and the posturing. At its height the mere thought of this match sustained every aspiration and conceit we cherished about the championship – the coiled intensity, the spleen of feud and familiarity. The billboards were writ with hurling's greatest marquee names: Loughnane, English, Daly, Leahy. Clare and Tipp was more than a match; it was a date that you carried around for months. One hyperbole would feed another until the match had no hope of fulfilling what we wished it to be, but, looking back, you wouldn't have swapped the anticipation for anything.

Before 1993 if there was any such thing as 'Clare and Tipp'

it was merely a Clare creation and a delusion of grandeur. Geography suggested a rivalry that history couldn't support. Tipp were bordered by eight hurling counties and while holy war raged continuously with two or three of their neighbours, Tipp's combat with Clare was prosecuted in skirmishes, brief and brutal. Essentially, Tipp didn't have Clare on their minds.

In thirty-four championship meetings before 1993 Clare had won only six. Between 1896 and 1955 Clare's only victory was achieved by an objection, overturning what had been a ten-point defeat on the field of play. Taking all the scores of all the games the average outcome was a nine-point victory for Tipp. In the 1993 Munster final Tipp doubled the average. In their hearts Tipp wouldn't have been surprised. That was how hurling worked before the revolution.

The Munster final of 1993 and Clare's revenge in the first round a year later must always be taken together. In the narrative of this rivalry those games stand as the Old Testament. Nicky English's smile to a teammate late in the game after a ridiculously easy point became the headline image in the Clare–Tipp iconography, and its power endured. According to Daly, Loughnane was still using it in 1999, English's first year as Tipp manager. The taste was still bitter on the tongue. 'It was used in a big way,' says Daly. 'It was just an unfortunate circumstance from Nicky's point of view. I read his account in his autobiography and I understand his explanation, but it definitely happened. We all saw it, and the television cameras picked it up. It was just perfect timing. If the roles were reversed he'd have used it too. But Loughnane really milked it. "Do ye want him laughing at ye again? Do ye want to crawl home again?" And he'd be looking over at me and Brian Lohan, deliberately. "I'll never forget it," he'd say, "sitting up in the stand in Limerick . . ." Oh, unreal.'

For the 1994 match against Tipperary, Clare had more

angles than a compass. They were scheduled to make three visits to the University of Limerick that year to have body fat and various other tests done. They knew that Tipp were undergoing the same process in the university, but when Clare made their second visit shortly before the Munster championship one of the testers happened to mention to Fergie Tuohy that Tipp hadn't been in yet and weren't booked to come until after the Clare match. Casual arrogance. Bingo.

They reflected, too, on the loss of their veteran corner-back John Moroney, who had died in a car accident during the winter. He had suffered with them in the 1993 massacre and their fondness for him was more coal on the fire. By match day it was a furnace.

'Once the draw was made all we thought about was that match,' says Daly. 'I was only after starting going out with Eilish that Christmas of 1993 and, you know, we'd go for spins down to west Clare for a drink and she'd say to me, "Are you having another one?" And I'd say, "No – May twenty-ninth." We laugh about it now. For months that was all she heard: May twenty-ninth. She thought she was going out with a fruitcake.

'I hardly ever cried after a Clare match, win or lose, but there were tears streaming down my face when we beat Tipp. That day was awful emotional. Coming off the pitch Jim McInerney said something about John Moroney and . . . oh, stop.'

Clare made mistakes in 1993 which shaped their outlook and changed their approach for ever more. The aggression that characterized Clare in their pomp can be sourced back to that day. 'Talk about lying down and letting yourself get a hiding,' says Daly. 'We couldn't do it again in 1994 and there was a fair bit of scutching that day. Eventually, years later, people gave out stink about that sort of thing, but we either had to do it at the time or stay the way we were, being nice and losing. We had to up the ante if we were to have any hope, and in fairness Loughnane recognized that.'

In the imagination of the hurling public 'Clare and Tipp' became a byword for murder and mayhem, but the reality was somewhat different. The Munster final and All-Ireland final of 1997 passed without malice, and so too did the drawn match in 1999. There were a few false strokes in the 1999 replay and Clare were narky a year later, jostling, bumping and goading as if they needed a flashpoint to ignite them on a day when they were empty. Generally, though, Clare prosecuted their matches against Tipp with the kind of aggression they reserved for any team in the championship.

'Ollie Baker hit me in the drawn game in 1999,' says Brendan Cummins, the Tipp goalkeeper. 'I'll never forget it. I tapped the ball outside him, he followed through and hit me a belt. I got up after it but it took me ten minutes to get right. The Clare lads in their prime would hit you so hard that it would knock five minutes out of you. That's how they wore teams down in the finish.'

In 2001 Clare purposely made the game into a war, but from 1993 until Sean McMahon's red card in the 2003 championship match there had only been one man sent off: Frank Lohan, during a ferocious league game in May 1997. In his book Loughnane described it as the 'toughest match' he ever saw. The Tipperary forward Michael Cleary remembered it as 'one of the toughest' inter-county games he was ever involved in. 'It was vicious the same night,' says Daly. 'There was no ball being played, by both sides. Loughnane really had us up for it. We kinda bullied them and got away with it.'

And yet the championship matches between the teams that summer delivered the best hurling this rivalry has produced.

The last forty minutes of the All-Ireland final was the apogee
of it all. 'We weren't consumed with roughing up Tipp,' says
Michael O'Halloran. 'We went out and fairly out-hurled
them in the Munster final. The Munster final burned up a lot
of the bile that would have been there, and in the All-Ireland
final we were the hunted. And that's how it panned out. We
were very flat in the first half and they were a lot more up
for it than we were.'

In their collective psyche that Munster final was huge. 'I
made sure the dressing room was locked,' wrote Loughnane
in his autobiography. 'The atmosphere inside was one of total
and absolute contentment. We're not supposed to feel it in
this lifetime. There was no need for a word to be said. The
downside was that you knew that there was never going to
be a day like that again, but it is a feeling that will last for
ever.'

Having to meet Tipp again in the All-Ireland final was
treacherous. Losing that game would have taken all the good
out of the Munster final. Remember how it finished: Tipp
got a goal to go a point in front with time nearly up; Clare
got two points to win it. In those days, at their glorious peak,
they didn't contemplate losing. Five years after that match
Brian Lohan could still remember exactly the mentality that
framed the performance. 'In the big matches that we played,'
he said, 'we always felt there was only going to be one result.
We felt we were stronger than anybody else. While the impression was there that Tipp had something over us we felt
ourselves that we had something over them. We felt we were
stronger than them and as a unit we were that little bit more
together than they were. I remember thinking in the 1997
All-Ireland final that if we'd ended level we'd have beaten
them by ten points in the replay. As individuals we were that
little bit stronger, mentally and physically.'

Looking back, both teams can identify watershed matches. For Clare there was another league game of seminal importance, this time early in 1995. Tipp were coming to Ennis with a full-strength team and Loughnane decided that this was the day to make a statement. Clare had won their first four league matches and Loughnane told the players that those victories meant nothing if they didn't beat Tipp. The visitors put out their strongest possible team, went to St Flannan's for a pre-match puck-around, and Loughnane convinced the Clare players that Tipp had come to blow them away.

In temper it was nothing like a league match. Declan Ryan and Seanie McMahon tangled with each other early on; Daly intervened and Johnny Leahy ran from the far side of the pitch to join in. Leahy gently questioned the validity of Daly's All Star from the year before and Daly raised some issues of his own with Leahy's selection. From this high pitch the match took its tone.

'I remember late in the game, we were winning and a Tipp free dropped wide and I let fly at English and [Pat] Fox. I told them they were finished, has-beens, they should hang it up,' says Daly, laughing at the memory of it. 'Nicky was a bit upset, but all's well that ends well. We're on great terms now. Sure, I brought his wife out dancing at the All Stars.'

For Tipp the watershed games came later, all of them under the guidance of English. A young team stiffened themselves for one almighty effort in the 1999 Munster semi-final only for a Davy Fitzgerald goal from a penalty in the last minute to force a replay. Six days later Clare wiped the floor with them. As a result of an administrative cock-up in Pairc Uí Chaoimh Clare and Tipp had been billeted in adjoining dressing rooms, and as Tipp were scheduled to take the field first they got their winding-up done first. As the decibels rose next door the Clare players couldn't help hearing. 'Nicky was doing the winding-up,' says Daly, 'and his last line was, "What do we do with wounded animals? Kill!" Well, when we heard that . . . Loughnane didn't even say anything. "Get out there," he said, "and give them their answer."' That day Clare delivered one of their truly outstanding performances, even though it was slightly devalued over time. Only five of the Tipp team that started the 1999 replay also started in the All-Ireland final two years later.

Later that summer, however, the rivalry finally got out of hand. At an U-21 match in Ennis the atmosphere was poisonous. Len Gaynor went there as a spectator. 'It was terrible, absolutely terrible. There was no need for it at all. An awful lot of people were very, very saddened with that and the things that were said and the things that were shouted from the terraces. For a couple of years there it seemed as if when you won you had a licence to say what you liked to the opposition. That U-21 game in Ennis was the lowest point. You could cut the air that night with a knife. I remember Tipp scoring a goal in the middle of the second half – a crucial goal; it was a very tight match – and I was afraid to even jump up and shout. I just felt it could start off something. I think Ger Loughnane spoke out afterwards and said it was time to put a stop to it, and it certainly was.'

The enmity wasn't discontinued, just moderated for day-time TV. Tipp came back and beat Clare by eight points in 2000, and in this relationship that was their watershed. A year later, though, was just as significant because Tipp beat them in a game played on Clare's terms – stern and suffocating. It was Cyril Lyons' first championship as Clare manager, but the dressing room contribution most remembered is Daly's. He was only a sub, togging out in a Clare jersey for the last time as it turned out. When he finished speaking some players were in tears. 'I felt Tipp were coming back to give us a good hiding that day,' says Daly, 'and maybe I went a bit overboard. I was a bit hyped myself that day. I was kinda bulling that I wasn't playing because I felt I'd gone well enough in the last weeks before the match. My speech mightn't have done any good to a couple of our fellas, and it mightn't have done any harm to a few others.'

The fear in Daly's mind came from 1993. Over time the wound of that defeat closed and the scar gave their face character, but in the life of that Clare team the memory of it never died. Coming back from 1993 was their journey to fulfilment. Tipp became their starting point and their destination.

In his autobiography, Ger Loughnane explained his philosophy at length and the thinking that underpinned it. A couple of principles towered above the others. One came from something he had read in a business journal called *Sloan Management Review*. The core of it was this: 'By breaking the rules of the game and thinking of new ways to compete, a company can strategically redefine its business and catch its bigger competitors off guard. The trick is not to play the game better than the competition but to develop and play an altogether different game.' If that principle came from capitalism, the other owed more to Marxism. 'So many people said and wrote so much nonsense about the secret of the Clare team, but they missed the fundamental point,' wrote Loughnane. 'When you came on to the Clare panel, you ceased to be an individual and became part of a team. There was such a unity there that the players themselves didn't matter. All that mattered was the team performing to the maximum of its potential. That was the ethos all the time.'

We asked Daly about this peaceful surrendering of egos. 'Codology,' he says. 'Sure fellas would be going demented.'

One offspring of those principles was the naming of 'dummy' teams. In terms of flouting authority, this was a white-collar offence. Nobody got hurt and still it fed into the perception of Clare as being punk in their attitude. Fifteen players would be named in mid-week, meeting Clare's obligation to provide a team for the match programme and giving the media something to report. The players, and soon everybody else, knew that the team to do battle wouldn't be named until the day of the match, and the forwards knew this more keenly than anybody. What 'dummy' teams came to mask was a wildly rotating forward line where six or eight players wondered from match to match if their number would be pulled from the hat to fill anything up to three or four contested positions.

You could argue that the practice started with Eamon Taaffe being named to play against Cork in the 1995 Munster semi-final and Ger O'Loughlin lining out instead, but really it began with the 1997 All-Ireland final. At the time it was explained as a means of protecting Niall Gilligan. He was just twenty-one, in his rookie season, and when they started him against Cork in the Munster semi-final he failed to deliver. They suspected that the occasion had affected him and he was replaced at half-time.

When Fergie Tuohy failed a late fitness test for the All-Ireland semi-final against Kilkenny, Gilligan was thrown in at the deep end against Willie O'Connor and swam. He was going so well in training before the final that he had to start, but they wanted to recreate the conditions of the semi-final where Gilligan wouldn't have time to fret. So they told Fergal Hegarty that he would be named in the team during the week but that he wouldn't be lining out. Hegarty was sworn to secrecy, but he confided in Daly. 'I wouldn't have been intimidated by Loughnane. Well, I would a bit – everyone was – but I wasn't going to go up to Loughnane and say, "You're acting the cunt here with Hego,"' says Daly. 'I did what I could. Hego got right thick. He was thick over not playing, number one, and then he had an uncle coming home from the States who wouldn't have been coming home if he thought Hego was a sub. It was a big issue with him.'

From the management, though, there was no sympathy and no compromise. When Clare next appeared in the championship against Cork nine months later, Michael O'Halloran and Conor Clancy were replaced on the day by Brian Quinn and Alan Markham. From then on the practice was established as a strategy. For the Munster final against Waterford that summer Clare took the strategy a stage further. During the pre-match puck-around and parade all of the players remained in their track suit tops so that the starting team would be indistinguishable from the subs until moments before the throw-in, prolonging the mystery and the deceit.

The players didn't have a problem with the delaying of team announcements until match day. A lot of the time they had a sense of how the team was shaping up from training, though their best guess wasn't always right. Justifying the practice to the players, the management said they wanted to take stock of their demeanour on the day of a game, they wanted to take account of the weather and they wanted to keep the opposition guessing. The players shrugged in resigned compliance.

Eventually, though, the players found the constant rotating of the team undermining and dispiriting. During the six matches of the 1999 campaign the carousel reached top speed. In Clare's attack only Niall Gilligan and Alan Markham started every match that summer; injury ruled James O'Connor out of the Munster final and he wasn't fit enough to start in the drawn All-Ireland quarter-final against Galway. In all, Clare used thirteen forwards, eleven of whom started in at least one match. 'Unless you were a really outstanding forward,' says O'Halloran, 'you had to be playing well every day, otherwise you were likely to be chucked out.'

Christy O'Connor joined the panel as a sub goalie in 1999 and he saw the reactions at close range. 'I know for a fact that a lot of people were pissed off over it. On the morning of the drawn match against Galway I was sitting alongside Barry Murphy at the breakfast table and he found out that he was dropped and he was half-shocked. He wasn't expecting it. It was easier for senior players to accept because they always knew they were going to be playing. I know it would have been a big bug-bear with Eamon Taaffe as well – on one day, off the next day. He felt he couldn't get a chance to establish himself. Like, Fergal Hegarty was started in the drawn match against Galway, was taken off after twenty minutes and wasn't even on the panel for the replay. He wasn't on the twenty-four so he would have had to make his own way to Croke Park.'

Fergie Tuohy was a peripheral player that year and endured a similar experience to Hegarty. 'For the first Galway game I was in the stand and had a few pints. For the second Galway game [eight days later] I came on as a sub. For the Kilkenny game [All-Ireland semi-final] I was back in the stand. You can't go from number thirty to number eighteen and back to thirty again. Forwards need continuity. I know you have to freshen it up if a fella isn't good enough, but around that time Loughnane thought he was Alex Ferguson.'

The greatest criticism of Loughnane was that in creating this Clare team he had failed to build a settled, dependable forward line. In 1995 five forwards started in all four championship matches and another, Stephen McNamara, started in three. It wasn't a devastating forward line, but they had an understanding with each other and they made do. Loughnane and everybody else knew that it had to be improved, and for the 1997 championship it was.

Two years later, however, Loughnane had a roster of more than a dozen forwards of inter-county standard to choose from but he couldn't make a coherent forward line. He had options but not enough harmony or structure. In the absence of stability he gave chaos a try and attempted to pass it off as a virtue. Some days the gamble worked, but ultimately the experiment was a failure. The practice went back to Loughnane's assertion that egos must be sacrificed for the good of the team. They weren't. Not all of them, and not all the time. Such a demand flew in the face of human nature. Players couldn't be stripped of their egos and inter-changed like mannequins without damaging consequences for their confidence and performance.

When they look back, the players can see that cracks were appearing in 1999. After the gruelling six-match campaign of 1998 the last thing they needed was another punishing summer, but that's exactly what they got – another six matches. They played really well in two games that summer and came from nine points down to force a draw against Galway in the All-Ireland quarter-final, but they couldn't put two good performances back to back. Those who had been on the road a long time were feeling the pace, and with it the slow erosion of self-discipline.

'There's a general acceptance among the senior players that there wasn't enough effort put in,' says Daly, 'in terms of lifestyle, eating, drinking. Fellas were that bit laxer than they were other years. There was a staleness there. Fellas weren't reacting to each other and not reacting to the management. I remember even [Brian] Lohan saying it to me. I nearly got a weakness. It might have been only one night with him that he let himself go but that would be in his head. I knew the fellas I was closer to were at it. Like, this was the fifth year in a row that we were at it. You know, you'd go to the Galway Races and you're looking at the Sheedys drinking porter and you want to enjoy the Galway Races too. We were definitely slipping a little bit.'

The grind was unreconstructed. In January 1998, at the first team meeting of the year, Anthony Daly raised the possibility of a change with Mike McNamara. On holiday the players had contemplated a fourth successive winter bleeding their guts in Crusheen and on the hill in Shannon, and the hamsters began to think that a different wheel might be nice. McNamara gave Daly his answer. 'I told them,' said McNamara, 'that if variety is what they wanted they should change their women. Or words to that effect.'

'He put us in our box fairly quickly,' says Daly. 'He said that Crusheen had served us well. There might be a bit of variety but basically it would be the same shit, different year, and if you don't want to do it you can fuck off. That kind of set the tone for the year.'

In the minds of the Clare management there was no other way for this team. In time their folly was exposed, first by the weariness of their own players and then by the wisdom of others. Tipp, for example, pushed themselves to extremes in training just to get over Clare, but after two years of that kind of preparation management realized that it was counter-productive and in the third year, 2001, Tipp won the All-Ireland by training less but in a more focused and enlightened way. Clare didn't make that leap. Crusheen had buttressed their minds as well as steeled their bodies, but once they had made the transition from losers to winners they didn't need Crusheen to give them a winning mentality any more. They didn't need to suffer in order to believe. Gratuitously, habitually, the suffering continued.

'Looking back,' says O'Halloran, 'it would be the one criticism that I would have, that the programmes were never tailored for individuals. Everyone did the same thing together. I pulled out in '99 but I'll never forget watching the All-Ireland semi-final against Kilkenny and thinking how heavy-legged the Clare players were. I know how fast Niall Gilligan was and David Forde and Alan Markham having marked them in training, and they literally couldn't get away from a player like Willie O'Connor. They just didn't have the same buzz in their legs.'

It was the last year that the original management served together. Loughnane brought in Sean Stack as a fourth selector, on the grounds that if he wasn't included in the Clare set-up Galway or some other county might grab him. Loughnane made no secret of his desire to groom Stack as his successor, and this cut the ground from under Mike McNamara. Eventually it became clear to Loughnane and the Clare players that Stack wasn't cut out to be the next Clare manager. So, at the end of 1999 Loughnane dissolved the management team and came back with new selectors in 2000: Louis Mulqueen and Cyril Lyons, the new manager-designate.

There was no serious falling-out between Loughnane and McNamara in 1999, but the cooling of their relationship was apparent to everyone on the panel. 'Bringing in Stack pissed off Mike Mac big time,' says Christy O'Connor, 'but Mac was willing to subjugate that level of frustration for the good of the team. A lot of the Clare boys would have massive time for Mac. I know some of the Clare players mightn't have been too impressed with the level of abuse that he might have given them, but Mac had that quality that you'd still respect him no matter what.'

'At the end of the day,' says O'Halloran, 'they're big egos – and I don't mean that in a bad way. What made them the type of men they were and the trainers they were was their ego. They wouldn't have been anything without it, but inevitably it was what was going to cause them to split. You hear of All-Ireland-winning teams where the players hate each other and are bitching about each other, but in our scene the players are still very close. We meet for a golf outing once a year and Mike Mac will always be there. Ger might come but he'll always be with Tony [Considine]. There'll be a bit of dinner afterwards and then they will go away and everyone else will nearly stay around. It's just a pity that the boys have taken their spat into the public really, especially in the last year.'

In his book, Loughnane says that he considered quitting again at the end of 1999 but Lyons told him that he wouldn't step in as manager without spending a year as a selector first. So Loughnane stayed and tried once more to light the fire. The league didn't go well in the spring – which was neither here nor there when Clare were at their peak. The big day would come and they'd be ready. Loughnane, though, was cranky after a league defeat to Limerick in Miltown Malbay, and whether his fury was staged or not he let rip in the dressing room.

'We'd a really big training panel in 2000,' says Christy O'Connor, 'and there would have been a lot of young guys on the panel, and they tortured them – literally. It was savage training. But I remember he went bananas after that league match. A few of the younger guys were in the dressing room and they didn't know where to look. They had this look of fright on their faces. This was the first they'd seen of the real Loughnane. The venom had been unleashed. He just felt that the rot was setting in then. We'd lost to Galway and we'd laid down basically against Limerick. I think it was just the manner of the surrender.'

St Joseph's Doora-Barefield were trying to defend their All-Ireland club title that spring, which tied up key players such as James O'Connor, Ollie Baker and Sean McMahon. Between club and county commitments those players hadn't enjoyed an extended break from hurling since the summer of 1996, and there was no relief in sight. 'In 2000 they got it hopelessly wrong,' says James O'Connor. 'We were involved with the club but we did some of the physical sessions with Clare, and I remember one night in Crusheen Ger said he wanted to see myself, Baker and Seanie. I was bollixed and sick of it, and I assumed he was going to say that we needed a break. Next thing he fucking tore into us about the way we were gone soft and lazy and wanted things easy, and all this kind of stuff. I was there with my mouth open. I remember coming back to the car feeling like I could burst into tears. The result of it was he drove us on harder in training. The thing was ceaseless. I couldn't understand it. Looking back now there's no question about it that it certainly contributed to Clare not getting as much out of us in subsequent years because of the way we were managed around that time.'

When Loughnane recalled the breakthrough of 1995 he spoke of 'driving the horse over the fence'. The problem was that five years later he hadn't discovered how to ride the horse any other way. Either the horse would be driven over the fence or it would fall. All or nothing.

In 2000, the horse fell in a heap.

After the last league match against Dublin the players were given a week off and then they embarked on an intensive programme of training that involved sessions on twenty-six days out of thirty-five. At the end of it they played Kilkenny in a challenge match, a fortnight before the Munster semi-final against Tipperary, and were blown off the pitch. They all knew that the tank was empty. They rested for the last two weeks but what had been lost couldn't be replaced.

In an interview for the All Stars history *The Chosen Ones*, Brian Lohan said that he took the field against Tipp weighing just twelve and a half stone – a stone and a half below his normal weight. 'We were supposed to be the fittest Clare team ever but we had trained too hard,' says Lohan. 'We didn't train smart. We just trained for the sake of training. It was stupid stuff. There was an awful lot of strength in a stone and a half.'

The thing that had made them strong in the beginning had drained all the strength from them in the end.

'Tipp beat us fairly well that day [eight points],' says Daly. 'Sure we'd nothing left. Even for the All-Ireland semi-final against Kilkenny the year before we'd very little in the tank. Loughnane would say something to motivate us but there wasn't much he could do. It was just wearing off at that stage.'

Loughnane announced his resignation at the next county board meeting. The great matador had left the bull ring. The bull ring was an altered place now.

A better place.

8. Old Money, Tiger Economy

Maybe you've forgotten how things used to be. For Cork, Kilkenny and Tipperary, hurling was their vast private estate. They didn't hold the deeds, exactly, but that didn't seem to affect their assertion of ownership. Every other county was either a trespasser or a poacher. At the end of the 1993 championship the Big Three had won seventy-six senior All-Irelands between them. Ten other counties shared thirty-one titles spread out over 106 years. Some of those titles were so old that they were part of antiquity. Relics. Tipperary once went eighteen years without winning an All-Ireland, Cork went sixteen years, Kilkenny went nine years a couple of times; but when one of the Big Three was down the other two prospered. In the history of hurling the Big Three had never gone more than two years without winning an All-Ireland.

And then, in the middle of the 1990s, the Big Three went five years without winning an All-Ireland. For three consecutive years, 1994 to 1996, none of the Big Three even appeared in an All-Ireland final. Here was the revolution. For the first time in the history of the game the Big Three weren't setting the agenda. They were left behind and challenged to catch up.

Sit down with a video of the 1992 All-Ireland final between Cork and Kilkenny and the 1999 final between the same two teams and the most dramatic period in the evolution of hurling is expressed before your eyes. In 1992 Cork and Kilkenny played the old game; by 1999 they had learned the new one. They had no choice.

I

It didn't matter that Tipperary had lost the 1997 All-Ireland final by a single point scored in the last minute of an epic match. It wasn't the beginning of anything or a staging post on the road to anywhere. On the first Sunday of the following June they were beaten by Waterford in the championship for the first time in fifteen years. The Tipp manager Len Gaynor didn't believe in the training methods that Clare and their admirers had embraced. He termed it 'commando' training and feared for the long-term welfare of players fed through the mincer of those regimes. So Tipp stuck to traditional principles and trusted in their hurling.

In 1997 it nearly worked; in 1998 it didn't. Tipp were unfit and off the pace. Gaynor stepped down; Nicky English stepped up. In hurling's new world Tipp were landed gentry in the big house, their status sustained by the past. Old money in a tiger economy.

When Tipp were cock of the walk under Babs Keating in the late '80s and early '90s English was the embodiment of their sophistication – svelte and smart. Slick forward play was the lifeblood of that team, and English was the pulse. Nobody who shared a dressing room with English doubted that he would manage the team one day; only the timing of his appointment caused surprise. The 1997 team was already in need of fundamental reform and the U-21 players who were identified as the raw material for change had been annihilated by Cork in the 1998 Munster final. Taking over only two years after his own retirement would mean confronting the decline of players he had soldiered with. Yet he accepted the job, and with it the biggest challenge of his hurling life.

He knew what was needed and he knew where Tipp

were lacking. As his own career drew to a close his attitude hardened. He privately confronted teammates about their contribution and spoke openly about deficiencies in Tipp's big-match nerve. Since Tipperary last won the All-Ireland in 1991 they had lost eight championship matches; seven of them by a goal or less, the other by four points. The trend was held up as a fault in the team's character.

English's only experience in management was with Dublin City University's Fitzgibbon Cup team, but it was a revealing trailer for the blockbuster to come. To toughen them up he introduced boxing gloves and tackling bags to training, just as Clare had done in 1995. There were training sessions at 8 a.m., and sometimes earlier at weekends. He challenged them and improved them with an irresistible zeal. They lost narrowly in the first round of the Fitzgibbon Cup but they won the Ryan Cup for second-division colleges, the first trophy in the history of the club.

With Tipperary his DCU methods were blown up to the relevant magnification. As part of a screening process he set up interviews with all of the players at the Anner Hotel in Thurles. Players were asked about their lifestyle and their goals, the formality of the exchange designed to give it weight. 'It was something that could have been done outside a dressing room,' says Brendan Cummins, a member of the Tipp panel since 1993, 'but he was showing us how serious it is.'

Physical tests were done on the players and those who didn't meet their standards for endurance or body-fat levels were given individual targets and told they wouldn't be considered until those targets were met. The 1997 captain Conor Gleeson was excluded from the panel for six months until he satisfied their requirements. Eugene O'Neill, Young Hurler of the Year in 1997, was jettisoned for even longer.

Tipp were drawn against Clare in the first round of the 1999 championship, but even without such an urgent focus Clare would have silently shadowed them that winter. Four years after their breakthrough All-Ireland this was a whole new phase in Clare's influence. It wasn't simply that they had demonstrated to all of the other oppressed counties what was possible. They had forced the powerful counties to examine themselves and accept that they couldn't win All-Irelands any more just by doing what they had always done. This was an intellectual leap for the Big Three because none of them had ever taken their cue from a breakthrough county before. Galway's running game in the 1980s, for example, was generally disdained by Cork, Kilkenny and Tipperary, and certainly not imitated. Clare's impact was altogether more potent.

Tipp needed to find a path that would take them to places Clare had been. They needed Clare's mentality, and to acquire it they needed to suffer. 'We were so far back in Tipp hurling,' says Cummins. 'We didn't understand what training to win an All-Ireland was about. I thought every year I was doing the right thing to win an All-Ireland. But when you play teams that have actually won it and see the look on their faces and the intensity they have, then you say to yourself, "Jesus, I'm only in the ha'penny place."

'It was never actually said that we had to do what Clare were doing, but it was implied all the time. Then it was said one day. "If ye want to win anything, ye have to beat Clare." They were the standard. If the Clare fellas were willing to go through a wall we had to go through two walls. If you could stand up to Clare you could stand up to anyone.

'Nothing against any of the other teams, but Clare was where we all wanted to be. It was where I wanted to be as a player anyway, at Clare's level. I didn't care whether everyone loved or hated me, I just wanted to win, and that's why everybody hated Clare at the time: because they were so successful.'

English brought variety and freshness. The squad had a session with a rugby league trainer and they had contact with a sports psychologist. Training began in November, only twice a week at first, but the Saturday session might be at 6 a.m. And then, about once a month, they went hill running on Devil's Bit. 'We weren't going up and down it as often as people said we were,' says Cummins, 'but it suited us to have people say we were.'

One session was different from all the others. English described it as a 'team-building exercise', something like the Lions rugby team had done before their tour to South Africa. At the Garda College in Templemore the team was delivered into the hands of Garda trainers and their limits ruthlessly explored. The players were told to bring three changes of gear and nothing else.

They did a five-mile run on the first night and were roused from their beds at four o'clock the following morning to run some more. Interminable laps of a small field with just a T-shirt and shorts to insulate them from the cold; they weren't even allowed to wear socks inside their running shoes. They were returned to their beds an hour later and disturbed again at 6.30, long before sleep could mature into rest.

They had breakfast first and then a meeting before they ran from Templemore up to Devil's Bit, a distance of more than five miles. On Devil's Bit they ran around a mucky field for an hour and then were told they would have to run back to Templemore again. A mile down the road, though, a bus was waiting to take them. Their legs didn't need the run and their minds had already processed the torture.

Back in the college they sat an aptitude test to gauge how their minds reacted under extreme tiredness, a laboratory simulation for the last five minutes of a championship match in the heat of summer. Against, say, Clare. Because it was Saturday night the players expected some licence to enjoy themselves. Instead they exercised some more in the swimming pool and were in bed by ten o'clock. At four o'clock the following morning they were wrenched from their beds again. Another run from Templemore to the Devil's Bit. Later that morning they had a meeting to discuss the value and purpose of the weekend, and at noon they were honourably discharged back into civilian life. Most of the players didn't make it to work the following day.

They didn't beat Clare that summer. They led by a goal with time virtually up but then Conor Clancy forced a penalty and Davy Fitzgerald buried it. Six days later Clare beat them by ten points in the replay. It was over in twenty minutes. Cummins kept pucking out the ball in double quick time, faithful to the plan that they would hit Clare like a whirlwind. Tipp's whirlwind, though, brushed against Clare's cheek like a summer breeze.

'Our game was going to be based on high intensity,' says Cummins. 'We probably thought that eventually Clare will get tired – and it never happened. We thought, "This is our bloody game," but we were the ones on the rack. It seemed to work in the first game because we doubled the intensity on them and we didn't leave them settle for a minute. We said, "Look, we'll match fire with fire and eventually the hurling will show out." We figured that man for man we had the better hurling team, so we'll get the physical part out of the way.

'In the replay we were boxing Clare. Under the Covered Stand in Pairc Uí Chaoimh a row broke out and a couple of players came from 50 or 60 yards to get involved. They had no business there. We lost the row. It was crazy. Clare were laughing at us, and they were right to.'

The practised stoicism, the artifice of calm, the months of contemplation, the seventy minutes of mind-bending concentration and strangling anxiety – all of it obliterated by one point and the final whistle. Tipperary 0–15, Clare 0–14 the scoreboard said simply, with exaggerated understatement.

English jumped. He clenched his fist and punched the air and ran and jumped. He bear-hugged one player, then another, and before he knew it he was facing the Open Stand in Pairc Uí Chaoimh, his arms spread like a priest at the consecration, a vision of demented bliss.

It was two years since the disastrous replay of 1999 and twelve months since Tipp had inflicted an eight-point revenge on Clare, but those matches hadn't resolved anything; they'd only heaped tyres on the bonfire. Clare were coming close to the end of their tether but they had a new manager in Cyril Lyons and Tipp knew that Clare would charge at them again in 2001. For this Tipp team it was make or break. The consensus that English had assembled the best Tipp panel of his three years in charge would be worthless in defeat. They had to win. They won.

For Tipp, the deeply satisfying part was that they had beaten Clare in a war waged on Clare's terms. A hard, grinding, suffocating match that went down to the wire, the kind of performance that was three years in the making. 'Eoin Kelly [making his championship debut] got hit that day and was turned up on his head,' says Cummins. 'He got up, drove the ball down the field and sprinted on like nothing was after happening. That showed all of the training coming together in one go. He had the physicality and the endurance to take the wallop and he had the mentality that what he had to do with the ball was the most important thing.'

Putting themselves in a position to beat Clare, reconstituting themselves to be capable of it, had brought Tipp on to a level where they could be seriously competitive again. But to win an All-Ireland they had to put Clare behind them. Since English had taken over the teams had now met six times in league and championship and Tipp had been beaten only once. In English's view, though, the team had dealt badly with beating Clare in 2000 and it undermined the rest of their summer. They lost a Munster final to Cork, shooting seventeen wides and missing two penalties; they lost an All-Ireland quarter-final to Galway playing badly. By the end of that summer Tipp were struggling to break even.

English recognized the need to change again. Runs up Devil's Bit were abandoned. The kind of training they had designed to beat Clare was self-defeating now. On the advice of Dr Liam Hennessy, the IRFU's fitness director, English acquired the services of Jim Kilty, an athletics coach. Kilty held the franchise in Ireland for a new kind of training called SAQ, which stood for Speed, Agility, Quickness. Its purpose was to build speed endurance, otherwise known as multi-sprint stamina. It also developed agility and sought to make every action on the field an automatic reflex. For hurling it was perfect. SAQ involved a specific weights programme but it didn't involve endless laps or a hard slog. Elite rugby teams in Ireland and Britain had embraced the practice, but in the preparation of a hurling team it was a new departure.

Hennessy had been Tipp's trainer when they won the All-Ireland in 1991, a year when the entire training programme was condensed into sixty sessions. He had no doubt that hurling teams were training excessively and failing to train smart.

By 2001 the group had a clear identity. Only eight of the team that started against Clare in 1999 were still in the first fifteen when Tipp won the Munster final two years later, but the team was settled now and structured. John Leahy and Declan Ryan were the only players left on the panel who held All-Ireland medals, and their influence was huge. Leahy wasn't fully fit for the first round against Clare in 2001 and started on the bench, but this in no way excluded him from Tipp's strategy. 'Our game plan,' said English, 'was pretty straightforward: go for as long as we could without John Leahy. And then, within thirty seconds of him coming on, he was gone.'

Leahy landed awkwardly near the Clare goal and damaged cruciate ligaments in his knee. His season was wiped out. Which left Ryan. Outside the group his importance was not fully understood. A bad experience with the media ten years earlier meant that Ryan didn't do interviews, so he didn't have the public profile of other players on that Tipp team. Anybody who met him would have said he was a quiet fellow.

In any case it looked to outsiders that he was finished in 2000. Injury had stalked him all year, and when he moved stiffly on to the pitch at Croke Park, a late addition to the subs for the All-Ireland quarter-final and nowhere near the team, we suspected that it was the last time we would see him in the blue and gold. But within the panel his presence had such an aura that English knew the value of rehabilitating him for one more season.

'He was huge for Tipp hurling over those years,' says Cummins. 'He was just a huge figure. He wouldn't say much. A couple of times all right when training was going bad Declan would call everyone in and say a few words. But I'd say he was the biggest figure I learned from. I used to sit with him before matches whenever I could. I never roomed with him, but one time I was feeling a little bit nervous before a game so I went into Declan for about an hour, hour and a half. No one said a word. "Well," I said going in. "Well," he said back. We just sat there watching television. Discuss the match? No. But I came out of the room on a high because the feeling you had around Declan was that everything was under control. Completely calm. This was only a game of hurling at the end of the day. You have the ability; you know what you have to do. He never said any of this, but the vibe you got when he walked into a room . . . The respect he commanded the very minute he walked in was just crazy.

'Players don't respect talkers, they respect doers, and at the end of the day he was a doer. On the field he had everything so right. When we played Clare everyone was going at 110 miles an hour but when Declan got the ball it all went into slow motion. He had so much time. Meanwhile there are five Clare players on his back and they can't get the ball off him.

'When we beat Clare in 2001 we were a point up with a minute left when we got a free. I looked up the field and Declan pointed to the corner flag so I drove the free up to the corner flag and Declan stood on it. He caused a row and it went out for a line ball. He stood over the line ball and wouldn't allow it to be taken. The Clare fella moved the ball up further and the ref moved him back. It just killed the whole thing.'

Tipp won the Munster final by a point. It was the first time in Cummins' career with Tipp that he had won a championship match by a point. In his eighth summer on the team it was his first Munster championship medal too, but they didn't allow themselves to get hysterical about it. He was home in bed before midnight. The All-Ireland was the thing.

Against Wexford in the semi-final they nearly blew it. Twice in the second half they went eight points clear but at the end they were hanging on. The referee blew for full time before all of the indicated stoppage time had been played, and it was Tipp who embraced the draw.

'The drawn match was the longest game of my life,' says Cummins. 'I'll never forget it. I even questioned what I was doing there. "Why are you here? Sure you're doing no fucking good to anybody being here if you're a bundle of nerves." Those things get into your head. Wexford got a couple of goals and at that point in the game I was hitting the ropes. Philly [Maher, full-back] was after hitting them. The whole full-back line had just gone to bits because I, behind them, wasn't going well either. We just collapsed. I remember after the game sitting down in the dressing room going, "Thanks be to God that's over." We escaped.'

They won the replay by eleven points six days later in a match destroyed by torrential rain, a disintegrating pitch and three sendings-off – two from Wexford and Brian O'Meara from Tipp. The referee reported O'Meara for striking and his suspension ruled him out of the final. Tipp were furious, but nothing was going to derail them. Not now.

'I remember the day before the final I was sitting at home,' Cummins recalls. 'My parents were gone up for the weekend and I was there on my own and I said to myself, "Fuck it, when I come back here I'm going to have an All-Ireland medal." It was as simple as that. Any time I got scared – and you do get frightened out of your mind before matches – I said, "Look, this is why you're doing it." The fear left and the confidence took over again.

'I was 100 per cent right for that game, never more in all my life. Nicky was very good at the mental aspect of your game. The key to getting inside a fella's head is that you don't let him think or feel that you're getting inside it. He appealed to everything that we wanted. You want to win an All-

Ireland? Yeah. Are you prepared to do anything to win it? Yeah. But are you really prepared to do anything? And eventually he got the fellas who were really prepared to do anything.

'For the All-Ireland final I didn't even notice the grass. I didn't know there was a crest in the middle of the field until I watched the video afterwards. I didn't realize the goalmouths were all mucky – and they were. But these things you don't take any heed of whatsoever because I was so right for it.

'I think it was probably the most mature performance to come out of that fifteen because there were times in it when we went four or five points ahead and they came back. At one stage it looked as if Galway were going to go three or four points ahead of us. But we always had it in control. We were in control of what we were doing.'

They had finished the year unbeaten – championship, league, challenge games, tournament matches. During the year that sequence had never been mentioned. The players were unaware of it until it was highlighted on *The Sunday Game* that evening. It was an unconscious expression of their excellence.

Three years after they entered the tunnel they had exited into the light. The tunnel had been the only way.

II

A video was made of Cork's All-Ireland weekend in 1999 with a handheld camcorder. The cameraman was a close associate of the panel and the tape was meant purely for private use, which meant that his access was hardly checked. What he produced is a priceless document, rough but intimate.

One scene stands out. After the final whistle Cork players

filtered back into the dressing room, hooting and hollering. Then Teddy Owens, the Cork trainer, appeared. Not the tallest man, Owens stood up on a bench to get the attention of the dressing room and held up a photograph. It was taken during Cork's sixteen-point mauling by Limerick at Pairc Uí Chaoimh in the 1996 championship and it captured the Cork management standing in the dug-out, devastation and bewilderment grafted on to their faces.

'Take a look at that,' roared Owens, 'and take a look at Jimmy now.'

The juxtaposition of those images framed the journey Cork had travelled under Jimmy Barry-Murphy. That defeat to Limerick was the first time Cork had lost at home in the championship for seventy-three years. Elders of the tribe checked the race memory and declared that it was the lowest point since 1965. Cork had bottomed out.

Limerick were one of the modern teams. They were fit and self-aware and driven, just like Clare had been in 1995 and like Wexford would be that summer. They had attitude and aggression and they didn't depend on their hurling alone to be competitive. Cork, however, still felt they could. That was the critical difference.

What history gave Cork hurling was a cockiness poorly disguised as everyday confidence. Since 1942 there had only been eleven years when they weren't at the top of hurling's roll of honour or tied for the position. They had come from nowhere to win their last All-Ireland in 1990, and in Cork there was a native conviction that this was possible at any time.

Yet there was a realization that things were bad. On the weekend that Tipp played Limerick at Pairc Uí Chaoimh in the 1995 championship Cork played Kerry in Tralee on the Saturday night. In the gents toilet under the Covered Stand one Cork supporter turned to another who had been in Tralee the night before.

'Will Cork get out of Munster?' he asked.

'Cork,' came the reply, 'wouldn't get out of Cork.'

Into this perishing climate Jimmy Barry-Murphy brought warmth, like the Gulf Stream. With him as selectors were Tom Cashman and Tony O'Sullivan, completing a management team that contained three of the most cherished Cork hurlers of the previous twenty years. The local press anointed them as the Dream Team. Optimism soared.

They blooded young guys and held on to old guys as scaffolding while the team was under construction, but they couldn't magic a team from thin air. By the time Clare hammered Cork at home in their final league game in March 1996, reality was biting hard. For the championship game against Limerick two months later pessimism capped the crowd at 20,000, fewer than half of it from Cork.

Barry-Murphy was shaken by the defeat and bruised by the reaction. He considered some of the criticism in the local media to be excessively personal and kept one newspaper cutting in his office drawer for years afterwards. Hostile letters were published with false addresses, and before he knew it he was questioning his own judgement.

The most important thing he realized was that he had been naive. In the beginning he had trusted too much in the perceived depth of Cork hurling and the elemental power of the red jersey. But Clare winning the All-Ireland in 1995 was like Year Zero. Limerick beating Cork by sixteen points in Pairc Uí Chaoimh only confirmed that hurling had passed into a new epoch.

In the first year Barry-Murphy and Cashman supervised Cork's physical training themselves. It was the kind of training they had done themselves as players, but it was an anachronism

now. For the following year Barry-Murphy enlisted the
expertise of the former Cork footballer Kevin Kehily, who
ran gyms in the city. Kehily, however, had to pull out for
personal reasons during the season and Barry-Murphy took
up the slack again. Barry-Murphy's next appointment was
Teddy Owens. They were in business.

'I'd never heard of Teddy Owens,' says Fergal McCormack,
who made his Cork debut in the Limerick mauling. 'I hadn't
a clue who he was, but Teddy Owens would drive the bus if
you gave him a chance. Teddy is the most confident man
that you ever came across in your life – which was great at
the time. He outlined exactly what we were going to do. He
had all these charts and we got tests done and you could feel
the difference. Teddy is principal in Glanmire community
school and we got the results down there. Dr Con [Murphy,
team doctor] said a few words and it was a big thing. We
were going places and becoming more professional. It was
only simple things. Ger Loughnane would have Clare training at six o'clock in the morning, so we went training on
St Stephen's Day – and so on.'

After 1995 nobody expected to win the Munster championship without beating Clare first. Clare had beaten Cork
in 1993 and again in 1995 with a last-minute goal, but neither
defeat threatened Cork's fundamental view of themselves or
where they stood with Clare. Against Clare they would
expect to win and blame themselves if they didn't. On the
week that the teams met in 1997 the Cork full-forward Alan
Browne suggested in an interview that Cork had more hurling
than Clare and wouldn't concede anything in fitness. In Cork
that wouldn't have been a minority view.

Clare ground them down, though, just as they did in the
Munster semi-final a year later. By then Cork had won the
National League and in beating Limerick had claimed a cham-

pionship scalp other than Kerry's for the first time in six years. Cork had hammered Clare in the 1998 league semi-final too, but the match meant nothing to Clare and their performance that day was worthless. All kinds of rumours circulated, including one that they had trained on the morning of the match. The reality was far less machiavellian. They hadn't tapered their training coming into the game and they weren't pumped up. Clare didn't have a high cruising speed for run-of-the-mill matches and they were unable to win in cold blood. In the championship match, however, normal conditions applied.

'We were confident enough going in against them,' says McCormack, 'but we were brought down to earth. There was a bit of a schemozzle early on. There were mini-duels all over the place and they got the better of them. They probably out-muscled, out-thought and out-played us in the end. After that we realized that we had to go that step further to progress.'

Clare bullied Cork that day. They played with the kind of menace that always accompanied their most potent performances, and Cork had no answer. In Cork the consensus was that Barry-Murphy would have to come back with a team built for combat. Barry-Murphy took the opposite view. He had no desire to build a team that could look Clare in the eye and stare them down. It wasn't the way he had played and it wasn't the way he wanted his teams to play.

McCormack remembers a league match against Laois the following spring when one of the Laois players struck him off the ball. McCormack squared up to his man but he didn't hit him back. Afterwards one of the Cork selectors rounded on McCormack for his pacifism. 'He fucked me from a height. "You'll have to stand up for yourself," he said, "You'll have to hit him back." And I could see Jimmy shaking his head.

Afterwards he called me over and he said, "Don't mind that. You were right not to hit him back." When we played Clare in 1999 we didn't want to become confrontational with them. That wouldn't have been Jimmy's thing. We were muscled out of it the year before and we didn't want to be muscled out of it again, but we didn't want to get into that kind of confrontational thing either.'

Looking back through the first half of 1999 there was nothing to suggest that Cork were going to be All-Ireland champions. In the spring a table was compiled of all the teams in that year's championship, calculating their ranking on a percentage of wins to losses over the previous ten years. On those rankings Cork came seventh.

In the autumn of 1998 the Cork U-21s had retained their All-Ireland title, but none of that impetus survived to the following spring. Defeat against Laois was the low point of a flat league campaign, and worse was to follow. A couple of weeks before they played Waterford in the championship they met Tipperary in two challenge games, home and away. Both ended in abject defeat.

'Things were just going horribly wrong,' says McCormack. 'There was no settled team and we had gone back a good bit again. We played Tipp in a challenge match and they were taking the piss out of us. Their fellas were having a laugh, and we felt we nearly deserved it because we were gone so bad. The first challenge game against Tipp wasn't so bad, but we were still well beaten. We could say we were away and we'd beat them at home the following week but then they hammered us at home and we were saying, "Jesus Christ, what's this?" This was only a couple of weeks before the Waterford match.'

Barry-Murphy was so despairing after the second Tipp match that senior players thought he was going to walk away.

He stayed, and for the Waterford match he gambled with everything he had. Six players were given their championship debut on a team whose average age was just twenty-three. If Cork failed that day Barry-Murphy's career as Cork manager was over. They won.

'I had faith in the players,' he said afterwards. 'I picked a team of hurlers.' A team of hurlers – that was his guiding principle. In hindsight, anything else would have been vulgar. Barry-Murphy simply couldn't have produced a team that depended on force. Yet Clare were next. How could they beat Clare without force?

They were fired up for Clare, there was no question about that. Everything about their approach to the Clare game was different from the year before. For years Cork teams playing in Thurles had taken lunch in the Anner Hotel on the outskirts of the town, even though there was no place for a puck-around and no chance of privacy. In 1999 they chose the seclusion of the Dundrum Golf and Country Club, a few miles west of Cashel and away from all the main routes to Thurles. They had a few pucks on a stretch of the golf course and had their team meeting in the clubhouse. A video had been pre-pared of selected moments from the previous year's meeting with Clare. Of Clare biting and Cork just barking back.

'After the Clare defeat [in 1998], we realized that we weren't mentally or physically at the right level,' said Fergal Ryan. 'We weren't expecting what was thrown at us.'

In 1999 Cork braced themselves for a storm that never came. As a championship team Clare depended on a needle or a cause or a slight, but they had no beef with Cork and no special fear of them either. Each of their last four champion-ship meetings had ended in a Clare victory. They hadn't beaten Cork in a Munster final since 1932, but that wasn't enough to get their juices flowing.

Cork had no such difficulty. Their shoulders were back and their chests were out. In the pre-match parade McCormack remembers one of the Cork players shouting across at the Clare captain Anthony Daly '27–3, 27–3!' broadcasting the latest score between the teams in the All-Ireland roll of honour. Daly looked over, a little perplexed. Cork's arrogance had a voice again.

Very few of that Cork team were capable of real aggression, but Fergal Ryan was one. He was booked early in the match and before half-time he might have been sent off. Niall Gilligan just evaded his block to score from the sideline, and as he was moving back to his position he met Ryan with a shoulder. Ryan interpreted the contact as an inflammatory gesture and tried to grip Gilligan in a headlock. Twelve months earlier none of the Cork players had shown such devil.

And still, Cork rode their luck. Injury had ruled James O'Connor out of the match and forced Ollie Baker to retire after half-time when he was dominating the game and leading Clare's fight-back. With a few minutes left David Forde missed a 21-yard free to bring the teams level, and only then did Cork pull clear to win.

Cork had impetus now. The summer was stretching out before them. Half of this Cork team had never played in Croke Park at any level but they went there for the All-Ireland semi-final against Offaly and played without fear.

Mark Landers was an outstanding captain that summer, but the key to everything was Barry-Murphy. He understood the game and believed in the value of its simplicity. He didn't want to complicate it. He didn't try to change players either. Rather, he gave them the confidence and the licence to express their talents.

Others looked after the minutiae. Owens analysed every

one of Donal Óg Cusack's puck-outs and gave him a print-out after every match, detailing the outcome of each. Cork had difficulty winning their own ball so Cusack, McCormack and Neil Ronan devised a strategy between them. They approached Barry-Murphy with their blueprint. 'In fairness to Jimmy,' says McCormack, 'he just said, "Look, ye're at liberty to do whatever ye want there. That's yer call."'

In Cork Barry-Murphy was an idol, but the players saw a side of him they never could have guessed existed. 'Jimmy was brilliant,' says McCormack, 'but he has no confidence talking in front of fellas. And then, when he spoke, he was fucking brilliant. I remember before the All-Ireland final that year, the footballers were in the All-Ireland as well and we were both training on the same day in Pairc Uí Chaoimh. We were in a huddle and Larry Tompkins [the Cork football manager] came down to us. He said his bit and Teddy says to Jimmy, "You'll have to go up there and say a few words to the footballers." "What'll I say, Teddy? Will you come up with me? Come on." They went up and I was talking to a couple of the footballers afterwards and they said it was the most uplifting few words they'd heard all year. That was typical. No confidence, but when he started speaking it was brilliant.

'I'll always remember before the match in the dressing room on the day of the All-Ireland final we were presented with our jerseys by Jimmy and it was a very emotional thing. There was a handshake and a hug. It was fierce spontaneous. I don't think anybody knew about it. Everyone was brought up with JBM as a hero and a legend and here you were up in Croke Park receiving your All-Ireland jersey from him. It was something else. You know, you'd like to win a match for yourself first, but you'd like to win it for Jimmy next. He was a great figurehead. He didn't upset anyone and he didn't like upsetting fellas.'

Barry-Murphy's approach was the opposite of Loughnane's yet, in the era that Loughnane defined, Cork were able to reach the All-Ireland final without beating anybody at Clare's game. They sucked what they needed from Clare's example and spat out the rest.

In awful weather the final against Kilkenny was an anti-spectacle, probably the worst final of the 1990s. Cork won it with a devastating surge in the final quarter and the identity of the match-winner was a glorious vindication of Barry-Murphy's philosophy. Seanie McGrath was the smallest man on the field, not blessed with power and not inclined to play the percentages. In the modern game he was an endangered species, and at half-time he could easily have been taken off. Cork kept faith, though, and McGrath's confidence was incorruptible. In the closing fifteen minutes he flashed over three points and Cork prevailed by one.

'We felt that it was going to happen and it just did,' says McCormack. 'Whether it was destiny or whatever it was, it was something that you believed was going to happen.'

On that day, it was almost as if the revolution had never happened. Almost.

III

Think of it now and let the memory sit for a minute. Kilkenny arrived in Parnell Park for the first round of the 1998 championship stalked by the fear of an upset. Dublin had rattled them the previous summer. They had stumbled through the league under new management and they were without a Leinster title in five years.

On the day they murdered Dublin. With the breeze in the second half they routed them by 3–14 to 0–3. As the summer went on, though, Kilkenny proceeded with a halting step. Laois ran them to a goal; the Leinster final was scrappy, decided by two frees that D. J. Carey smuggled into the Offaly net; Waterford seized up in the All-Ireland semi-final and Kilkenny mugged them by a point, 1–11 to 1–10 – a bad football score. That was the way they were. You looked at the caterpillar and couldn't picture the butterfly.

They entered the All-Ireland final as uneasy favourites, their status underpinned by the hackneyed wisdom – or superstition – that Kilkenny would be different in an All-Ireland final. They weren't. Not that Kilkenny team. Not yet. Offaly did them.

'We didn't seem to be going anywhere,' says Willie O'Connor. 'The training that year was up and down a bit. There were a lot of old lads there and there were new lads coming and maybe it was just an in-between time. We were very lucky to even be in that All-Ireland because Waterford should have beaten us in the semi-final.

'We weren't convincing. Probably our heads weren't right going into the All-Ireland, but there was no excuse. There were a lot of question marks over that team and they were answered that day. Then Kevin Fennelly [manager] left so he mustn't have thought we were going too far either.'

The record breaking six-in-a-row in Leinster started that year, without fanfare or presumption, and seven of the Parnell Park fifteen won an All-Ireland two years later.

To make their wine, the sour grapes of 1998 needed to be crushed. That was the beginning.

Winning is necessarily the measure of that Kilkenny team's greatness, but it was losing that made them. When you consider the pivotal, formative matches in the life of that team the only victory that springs to mind is the 2002 All-Ireland semi-final against Tipperary, but by then they had been through the furnace of their worst defeats. The All-Ireland final of 1999 forced them on to another level; the All-Ireland semi-final of 2001 goaded them on to the highest level.

What killed them about 1999 was that they threw it away. With seventeen minutes to go Kilkenny were four points up in a match where every score was a military operation. In the previous forty-five years only two finals contained fewer scores and still Kilkenny were overtaken without conceding a goal. 'When I look back and I think of what we do now psychologically,' says Johnny Walsh, a selector between 1999 and 2004, 'we weren't as prepared for that match as we would be now. When Cork came with a run we gave up meekly enough. You learn about players, and we learned that we weren't mentally tough enough.'

Everything else about that summer had been the opposite of the summer before. They breezed through the championship, killing teams without once resorting to a blunt instrument. Thirteen goals in three matches. Teams were whacked and body-bagged before there could be a mess on the floor. 'We'd played so much good hurling we were probably a bit cocky going into the All-Ireland final,' says O'Connor, 'which is a disaster when you're going in against Cork.'

Everybody sensed that this was a crossroads in the life of this team. Mick O'Flynn has been the Kilkenny trainer for fifteen of the past sixteen years and he knew what defeat was, but this had a rawness he hadn't experienced before. 'It was an absolute morgue after that match. It really was a case of huge question marks. Like, is that it? The first time round [1998] there's always that feeling that, "Jesus, next year we'll get back there and do it." But the second year round there was silence. People questioning within their own minds.

There was nobody talking openly about next year. There was a numbness, a questioning of your own ability, personally and as a group.'

No team had ever lost three All-Ireland hurling finals in a row, though Cork in 1984 and Kilkenny in 1947 had stared into that abyss. According to O'Flynn they considered using a sports psychologist in 2000. In the audit of where they were going and where they had come from, nothing was dismissed without consideration. In the end they used their own flash lamps to enter the minds of the players.

'We spoke about it [losing three in a row],' says O'Flynn. 'We worked on that side of it. We had a good few honest-to-God sit-down chats with everybody and everybody said what they wanted to say. You put yourself in the situation that you're here, it's the day after the match and you've lost. Are you going to be in a situation where you're going to have to cope with that? And the realization of what an awful tragedy it would have been for them individually if it did happen. When you confront these things people begin to cope with them.'

As the 2000 final came closer they did what they could to shelter the players. Training was moved out of Nowlan Park some evenings to put an arm's length between the players and the public. But the players knew there was no hiding. 'After the All-Ireland semi-final,' says Canice Brennan, a Kilkenny player for a decade, '[Manager] Brian Cody didn't need to be there because the team trained itself. The intensity in training was just ferocious. They could have picked the best fifteen from the rest of Ireland and they wouldn't have beaten us in the All-Ireland final.'

And then winning made them soft. It was as if they rolled up a huge joint and puffed it until they were mellow. There was nobody in Leinster to give them a game in 2001, but that wouldn't have been a problem if the demands they made on themselves in training hadn't slackened. But they had.

'After winning the All-Ireland in 2000 there was great hype about us,' says Henry Shefflin. 'We thought we were great lads. We probably didn't think we'd have to put in the hard work and we definitely didn't put in the hard work. Training was very poor and you could feel in training that it wasn't going well.'

Galway didn't just beat them in the All-Ireland semi-final, Galway went through them. Offaly had tried to hustle Kilkenny with aggression in the first round that year too but they didn't have the guns to wound them. From the moment a nineteen-year-old Richie Murray floored Brian McEvoy at the throw-in, the mood of Galway's performance was set.

'Against Galway we were horsed out of it, simple as that,' says Shefflin. 'We weren't hungry enough. We weren't able for the physical battle.'

'Galway dragged us down that day,' says Johnny Walsh, 'and we didn't cope well with it. Galway roughed us out of that game and you had certain players getting involved and arguing with them and looking for protection from referees and umpires. We swore after that that this would never happen again.'

In Brian Cody's management career it was a watershed too. He blamed himself for the performance and for the conditions that allowed it. Those conditions were identified and eliminated. 'Brian's attitude changed after 2001,' says D. J. Carey. 'He was really gutted that day. On that occasion he would have felt that his mind was soft. Andy Comerford was concussed the Tuesday night before that match in a training session, Brian McEvoy was injured, I'd been out for a few weeks, John Power hadn't trained for a similar length of time,

Peter Barry was the same – but he went with everyone. He left guys out that were fit and played with the regular fellas, who hadn't done that amount of training, instead of turning around and being rude to them and saying, "Well, there's guys here who were training and training well." That's the way he looked at it after 2001.'

Things were done differently the last time Kilkenny had a great team in the early 1990s, in the days before hurling's uprisings. In 1991 Mick O'Flynn was the first physical trainer ever introduced by Kilkenny, and he remembers how much scepticism greeted his appointment. As a county Kilkenny were comfortable with their tradition and with traditionalism as a means of proceeding. Then along came Clare and Wexford and Limerick, and with them a culture of penal suffering on the training field. Kilkenny, like the other establishment counties, were challenged to change or be eaten alive.

O'Flynn was an international athlete in his youth and a PE teacher by day and it wasn't in his nature to panic about new fads in physical preparation. 'There would have been a lot of, I wouldn't call it pressure, but opinion suggesting to me that I find a hill, 100 yards long at an angle of two-to-one, and that this sort of thing was the answer. I stuck to kind of believing that what we were doing was adequate. We did the sort of work I did myself as an athlete.' He did find a little hill, behind the GAA field in Bennetsbridge, 'but it wasn't a slog. You never lost the form of actual running. You were still motoring when you got to the top.' For variety he brought the squad to the undulations in the middle of Gowran Park racecourse, terrain that is a golf course now, and to St James' Park in the city. Over the years he assembled a collection of light weights in Kilkenny CBS and the squad would do some circuit training there without ever becoming slaves to gym work.

When Tipperary won the All-Ireland in 2001, espousing the virtues of Speed, Agility, Quickness (SAQ) training, O'Flynn bought the equipment and made himself familiar with the techniques but used them only in moderation, blended with his own fitness templates. Kilkenny didn't follow fashions; they made their own arrangements. They provided a masseur for their players at every match and training session long before the Cork hurlers won this concession through strike action in 2002. In 2000 they acquired the services of a dietician and embraced a little more of the available science. But they passed on the Nutron Diet that Waterford adopted and the training sessions at daybreak that Clare swore by. The pressure to do as Clare did wasn't as immediate for them as for Cork or Tipperary because Clare didn't stand between them and a provincial title. But that doesn't mean they ignored Clare. After 2001 they leaned more and more towards the Ger Loughnane model.

They made plans but they rarely made self-important strategies. They had no truck with dummy teams, or delaying team announcements until late in the week. In the 1999 championship they employed a tactic of constantly rotating their forwards during a match, all pre-programmed to move every couple of minutes; but in the end they recognized it as a gimmick and ditched it. When Clare employed a sweeper against them in the 2004 championship Kilkenny replied in kind for the replay, but they were happiest in conventional warfare.

A culture evolved around the team and the management which clearly dictated terms to everybody. After 2001 training was characterized by what O'Flynn describes conservatively as an 'edge'. The stories emerging from Nowlan Park were that Brian Cody blew the whistle to start practice matches and then swallowed it, like Ger Loughnane did with Clare in the 1990s. 'You had to make sure that your preparation was just tougher and harder and was going to be geared for whatever challenge was there,' says O'Flynn.

Consciously or not, the Kilkenny regime came to resemble Clare under Loughnane. In an interview with the *Irish Examiner* in February 2004, Loughnane identified the parallels. 'People were giving out about Clare in the 1990s,' said Loughnane, 'but now Kilkenny are playing the same way as Clare did, that aggressive, relentless style of play. Cody found out that's what Clare did and he copied it.'

In the following day's *Examiner* Cody rejected the comparison in diplomatic language, but it was undeniable. Some of Kilkenny's tackling and lust for bodily contact came to occupy that blurred area between lawful and lawless that Clare had colonized in the 1990s. At half-time in the 2003 All-Ireland final the Cork management protested to the referee Pat O'Connor about the number of head-high tackles being committed by Kilkenny players. A year later, when the teams met in the All-Ireland final again, Cork didn't expect protection; instead they drilled themselves to cope with head-high tackling.

Like Clare in their pomp, Kilkenny depended to a certain extent on permissive refereeing. But Kilkenny's iron fist was housed in a velvet glove. They had so many accomplished players, so many deadly forwards, that their reputation as a hard team was suppressed in the public's perception. Yet it was critical to their rehabilitation after 2001. They didn't just beat teams, they overpowered them. They played with the inner conceit of winners and the humility of underdogs.

They leaned towards big men, self-sufficient players who could win their own ball and stand their ground. From that base they dominated teams in the air. Between 2002 and 2004 if you didn't have a puck-out strategy against Kilkenny you had no chance of controlling your own possession. 'You were relying on your guys to be strong enough under the dropping ball,' said Brendan Cummins, the Tipperary goalkeeper. 'People up in the stand would say to you, "Why don't you just put it in the space in front of the half-forwards?" But from ground level where I am all you can see are six-foot-three guys in Kilkenny jerseys across their half-forward line and centre-field. You can't see the space.'

You couldn't ad-lib against them. You needed a plan, and the plan needed to be good. In the 2004 championship Galway were the only team to engage Kilkenny in an ortho-dox fashion with no discernible plan for ball management, and they were hammered.

Even if you matched them for possession they had other means of killing you. Goals were the poison in their bite. In thirty-nine championship matches between 1994 and 2004 they were held goalless on only four occasions, and three of those ended in defeat, two of them All-Ireland finals against Cork.

They always felt that they could get goals. They knew it, their opponents knew it. 'When a Kilkenny player is coming in with the ball you know he's going for a goal,' said Liam Dunne, the former Wexford defender. 'They're going for the jugular. Eddie Brennan and D. J. Carey and these guys are not happy with a point. Brennan missed two chances against us in 2003 but still, the first ball he got after half-time he went straight for goal again and got it.'

At half-time in the 2003 All-Ireland semi-final against Tipperary they trailed by two points in a game where points were precious. Yet they came out in the second half looking for goals. Against Brendan Cummins, the best goalkeeper in the country in the form of his life, they ruthlessly pursued the goals they knew would break Tipperary, and they got them. 'DJ emphasized that at half-time,' says Johnny Walsh. 'He emphasized goals. I remember well. I remember him saying that – it was his call. "There's goals there. We'll bury them." He put it into their mind. DJ is a great fella to talk to fellas and get them worked up.'

Clare at their peak didn't have the power of goals. In the evolutionary process, Clare were the mobile phone; Kilkenny were the mobile phone with picture messaging and internet access.

In the post-2001 reconstruction, reputation and sentiment were buried. Charlie Carter and Phil Larkin both lost their places on the team while they were sitting All Stars. Pat O'Neill and Eamon Kennedy went from being the championship centre-backs one year to losing their places on the panel the following year. Of the team that lost the 2001 All-Ireland semi-final to Galway, six were cut from the first fifteen for the following year's All-Ireland final. Every year the team was refreshed and every year the same threat of exclusion hung over the tired or the weak.

'I suppose there are players who went by the wayside,' says O'Flynn, 'and a lot of people's jaws would have been dropping on account of it, but there's a time when things have to move on. In some cases it wasn't a total loss of form, but there comes a time when you have to wield the axe. Brian [Cody] is very good at seeing a player in decline. It's a tough call because you're talking about players that have been loyal to you and that you've had a good relationship with in a lot of cases, but you just have to say, "Okay, right, this is it." You could go on for another year with this player but at the end of the day you could be sorry.'

Cody isn't close to the players, like Liam Griffin was in

Wexford or Jimmy Barry-Murphy was in Cork. Affection isn't a dynamic in his relationship with the squad. He is a serious-minded fellow carrying out serious business in a hard-headed fashion. 'Someone like Ollie Walsh [Kilkenny manager, 1991–5] was always enjoyed by the players and was friends with the players, but Brian Cody is a different kind of man,' says Eddie Brennan. 'He wasn't as friendly to the players as other managers, and I think for some of the older players that turned them off hurling for him. But there were so many players coming through it didn't matter. He could pick who he wanted. There's a ruthless streak in him to win. The only thing that drives him is winning.'

The ideal was that the team would be picked almost by a process of natural selection. Whoever prospered in the crucible of Nowlan Park on training nights earned their right to the jersey on championship day. New players arriving on the panel knew what was demanded. Young Tommy Walsh is a wizard but he's small, and when he broke into the team in 2003 he was inclined to mix it with big players, as if to demonstrate his courage. Eventually they had to tell him to relax. They knew he was brave but they didn't need him to play like a big man; Walsh didn't feel he could take that chance.

With Cody's style there were bound to be casualties. In June 2003 Charlie Carter, darling of the galleries, quit after a public stink. Over a period of time, management had lost confidence in him. His attitude to training and his work-rate on the field didn't fit their post-2001 imperatives. He lost his place for the 2002 championship, regained it, and lost it again. Then his club won the county championship and made him captain for the 2003 season. He resolved to give his all and trained hard over the winter, but by then management didn't see him as a seventy-minute player and Carter didn't see himself as an impact sub. Enraged sections of the Kilkenny public saw Carter's retirement as constructive dismissal. In similar circumstances, Brian McEvoy went with him. Cody didn't blink.

'The players were never going to win,' says Johnny Walsh, 'because if they won there'd be no point in us being there. What they did was dig their own graves. The way they were behaving, saying they should be playing, it wasn't a wise thing to do. What Charlie should have done was bide his time and he could have lifted the MacCarthy Cup if he had behaved differently. He chose not to, and it's history now. I felt sorry in a sense for him.

'We felt we did what we believed in, and of course if we didn't win [the All-Ireland] you had a lot of Charlie Carter fans in Kilkenny who were just baying for us. There were phone calls into Kilkenny radio saying that the management should go and all of this. We listened, we said nothing and we brazened it out. What else could we do? But it wasn't easy.'

They found the people they wanted. They spotted Derek Lyng, a player with no under-age pedigree, from a small, powerless club in the north of the county and turned him into an All Star centre-fielder. They took a good player such as Peter Barry and made him the pillar of their team. 'There were players on this Kilkenny team,' says Walsh, 'and there were better players who weren't there. We had guys you could depend on. Take someone like Peter Barry. He isn't the greatest hurler ever but there's nobody stronger in mind. He might be playing badly but he'd still be in there and his head will never drop.'

More than any other player, Barry expressed Cody's vision.

★

You will see in the record books that Kilkenny had achieved three All-Ireland titles in a row once before, 1911–13, but one of those titles was granted in the committee room and Kilkenny people don't boast about that feat. For this Kilkenny team, the summer of 2004 was their shot at immortality.

In their time together, so many barriers fell before their relentless march. Kilkenny had beaten Tipperary in the championship only once in eighty years; this team did it in successive years, the second time a humiliating rout. No team had won back-to-back All-Irelands for a decade, and in hurling's new pluralist society people doubted it would ever be done again. They did it.

For twenty years Offaly had haunted Kilkenny. In a *Kenny Live* interview on the night before the 1998 All-Ireland final Kevin Fennelly said that Offaly 'were the one team that took a lot of dreams away from me'. Him and plenty more. Offaly believed that if they were within four or five points of Kilkenny with fifteen minutes to go in the 2000 All-Ireland final Kilkenny would be so spooked that Offaly would take them. In the event Kilkenny finished the game in the first ten minutes. In their five championship meetings between the 1998 All-Ireland final and the 2002 Leinster semi-final Kilkenny beat Offaly by an aggregate of fifty-five points. Buried them.

The bar kept rising. Three-in-a-rows had been done before, but not in championships as deep as this one. This time it would have been a world record. But they clipped the bar with their trailing foot and it joined them on the landing pad.

Wexford unsettled them with an applied and clever performance in the semi-final of the Leinster championship and suckered them with a goal in the last seconds of stoppage time. Kilkenny were diverted on to the back roads of the qualifiers for the first time, and instead of easing into the All-Ireland semi-finals in August with a handy provincial championship behind them they were forced to spend some of their reserves in mid-summer. Instead of taking two matches to reach an All-Ireland semi-final, they took five.

'The one year that Kilkenny didn't want a long run in the championship was this year [2004],' says Carey. 'There was a huge deflation after winning the Waterford game [All-Ireland semi-final]. For the previous four or five weeks we had been playing every week; we might have had one week of a break. The lads were kept right, they were kept motivated, training was very light, a recovery session on the Monday, a puck-around of a Tuesday. After the Waterford game we knew we were in the final. There were four weeks left and I know myself I didn't recover for ten days after the game. Just didn't recover. Motivation was gone mentally. Physically the soreness was there.

'Now, we didn't train. I think we had two rounds of club matches, but I can remember playing in one of them with no interest in hurling at all. It was the one year that we didn't need a long run. Even though we played pretty well up to the final and things looked right for the final, it just didn't happen.'

They led by a point at half-time but failed to score for the last twenty-four minutes of the second half. Cork reeled off nine points without reply. For the most potent team of their generation it was a stunning eclipse.

'We were playing teams all year who were coming out with plans against us,' says Carey. 'Once Cork got ahead they were always going to block it up. With fifteen minutes to go they were able to block up the whole thing, so tactically they got it spot on. What could we do? You know, these tactics can work.'

As Clare learned in the late 1990s, you set the standard and some day somebody else meets it. In the chase, though, hurling had been taken to a place it had never been before.

9. McCarthyism

At half-past nine on the morning of the 1998 Munster final, Dave Walsh loaded himself and ten other pilgrims into his Toyota Previs and left Dungarvan for Thurles. Sunday, at last. The family holiday in Kerry wasn't supposed to end until Saturday but they were home by Friday. Walsh's nerves couldn't stand the dislocation any longer. He needed to be at home where he could see a reflection of the match in every like mind and familiar face.

It had been nine years since Waterford last contested a Munster final, thirty-five years since they had been Munster champions. For all of that time Walsh had lived his faith. Before the supporters' club disbanded he was at the head of it. Afterwards the Waterford hurlers continued to enjoy his largesse. He described himself as a friend of Waterford hurling and cherished the friendship. On the night before the match he rang most of the players. A few days earlier he had written to the Waterford captain, Stephen Frampton, thanking him for what the players had done for the county and trying to express the swelling in his chest.

'I said in the letter, if he could only see how proud my kids were to be from Waterford,' says Walsh. 'When we were down in Castlegregory [County Kerry] they insisted on having the Waterford colours on the caravan. There was blue and white on the car. It's not just them. It was everywhere. In my shop if I went out to the counter I'd be fecked because I'd be caught talking about the match. If I went outside the door I'd be caught for an hour sitting on the window talking about it. If I walked down the street twenty people would stop me and want to talk about it.'

Terry Dalton travelled with him that Sunday. He was a selector when Waterford won the Munster title in 1963. Walsh was ten years old when his father took him to that match. Thirty-five years later six of Walsh's eight children came with him, from the five-year-old to the fifteen-year-old. They were in their seats a quarter of an hour before the minor match so that every vapour of Munster final day would catch their breath. The senior match was a draw and a classic.

'We got home that evening at nine o'clock. It was half-time in the World Cup final and for the two weeks that we were in Kerry we watched every match of the World Cup, but all the kids said when they came in the door was, "Mam, have you the [Waterford] match taped?" They put it on straight away and watched it. They got up again the following morning and watched it again. And watched it again that evening.'

Walsh went to bed at about one o'clock but sleep wouldn't come. When he closed his eyes the day refused to be still or quiet. As dawn seeped through the curtains he turned out the light.

Before the dawn, darkness stretched back for as far as the eye could see. Waterford regarded themselves as a hurling county and that status was recognized by their peers in hurling society, but it was an unequal society and Waterford were condemned to its margins. They hadn't won a senior All-Ireland since 1959 and in the Munster championship they mined glory from occasional acts of giant-killing. That was their rank. Like so many other downtrodden counties in hurling and football it was said of them that on their day they were a match for anybody. It was a patronizing remark disguised as a compliment, and they accepted it in better spirit than it was given. They didn't rail with a fury against their oppression.

Waterford had reached three Munster finals in the 1980s and each had ended in annihilation, the aggregate margin of defeat soaring to sixty-one points. Trainer Shane Aherne played in the 1989 defeat to Tipperary in Pairc Uí Chaoimh. It turned into a spiteful match and a massacre on the scoreboard, 0–26 to 2–8. He remembers going to hospital the following day for treatment on a hand injury and meeting another Waterford player being patched up. 'He said to me, "Sure, I knew we weren't going to win anyway." To me that was like being shot in the heart. It was awful. I was saying to myself, "What the feck am I doing here?" That's what you were dealing with.'

In the early 1990s Waterford were relegated to Division Three of the National Hurling League, and in 1993 they bottomed out. Kerry came to Walsh Park for the first round of the championship and won – one of the biggest shocks in the history of the Munster hurling championship. Before that match Waterford were regarded as a team with prospects. They had won the 1992 All-Ireland U-21 championship and been beaten in the minor final. The stock of Waterford hurling was at its highest value for a generation. And then this.

Stephen Frampton was in his fifth year on the panel and he could see the train coming down the tracks. Attendances at training oscillated in and out of double figures. Organization was poor. Attempts at serious preparation were superficial and sometimes comical. They didn't get meals after training, but he remembers one night when a county board operative was dispatched to Kentucky Fried Chicken downtown and returned with his car boot full of snack boxes. Waterford Crystal had donated money to kit out the team in blazers and on the day of the Kerry match they were photographed in their shiny new uniforms. As an indication of professionalism it was a feeble pretence. When the Kerry players arrived they were greeted by the sight of the Waterford players posing on the little green outside the dressing rooms. For the Kerry management rallying speeches were almost superfluous.

'It was a farce of a year, crazy,' says Frampton. 'We were going out to play a championship match and our preparation was just absolutely terrible. Really bad. We were on a hiding to nothing. I remember one night that year the physio stood into goal to make up the numbers in training. I had broken my arm the November before and I just made it back for the Kerry match. I only had my cast off a couple of weeks. I shouldn't have been playing, but that's the way it was. Just crazy.

'They had a few good hurlers, in fairness. I was marking a guy called D. J. Leahy and he was good now as well. He got one ball and I'd say his arse was rubbing off the corner flag. He didn't look, he just turned and hit this ball over his head, and it went over the bar. Don't ask me how he could get a point from where he was but he did. It was just one of those days where everything happened for them and nothing happened for us. After losing that match the abuse we got leaving the pitch was savage.'

But the Kerry defeat didn't ignite a revolution. A year later Tom Feeney joined the senior panel for the first time and he remembers 'seven or eight' players showing up at training less than a month before the championship. There was still no anger at the prevailing culture, no will to overturn it. In the early 1990s Brian Flannery came to study in Waterford IT and in 1995 he won an U-21 All-Ireland with Tipperary. He had transferred to the Mount Sion club in Waterford city by then and a couple of years later he declared for the county, but for a while he watched from the outside.

'Club hurling in Waterford was too strong,' he says. 'I remember one night the county team were training below in Walsh Park and Mount Sion had a challenge game up in our field which was two minutes up the road. All the Mount Sion players came up and played the challenge match with the club. I remember thinking to myself, "Jesus, this would never happen in Tipperary." Your club would be so delighted that you'd get a chance of playing with the county and it would be such a big deal that you wouldn't even think of not going training with the county. That was one huge difference.'

In marginalized counties it is a common symptom of the losing condition: players with drive invest their ambition in their clubs. In the 1990s Ballygunner were a serious team with aspirations to win the Munster club championship. Their best players were critical to Waterford, but on the night that Gerald McCarthy was introduced to the county panel as their new manager in the autumn of 1996 the Ballygunner players were absent. 'They were preparing for a Munster club match,' says Tom Feeney, 'and they were completely focused on the club. It showed how focused Ballygunner were compared to the outlook of Waterford. They were taking care of themselves and they had brought Waterford club hurling up to a completely new level.'

The lazy assumption was that the outstanding U-21 players of 1992 would rescue Waterford hurling, but nothing of the sort happened. They were a talented bunch, but within the group there existed a mixture of mentalities and diverse outlooks. As U-21s they were superbly marshalled by Tony Mansfield; at senior level they needed a firm hand and enlightened structures. Those conditions finally arrived with McCarthy, but it was already too late to save everyone.

Of the best six players from the 1992 U-21s only three made it on to McCarthy's first championship fifteen in the summer of 1997: Tony Browne, Fergal Hartley and Paul Flynn. By then the best five Offaly players from the U-21 team that Waterford had beaten in the 1992 final were already the holders of senior All-Irelands, and only John Troy was waiting for his All Star; Brian Whelahan, Hubert Rigney, Johnny Dooley and Kevin Martin were the others.

The experience of Sean Daly illustrated the potential difficulties. In 1992 he was the star full-forward on the U-21 team, uncontained and devastating. He scored four points against Cork, five points against Clare, three goals against Antrim and three goals against Offaly in the drawn All-Ireland final. All from play. What you must remember too is that his tallies against Offaly and Clare were plundered from Kevin Kinahan and Brian Lohan, the two outstanding full-backs of the 1990s. Index-linked, imagine what those totals were worth around 1997?

It was not possible for all of the Waterford U-21s to have successful senior careers, but Daly was marked down as a certainty. The transition never really happened. Right after the U-21 victory he played for the seniors in losing years. In those days he played a bit of soccer and took the odd liberty. People were fond of Daly and quick to forgive him. He was good; they needed him. But McCarthy's regime was short on allowances, regardless of who you were or how good you were. Early in 1997 Daly was cut from the panel, one of four players culled by McCarthy for disciplinary reasons that winter. In Daly's own words, this is what happened. 'We had a training weekend in Clonea. I trained on the Friday night, I trained on the Saturday. On Sunday the point-to-point [races] were on in Dungarvan which was only three miles away. We were training that day but I headed off to the point-to-points. I fell out with Gerald McCarthy over that. You couldn't blame him.'

Daly apologized, but Waterford pressed on without him. He waited fifteen months to be invited back on to the panel and he didn't start his first championship match under Gerald McCarthy until the end of July 1998. By then the show was on the road, but so much time had been wasted. Daly was gone again in 1999 and never played in a senior championship afterwards.

'If you think about it,' says Feeney, 'we beat Clare in a cracking Munster U-21 final in 1992 and we beat Offaly in the All-Ireland. Players from both of those teams won two senior All-Irelands afterwards. They had their structures sorted out. They had Eamon Cregan and they had Ger Loughnane. If we'd had Gerald McCarthy around 1993 or 1994 we could have won a senior All-Ireland too. But the team changed and people changed. The structure wasn't there. The management wasn't capable enough of directing a group of wild cards, shall we say, and bringing a cohesive effort together.

'Looking back on it he [McCarthy] had a lot of shit to straighten out. He had to cut out the bullshit, and bullshit within every player. There was strict discipline, like we'd never seen before. What would have happened before was if a very important player went on the piss on the night before a game he would still have been playing. Whereas with Gerald, no way.'

As a player McCarthy had won five senior All-Ireland medals with Cork, and when Cork won the All-Ireland in 1990 he was the trainer and assistant coach. He was coach too when Cork reached the All-Ireland final in 1982, and but for a bureaucratic veto and a tangle of by-laws he would have been appointed Cork manager in the autumn of 1993.

Instead he was available, and Waterford chased him down.
The All-Irelands of 1995 and 1996 had been won by Clare
and Wexford, two counties who had started out from the
same ghetto of hurling society that Waterford still inhabi-
ted. Appointing McCarthy was Waterford's declaration of
ambition.

McCarthy presented the players with a ladder he believed
they could climb. In year one they would target a good league;
in year two they would win the Munster championship; and
in year three they would be All-Ireland champions.

In year one they failed to win promotion from Division
Two of the league, were beaten at home by Dublin in the
spring, and a spineless performance against Cork resulted in a
ten-point thrashing at Pairc Uí Rinn. In the 1997 championship a Limerick team in decline beat them by six points at
their ease. McCarthy's eyes were opened. Hurling had moved
on and Waterford had been left behind.

Waterford trained hard in 1997 and McCarthy was careful
to nourish the self-esteem of the players. They were looked
after in the recognized currency of the amateur game. Each
player was given two pairs of boots, for example, one multi-
cog, one with long studs. It was accepted practice in a lot of
successful counties, but in Waterford it was a novelty that an
experienced player such as Frampton had experienced only
once before. They did some early-morning training in 1997
too, recognizing that this was the new expression of absolute
commitment. But in 1998 they moved on from that base and
pushed new boundaries.

Aherne was McCarthy's trainer and assistant coach, and
from his days as a League of Ireland soccer player with
Kilkenny City he was familiar with a killing stamina run
around the sand dunes in Tramore. They first went there on
the last Sunday of December 1997 and revisited their own

private hell for six Sunday mornings in a row. The shortest route that Aherne knew in the dunes lasted an hour; the deluxe version stretched out for two hours. 'I remember we were down there one Sunday morning,' says Aherne, 'and it was January and there were sea-rescue helicopters going out over our heads to rescue people from trawlers that were being blown by the weather. And here we were, mad idiots running up and down sand dunes and no helicopter to save us.'

The sand dunes, though, were just the most exotic manifestation of a whole new regimen. From September to Christmas the players worked alone in the gym on a personal weights programme, and then the pace picked up. 'I have never trained as hard before or since as I did in 1998,' says Brian Flannery. 'In effect we used to be doing two training sessions per night. We would do a session of circuits and weights in St Augustine's in Dungarvan from 6.30 to 7.30 in the evening. We'd drive from there over to Fraher Field for eight o'clock and do another full hour or hour and a half of running. We did huge volumes.'

In the search for an edge, the management came up with the Nutron Diet. It had physical benefits but its greatest value was psychological because the sacrifices involved were significant and daily. Away from training the Nutron Diet was asking the players to make a conscious commitment to Waterford at every meal time, at every snack time, every time their tummies rumbled. It was their conscience. Everything that their hands brought to mouth involved a choice and a dilemma: 'Is this for Waterford or is this for me?'

The Nutron Diet was designed to shed weight and increase energy. At the beginning of the diet each player had his blood analysed to determine what foodstuffs suited him best and what foodstuffs were a drain on his system. Each player's programme was individually tailored, but some substances were common to all banned lists. Alcohol was one. The discipline involved was extraordinary.

Sean Cullinane's programme didn't allow him to drink anything except water. No tea, no coffee, no milk, no alcohol. From January to August that year, water was the only fluid that passed Cullinane's lips. For two months he couldn't eat anything that came out of a tin either. Naturally, Cullinane lost weight. His thighs shrank, his face tightened. 'Everybody thought I was dying,' he says. 'There were people saying, "Jesus, are you all right?" I never felt better. I felt I could jump over a roof I had so much energy, it was unbelievable. Once I got my second wind in a match I never got tired.'

Looking back, players wonder about the physical benefits of the diet. The post-training intake of food was entirely fruit when nutritionists would say that carbohydrates are a priority to begin the refuelling process. Frampton felt that by the end of a long year the team had run low on fuel and maybe the downside of the Nutron Diet had kicked in. But as a bonding agent it was invaluable. This was their Crusheen. Would you do this for Waterford? Could you do it for Waterford?

'The four selectors went on it as well,' says Aherne, 'and I remember driving to training with a few players in the car and we'd be talking about how to cook a certain rice. Everyone was talking about how do you cook this, how do you cook that? A lot of them were still living at home and trying to re-teach their mothers how to cook. I used go into the Nutron Clinic in Waterford every week and check who was coming in for their check-up and sit down with your woman for an hour and go through every player. What were they doing, what were they not doing, who needs a little chat.

'But we were winning matches in the league and everyone was buying into it. We all went off alcohol for six weeks at the start and when that six weeks was up we said, "Look, lads, there's another two matches coming up. Let's keep this going and then you can drink away for a week or two if you want." It was all short-term goals. If you tell a fella he can't drink for six months he'll break it.'

Waterford were that summer's hurling romance. They were the coming team. They reached the league final against Cork, and that day in Thurles had the mood and atmosphere of a championship match. Waterford lost, but it didn't derail them. They met Tipperary in the Munster semi-final and came from five points down at half-time to win by three. Waterford hadn't beaten Tipp in the championship for fifteen years. On they went, surfing the wave.

'You could see it around the town, around the county,' says Frampton. 'We were starting to win matches and they were coming out of everywhere to support the team. Hurling was starting to become cool and trendy. Young fellas thought it was cool to be walking around with a hurley. We became mini-celebrities where a few years previous nobody would have known you.'

Flannery remembers going into supermarkets to do his shopping and mothers bringing their kids over to ask for an autograph. He remembers coming home after the All-Ireland quarter-final win over Galway later in the year when a couple of thousand people were waiting on the quay in Waterford to greet them. A pub in town called Muldoon's had cordoned off the third floor for the private use of the players and their guests. At training sessions before the All-Ireland semi-final it took some players half an hour to leave the pitch, wading through the quicksand of autograph hunters. Hurling was sexy in a way it never had been before, and here were the symbols of that sexiness. (Sex symbols, you understand, would be a different thing.)

But at the end of the year they had no prize to show for

it. With injury time running out in the drawn Munster final against Clare they had a chance to win a game that they had trailed by eight points at half-time. With a breeze at his back Paul Flynn lined up a free 100 metres from the Clare goal and launched it. 'I was standing there watching him,' says Frampton, Waterford captain that year, 'and I'll always remember thinking to myself, "If he puts this over, we're Munster champions." If there was one fella I'd pick on the field to hit this free it would be him because I've never seen anyone strike a ball as well as he can, and he's got a neck like a jockey's bollocks. "He won't even feel the pressure," I said to myself. I could almost see myself going up the stand in five minutes' time to accept the cup.' The free, though, drifted to the right and wide.

In the replay seven days later Waterford were swept up in the vortex of Clare's fury and lost by twelve points. The extraordinary thing was their response. A week later they met Galway in an All-Ireland quarter-final, the first appearance by a Waterford team in Croke Park for thirty-five years, and they blew Galway off the field. 'We were in bits after the Clare match,' says Feeney. 'On the Monday we had a team meeting and Gerald calmed us down because we had felt very disappointed in ourselves that we were beaten by so much. We were saying, "Ah fuck, maybe we're not good enough." "No," he said, "this is what happens when you give a little bit of space to each player." On Wednesday night we had our only training session and our bones were aching, to be honest. Then the weekend came. On with the jerseys and out you go. That was one of the great days.'

The semi-final against Kilkenny, though, wasn't. It followed a pattern that stretched back to the league semi-final in April. Every good Waterford performance was followed by an inferior one. They had even struggled to beat Kerry in the Munster championship a week after the league final. Kilkenny were vulnerable that year. Ordinary. D. J. Carey was enduring the worst season of his career, John Power was in bitter exile and Henry Shefflin hadn't come along yet. Kilkenny were there for the taking. Waterford couldn't do it. Kilkenny got a flukey goal just after half-time and as the second half wore on Waterford lost their shape in a gathering fog of panic. They were beaten by a point.

'You have to perform on the day, and we didn't,' says Feeney. 'At times like that you need key men to stand up and say, "Look, I'm going to grab this and we're going to do it." We probably didn't have it, whereas Clare did have it. Certainly in terms of Lohan, McMahon, Baker, Jamesie – key men who were willing to drag games by the scruff of the neck. They possibly shouldn't have drawn the Munster final with us, but they did. When it was slipping [in the second half of the All-Ireland semi-final] did the characters really come out to say, "Look, we're in trouble here – we have to do something"? We were aware enough. If you compare ourselves to Clare, did we stand up that day and be counted? I don't think so.'

The comparison with Clare was valid. Their provenance was no different. They had come from the same neighbourhood, carrying the same baggage of defeat. At the beginning of 1992 it took two matches to separate Clare and Waterford in the first round of the Munster championship. By the end of that year Waterford were the team with a golden generation of young players to underwrite the future. They were the county with momentum. At some point, though, Waterford and Clare took different paths.

Compare the Clare team that won their breakthrough All-Ireland in 1995 with the Waterford team in 1998 and you could not say that Clare were more talented. It would be

easier to argue that Waterford had better players. For certain
they had better forwards. Yet Clare succeeded and Waterford
faltered.

The critical difference was this: Clare's best players were
also outstanding leaders. Most of Waterford's leaders weren't
their best players, and their best players weren't necessarily
leaders. Fergal Hartley and Stephen Frampton were about the
only players who fitted comfortably into both categories, year
in, year out through the 1990s. Ken McGrath was still young;
Tony Browne and Paul Flynn were inconsistent, bordering
on unreliable. Clare, though, had half a dozen players with
the qualities and status of Hartley and Frampton. The deficit
in Waterford's performances was not a hurling issue alone.

'The door opened for Waterford three times in 1998,'
wrote Ger Loughnane in his book, 'and they couldn't go
through it.' The league final, the Munster final, the All-
Ireland semi-final were all squandered. At the time the Waterford players didn't feel so bad about it. Gerald McCarthy had
dressed them up and taken them to all of hurling's best parties.
In Flannery's estimation he had taken them forward 'ten years
in two years'. The summer had been such an adventure that
there were enough endorphins in their system to strangle the
pain. 'For a lot of us,' says Flannery, 'it was probably the time
of our lives.'

But the serious questions would have to be answered soon.
In hurling's enchanted new world fairytales just didn't happen; you had to make believe first and then make it happen.
Clare had returned from two crushing Munster final defeats
to become champions. What kind of Waterford would return
in 1999?

The answer wasn't good. They went to the sand dunes
again in Tramore but management quickly realized that the
players were bored and the long runs were switched to a

wooded area in Portlaw. The Nutron Diet was embraced
again, but it was a cold embrace. Some players had worked
out short cuts and that defeated the purpose of the exercise.
Without discipline, where was the sacrifice? Flannery was
captain that year and he could see the slippage. By June they
were out of the championship.

'Because we had a lot of young players on the panel maybe
we needed to be tougher with players,' Flannery says. 'We
probably took corners that we didn't do the year before. You
can have players in training twenty-four hours a day but if
they're not putting in the effort they may as well be at home.
We probably thought we were better than what we were.
We got an awful lot of attention and maybe we weren't able
to detach ourselves enough from that. We weren't able to
pull ourselves away from it the following year and realize
that life doesn't always run that smooth. It was a different
atmosphere. We weren't focused. And we'd won nothing,
which was very relevant. The champagne was out one night
[in 1998] having won nothing. When you're that close on a
panel everybody knows everything. The players will know
who's not putting it in quicker probably than management
and you had players upset with other players.'

Management, though, were aware of the virus in the system
and tried to treat it. One-on-one meetings were held with
every player in an attempt to galvanize them. Tony Browne,
Hurler of the Year in 1998, was one player management
were unhappy with and they confronted him head-on for a
Saturday league match against Cork in March 1999. He was
selected to play but he failed to show up for a Friday-night
session, and on the following day he wasn't given a jersey.
Nothing was made of it in public and it wasn't reported at
the time as a disciplinary issue, but that is what it was.

It wasn't only Browne. It was a general issue, and it was an

ongoing issue. As a group they weren't as driven or as motivated as Clare who, in the late 1990s, were still the team
everybody had to beat. A massively gifted player such as Paul
Flynn wasn't typical, but he reflected the problem.

Over the years Flynn's admirers always needed to be
defenders and sympathizers too because so many of his performances didn't amount to self-defence. For over a decade
a bristling tension existed between the player Flynn promised
to be and the player he became. He finally won an All Star
award in 2004, but by then he should have had two or three,
such was his talent. The pattern with Flynn was that every
season there would be one or two days when he was absolutely
faithful to his talent. And too many days when he wasn't.

He wasn't an enthusiastic trainer. He was diligent about
showing up but he didn't tend to burst himself when he got
there. Under Aherne, players who cut inside the cones that
marked out the training laps were made to do press-ups. It
was no deterrent to Flynn, though, and eventually the conditions were changed: if Flynn cut inside the cones, everyone
did press-ups. Another trick that the other players noticed
was that he would linger on the treatment table getting a rub
until the warm-up was finished. He struggled with his weight
at different times and in reality he should have been working
harder in training than the others just to keep up; but his
nature was to do less.

'He'd do anything to avoid training,' says Flannery, 'but
what a phenomenal talent, and what a free-taker. You'd be
shaking on the line when Flynner would be hitting frees at
you.' That was at the core of it. They couldn't be without him.

Down the years Waterford managers used the carrot and
the stick to tease what they could from Flynn. Results were
mixed. When he was dropped from the team late in 1995 he
wrote to the manager saying that he was quitting the panel;

six weeks later he phoned to say he was coming back. In the spring of 2001, during Gerald McCarthy's last league in charge, they were desperate for Flynn to get out in front of his man and contest the ball more vigorously. When they tired of pleading with him they left him out. He was recalled for the next match against Tipp and reeled off 1–4 from play. That was Flynn. With his ability and his status he should have been a driving force in that Waterford dressing room, but it simply wasn't in his nature to lead.

Aherne quit as trainer at the end of 1999 and Colm Bonnar took over for the next four years. By then they were a reasonably mature and established group, but the problems that faced Bonnar were the same ones that faced Aherne.

'The first year I was in with them,' says Bonnar, 'I noticed that they were just going from session to session. A lot of them were coming to training because we called training. Go through the motions, go home – no real purpose. Never analysed what they had done. Could they have done it better, could they have done more, did they improve anything in the session, did they improve on any individual goal that they had? You could see several of the younger lads getting into bad habits. Training with a bad attitude and with no real purpose and no real commitment to what they were doing. Very good hurlers depending totally on their hurling, but when the shit hit the fan in big games they started getting frustrated with themselves and then with other players and with the referee, and it just accumulated into arguing with everything then. I asked the question one night at training: "Honestly, lads, who here believes we're going to be Munster champions at the end of the year?"' This was in February [2000]. I think two lads put up their hands. Peter Queally and somebody else.'

It was clear that there was a weakness in their mentality.

When Mount Sion were pushing for the Munster club championship in 2000 they enlisted the help of a Dublin-based sports psychologist, but Waterford didn't go down that route. Bonnar and Gerald McCarthy tried to access the players' minds by their own means.

'A lot of what was holding them back was mental,' says Bonnar. 'When you've been down for so long doubts will always come in. The attitude of other teams against them would have been, "Keep going, keep going and you'll get on top of them in the end." That would have been Cork's mentality, and Tipperary's. Even Dublin playing them in the league would always believe they could beat them [once under Gerald McCarthy, twice under Justin McCarthy]. Waterford would struggle because they were always meeting players who thought they could beat them.

'I just felt with some of the Waterford lads their heads dropped when you moved them. They weren't mentally tough enough. This is one of the things we were on to them about. If you're moved it's a new challenge. It's the same ball you're going for. Like, Eoin McGrath. Eoin would have played corner-forward in his first year [2002] and the following year all he wanted to do was play midfield. And when you moved him to corner-forward his attitude was, "I'm not a corner-forward."'

The reality for Gerald McCarthy, though, was that he couldn't discard players and start again. The big turnover in the panel every year was never in the first fifteen, it was always in the next fifteen. Players who auditioned for bit parts and joined the cast as extras.

In that respect Justin McCarthy got lucky.

Gerald McCarthy finally walked away after the 2001 championship. His team had surrendered an eleven-point lead to

Limerick in the Munster semi-final and lost by three. Once more the championship had showcased their brilliance and revealed their weakness. Gerald McCarthy had made them contenders but he couldn't make them champions.

All the improvement he had wrought, all the impetus he had generated was suddenly at risk. If Waterford erred in the appointment of his successor they faced stagnation or worse. The Waterford chairman Paddy Joe Ryan and Justin McCarthy had known each other a long time. They were in the same business. McCarthy was sales manager for an oil supplier, Ryan owned an oil distribution company. It was sixteen years since McCarthy had last been involved in senior inter-county management and outside Cork his profile had declined far below his standing. In Waterford a vocal caucus wanted to appoint from within the county, and Brian Greene's father Jim ran a vigorous campaign. Ryan, though, stuck to his guns and Justin McCarthy accepted the challenge.

The bullet points of his CV were hugely impressive. Hurler of the Year as a twenty-one-year-old in 1966, he coached Antrim to their first hurling All-Ireland, an intermediate title, in 1970. Five years later he coached Cork for the first time, and he held the role again when they won the All-Ireland in 1984. Along the way he coached Clare to win two National Leagues in the late 1970s and so nearly master-minded their championship breakthrough. But that was all in the past, only half-remembered. His reputation would have to be forged again.

Gerald McCarthy and Justin McCarthy had been room-mates on the 1963 Cork minor team and they remained friends for many years, but their approaches to management were very different. Gerald had embraced the modern imperatives of hard physical training, he had an awareness of sports science and he had a sense that players needed to be handled according to their individual needs and sensibilities. He was straight and he could be tough, but none of the players would have felt he was unapproachable. And though he spent five years in that dressing room he never lost the capacity to affect those players. Flannery remembers his speech before the 2000 championship match against Tipperary, which had some players in tears. He also remembers a little ceremony before the 2001 match against Limerick when he presented the players with their jerseys after their puck-around in St Finbarrs' club ground. He hadn't done that before and it worked. He had reached inside them again.

Justin had a different outlook. He was a coach in the strictest meaning of the term. He watched players, assessed them, improved them. He had no desire to be a father-confessor or a confidant to the players. He didn't necessarily want to be their friend. He arrived at training and left after the meal. In between he guaranteed them the best hurling sessions known to man.

Some players didn't like Gerald for the home-truths he plainly expressed to them, but that would have been a minority view. They all knew that if they found themselves in Gerald's company over a pint they would have a laugh. Justin didn't drink. At meals he tended to sit with county board people. There was a distance that Justin had no apparent desire to close.

Colm Bonnar worked with each of them for two years and witnessed the contrast. 'Justin's not really into man management. He feels – coming from Cork, and I'd be of the same opinion coming from Tipperary – that players on the county panel should have a purpose and they should know why they're there. They come, they train properly, they go away. Justin had been coaching for so many years that he'd just come and say, "We'll do this and we'll do this." Gerald would have it all written out. Very specific on what he wanted to achieve. He used to let me do a lot of the coaching and he'd take a step back. He'd go to the players he felt he needed to talk to and take them aside. He commanded a lot of respect. I wouldn't say players were afraid of him but they wouldn't cross him.

'Justin would be very good to read players and read the opposition. He would go through each player and tell them about their opponent and why he would get on top of him. Gerald would tell them what to do as well and what system we were playing but he was very passionate with it and have the lads fired up. He would give a very, very passionate speech. Let it fly, let it rip. Your heart would be pumping. Lads would be very emotional about it. Justin would be more into having the lads focused. To know they were going out to do a job.'

When it came to hurling, a deep knowledge sponsored Justin's convictions and floated his confidence. He didn't invite questions or debate, and that didn't always sit well with the players. A couple of nights after the 2003 Munster final the panel had a meeting in Walsh Park. Waterford had led by eight points at one stage with the breeze in the first half but their second-half performance hadn't been good enough and in defeat the Waterford management had performed poorly on the sideline. 'The players were all sitting in the stand,' says Flannery, 'and the selectors were there. They preached for about an hour on how we didn't win. John Mullane actually turned around to the selectors and told them, "Lads, you'd want to look at yourselves." A guy who normally wouldn't be terribly articulate, but he had scored 3–1 in the Munster final and he was the ideal person to say it. Every player was probably thinking it. I can't imagine Gerald standing in front of us for an hour and lecturing us without some sharing of the blame or whatever. But that wouldn't be Justin's style anyway.'

When he first arrived he brought the courage of his convictions. His methods and principles pre-dated the fitness revolution but he saw no reason to amend them. For nine-tenths of each session hurleys didn't leave players' hands. He was a fundamentalist. McCarthy's superb autobiography *Hooked* was published early in 2002, and in it he outlined his creed. 'There is a popular theory now that hurling is a young man's game, but why's that?' he wrote. 'Because there has been an overemphasis on physical fitness. We won't be making that mistake in Waterford. I want our players to have a balanced lifestyle. We've stressed to our players the importance of time management so that they're focused enough for hurling. We're focusing on quality rather than quantity. Come the championship we'll be hurling fit.'

Under Gerald McCarthy extreme physical hardship had been the base camp for every climb. The players had become accustomed to it, and in a perverse way it was a comfort. It was as if any perceived deficiencies in their hurling or their mentality could be addressed with more hard labour. Justin McCarthy took a different view. He knew that Waterford players had issues with mental strength but he planned to reinforce their minds through their hurling.

The players were exposed to McCarthy's brand of holism. In his doctrine, hurleys are the first principle. He laid his hands on every hurley in the panel. One by one he picked them up in the dressing room after matches or training and took them away, permission assumed rather than sought. Every one of Flannery's hurleys for the previous ten years had come from the same template, but the stick was kidnapped one night and returned in an altered state. With every team McCarthy ever coached he tended to the hurleys in his workshop at home as a matter of urgency. 'You'll never know a good hurley until you have one in your hand,' wrote McCarthy. 'It can add 15 per cent to your game.'

With Waterford, every fraction of improvement was indispensable. The margins were too tight. If a player fluffed one pick-up in five because the heel of his hurley was too thick, that was one too many. They needed to be better hurlers. They needed to feel like better hurlers. They needed to believe they were better hurlers. He had to make them better hurlers. That's what every training session was about. In his first season the only running the players did outside the approved context of hurling drills was shoehorned into fifteen minutes at the end.

'We practised stuff in training that I hadn't done since I was under-age,' says Flannery. 'We did drills for hooking, blocking, protecting yourself. Most managers wouldn't be bothered with those kind of skills. It would be taken for granted that you had those basics. I mean, I'd be his biggest critic, but his hurling training is very, very good. Very good. That's what he's best at. You'd say if you could have him doing the skills and Gerald managing the team you might have the ideal combination.'

The players were sceptical about his approach at first, and after a league defeat to Dublin in March 2002 doubt exploded into dissent. The whole day had been a disaster. The match was fixed for the Bank Holiday Monday of the St Patrick's Day weekend and two players had lined out for their club in a tournament match in Cork the previous day without management's knowledge or permission. According to Bonnar, other members of the panel had played a soccer match. A luxury bus was laid on to transport the players to Dublin but about eight of them decided to make their own way. Flannery drove, got lost on the way to Parnell Park and arrived late. After the match, tempers flared. Players expressed the view that they weren't fit enough, but it was more than that. Discipline had slipped again and attitudes were slack. 'There were hurleys flying across the tables and things were lively,' says Flannery. 'Players were saying, "This isn't fucking good enough. Why am I bothering my arse?" Having a go at each other.'

McCarthy held firm. The hurling drills were demanding and he believed that honest commitment to the drills would give them the fitness they needed. To ease their minds they were given more running in training for a couple of sessions after the Dublin defeat, but there was no shift in policy. And then by April players started feeling better. They beat Cork by a point in the Munster semi-final and nobody mentioned fitness again. They won the Munster final for the first time in thirty-nine years and all of a sudden McCarthy's way was hailed as the enlightened path.

In other counties there had already been a broad acceptance that the extreme fitness regime pioneered by Clare and copied by most of their pursuers was unsustainable, but McCarthy had taken the counter-revolution to a new level. Ultimately, however, the counter-revolution was unsustainable too. The belief that any elite team could compete and prosper on a diet of high-class hurling drills performed at pace was a romantic conceit. There had to be a middle point.

When Clare beat them in the 2002 All-Ireland semi-final with a typically grinding performance, Waterford players wondered again about their physical condition. 'At half-time we were out on our feet,' says Flannery. 'I've never seen so many men out on their feet, myself included. It was a hot day, yeah, but we were living on our balls because we hadn't the fitness. The training we had done in '98, '99, 2000 and 2001 probably carried us through 2002 because we did fuck all training in 2002. You still need to do pre-season training.'

They trained a little harder in 2003 but not significantly, and then a pattern emerged. In three of their four champion-ship matches that summer they built up a commanding early lead and lost it. Counting the 2002 All-Ireland semi-final loss to Clare, that amounted to four championship games out of five where they couldn't maintain their early pace. By the end of 2003 the players had returned to the view expressed in Parnell Park eighteen months earlier.

'I understand what he was saying about the hurling,' says Feeney, 'that what will win matches and lose matches is hurling mistakes. Our hurling was our problem, our speed of striking. You don't want a set of greyhounds. There is a balance. There has to be. You do need to be fit as well these days. Do you need the kind of dogged running to bring discipline and psychology into it? When the shit hits the fan in Thurles, where do you dig deep to when maybe you mightn't have dug deep in training – even though you would have worked very hard? There's a question mark over 2003. The second half of every match we seemed to die a little bit. Were we fit in certain matches? I don't know.'

In fairness to McCarthy, he accepted the need for compro-mise. Bonnar quit, Shay Fitzpatrick replaced him for the 2004 championship and physical training was significantly increased. A handful of senior players were let go, new players were blooded and the team was reshaped. What followed was their best year.

A league final defeat to Galway was shrugged off seven days later with a devastating win over Clare. They toughed it out against Tipperary, conjuring a late winner in a bobbing finish. The extraordinary thing was that Ken McGrath, Paul Flynn and Tony Browne weren't on the field when the winner was conceived; at any other time in the life of this team that would have been inconceivable. To beat Cork in the Munster final while only having fourteen men for most of the second half – and the breeze in their face – would have been unthinkable at any time in Waterford's history. Here was the mental toughness that Gerald McCarthy had aspired to eight years earlier. At last.

They lost another All-Ireland semi-final, this time to Kilkenny, but they did so narrowly and with honour. They didn't produce their best hurling but their nerve didn't fail them either, or their legs. Leaving Croke Park that day there was a clear sense that this was a team that could win an All-Ireland, even in the most competitive championship hurling had ever known. After the revolution and the counter-revolution and the treaty of compromise, here was a serious team and a modern team.

They reached higher in 2004, but the Munster final of 2002 remains the day of days. By 2004 they knew that they could be Munster champions; in 2002 they still had to convince themselves and challenge the doubt inherited from generations before them. Laois and Dublin had fallen so far off the pace in Leinster that Waterford winning the Munster championship was the last feasible breakthrough that hurling's era of liberation could give us. Gratefully, we accepted.

McCarthy identified a weekend away in Antrim two weeks before the Munster semi-final as the turning point of the year, and Flannery agrees. 'The Antrim trip saved us. Talk to anybody now and they'll tell you that. The Antrim trip saved us. The players weren't happy. They weren't happy with management, they weren't happy with each other. Everything was wrong.'

The journey tested their morale even more. They assembled in Waterford at 3 p.m. on a Friday afternoon and arrived in north Antrim late that evening, conveyed by two trains and a bus. 'We weren't supposed to be drinking on the Friday night because we were playing Antrim in a challenge match the following day,' says Flannery, 'but we were so pissed off we were going drinking and that was it. So we found a nice quiet pub in Ballycastle that was still open. We were all in there together. We had a right good session and everything seemed to take off from there. We went sight-seeing the following day and then we had another session on the Saturday night. The whole hog. It was just a great weekend.'

By Munster final day on the last Sunday of June they were in the form of their lives. Primed to go off. On the previous Thursday night McCarthy had ended a training match after just twenty minutes. When they pleaded for more he'd told them to keep it for Sunday. The work was done. 'Don't be afraid,' McCarthy told them, 'take risks, take chances, go for it.'

The team had also been galvanized by the fearlessness of youth. Seamus Prendergast and John Mullane were only in their second full seasons, and Mullane had just twenty minutes of the previous year's championship in his legs. Eoin Murphy, Eoin Kelly and Eoin McGrath were all rookies. Four of Waterford's forward line were twenty-one years of age or younger. 'Gerald hadn't the same group of players that Justin had when he came in,' says Bonnar. 'That definitely had a big part to play.'

On a fresh canvas they painted a new picture. When Waterford lost to Limerick in 2001 they had abandoned the game plan. They knew that they couldn't allow that to happen again. In their outlook and demeanour they were ready to execute a strategy. 'We talked a lot among ourselves in the week of the match,' says Peter Queally. 'We knew

how hard it was to get to a Munster final. We thought that
what happened in 1998 would bring us on a lot and still we
had to wait four years to get to another Munster final. We
were back there now and we weren't going to let it go.

'Colm [Bonnar] went into the psychological side of things
with us. That was important too. The first place you give up
is in your mind. There was no major thing, just a number of
small things. The approach had been a lot about calmness.
We often went into games where the performance came
more from the heart than the head, but you can't be going
bald-headed for everything.'

It was expressed in their use of the ball. Waterford players
repeatedly composed themselves in possession and delivered
low ball to the forwards – diagonal ball, fast ball, considered,
directed, deliberate. They hurled out of their skins in the first
half, and with the wind to come they were only a point down
against the All-Ireland champions. The game was theirs to
lose.

'Just before we left the dressing room,' says Queally, 'Brian
Flannery shouted out, "Come back here a second. Remember one thing: we're still losing this game."'

But they couldn't lose it. They drove sixteen wides, conceded three goals, allowed Tipperary back into the match
twice, three times, and still they blew them off the field with
the beauty and sweep of their hurling. Slowly, the suspension
of disbelief melted in the face of reality. On Waterford local
radio, WLR FM, the match commentator Kieran O'Connor
delivered the lines he had prepared in the event of a sensation.
'Generations have gone by,' he said. 'The currency has
changed twice. Seven Taoisigh have changed [since 1963],
but Waterford are back in the year of 2002.'

After the final whistle supporters were excluded from the
pitch, but Dave Walsh penetrated the cordon. He opened

negotiations with a Garda and pushed his pleas beyond diplomacy until his passage was secured.

That evening he fell into bed around one o'clock, but it
was a restless sleep and he woke again at four. He made tea
and wondered how much longer before the papers would hit
Dungarvan. At seven he went searching.

There it was. In black and white. The dream he had
dreamed.

10. Strike

By the last Thursday of November 2002, the Cork hurlers
had talked themselves into a situation where words had
lost their value. They had tried megaphone diplomacy and
committee-room bartering. They had fixed the county board
with a stare and shaped for a fight. The county board looked
at its hand again, unable to see how its picture cards could be
trumped. The county board didn't say that the players were
bluffing, not in so many words; but that was the belief that
underpinned their smugness.

A corner of a function room in the John Barleycorn Hotel,
five miles from Cork city, hosted the Cork panel and their
dilemma that Thursday night. The twelve players who had
represented the panel in direct negotiations with the county
board convened at six o'clock and the rest of the panel joined
them an hour later. Once more they examined their position
and what prospects remained for its improvement.

Since their last meeting with the county board exactly
three weeks earlier, written correspondence had been the
only means of communication between the two sides. In their
letter the players expressed their disappointment with the
board's reaction to their demands on a range of basic welfare
issues, but offered the possibility of another meeting. The
board's response offered next to nothing. They pleaded in-
capacity, bound by Central Council guidelines. The players
refused to buy it. In earlier meetings the board had acknowledged to the players that they were already in breach of
Central Council guidelines on the issue of gear allocations.

The board suggested further meetings with smaller delegations. Conceding to a fragmented negotiating process dictated by the board was out of the question. For the players, their strength was in numbers.

The players examined their consciences one more time. They didn't believe that any of their demands were unreasonable or excessive. They wanted to be provided with appropriate gear before pre-season training commenced with a top-up before the championship. They wanted gym membership for every member of the panel and better meals after training. They wanted a doctor at every Cork match and more efficient settling of medical expenses. They wanted an increase in their allocation of complimentary match tickets for championship matches involving Cork and the opportunity to buy more tickets. They wanted a better mileage rate and the guarantee of a team holiday, funded by the county board.

The core issue, though, was far greater than the individual demands. What the demands amounted to was a plea for respect. For their efforts to be acknowledged in a tangible way.

The magnitude of what they faced was clear to all of them. In the history of the GAA there had never been a players' strike. There had been tiffs and stand-offs but no county panel had ever withdrawn their services. The players knew that their adversary was the most powerful of all county boards and that the board secretary, Frank Murphy, was one of the most experienced and skilful of all GAA politicians. They couldn't be sure which way public opinion would swing and there wasn't time to seek the support of their own clubs.

They felt, though, that they had the moral authority to consider this course of action. Ten years earlier, when Cork teams trained a couple of nights a week and didn't burst themselves during the winter, a strike would have been inconceivable. Those days were gone. The revolution came and personal sacrifice was the new starting point for inter-county teams with ambition. Training and matches and self-denial were imperatives around which players arranged their lives. Such a life, however, required the comfort of certain conditions, and in Cork those conditions didn't exist. The strike was born of special circumstances but it was also a product of its time. Without the profound changes in hurling the strike could not have happened.

For these Cork players the time was now. Either they made a leap of faith or they abandoned all hope of a breakthrough. That was the choice.

It was no choice.

When things started to happen, they happened all of a sudden. At training one night in March 2002 membership forms for the Gaelic Players' Association (GPA) were distributed among the Cork players. The Cork footballers had embraced the GPA from the beginning, but most of the hurlers had stood back at first and for years had shown no signs of closing that distance. When both teams reached the 1999 All-Ireland finals twenty-seven of the football panel were paid-up members, but only Brian Corcoran and Donal Óg Cusack from the hurling panel were in the GPA. 'I know there were a few hurlers approached about joining,' says the former Cork footballer Ronan McCarthy, who was a GPA rep in Cork, 'and they thought it was absolutely hilarious.' By the spring of 2002, however, leading members of the hurling panel had come round to a different view.

Instantly and accidentally there was friction. The Cork manager Bertie Óg Murphy had tried to enter the dressing room while the players were discussing the GPA and found the door locked. He later established the reason and skipped the post-training meal at the Commons bar on Cork's north

side. The players sensed that Murphy had mistakenly interpreted the meeting as a threat to him and sought to address
this immediately. Four of the panel, including former captain
Mark Landers, tried to ring him from the car park of the
Commons to put his mind at ease, but it was never going to
be as simple as that. Murphy would have known the hostility
of the Cork establishment to the GPA and it was a complication he didn't need.

Other issues had surfaced by the end of that evening. On
the following Saturday Cork were away to Derry in the
league and the players were told that the bus would be leaving
at 1 p.m. on Friday. Two years earlier Cork had flown to the
north on the morning of a Saturday match against Derry, but
this time they were being asked to take time off work and
face a gruelling 300-mile journey in a coach. They refused to
accept it and they attempted to make a stand: if the bus was
leaving at lunchtime they demanded €100 for every player in
compensation for lost hours at work. The board didn't blink.
They later claimed that they had sought to charter a plane
but the cost was prohibitive. In the meantime the travelling
arrangements were simply adjusted: the bus would now leave
at 5.30 p.m. which meant they didn't arrive at their hotel in
Monaghan until 1 a.m., leaving a ninety-minute journey to
the venue in Swatragh on Saturday morning. The players
were forced to swallow it.

Worse was to follow. Niall McCarthy suffered a terrible
gash to his face during the match and though he was treated
at the ground by the Derry doctor it was clear that McCarthy's
wound required further treatment. The Cork doctor, Dr Con
Murphy, had been unable to travel and in his occasional
absence from away fixtures it was common practice for the
county board to depend on the other team's doctor. An
eight-hour bus journey was the last thing McCarthy needed

in his condition and it exacerbated the players' displeasure with the whole trip.

In the first week of April thirteen of the Cork panel joined the GPA. Quietly, management made it clear to a number of young players that it would be in their best interests to decline membership and, naturally, the young players regarded this advice as a warning. Frank Murphy was a hurling selector that year and it was known that he was opposed to the GPA. The Browne brothers, Alan and John, and the O'Connor brothers, Ben and Jerry, were prominent absentees from the roll of GPA members but most of those who joined were hardened campaigners and the core of the team.

Cork reached the league final against Kilkenny on the first Sunday of May, eight days after the GPA held what was regarded as a make-or-break EGM in Portlaoise. The AGM earlier that year had been poorly attended, Croke Park still refused to recognize the GPA as a legitimate players' union, and the perception was that the GPA was wounded and losing blood. They needed a big attendance in Portlaoise, and they got it. Six Cork hurlers travelled: Landers, Cusack, Wayne Sherlock, Fergal Ryan, Diarmuid O'Sullivan and Alan Cummins. The meeting turned out to be a watershed.

Cusack and Landers had worked on a speech which Cusack delivered to the EGM, taking fifteen minutes to complete it. Later on Landers got to his feet and improvised, suggesting a protest before the league final. 'I basically said that we were going around in circles,' says Landers. 'We had the GAA on one side, we had the sponsors on the other side and we had the players in the middle. The GAA were creaming off the sponsors, the players were getting fuck all from it, so who were we going to hit? We'll hit the sponsors through the GAA. Charlie Carter, Andy Comerford, D. J. Carey and Brian McEvoy were there from Kilkenny and I said, "If ye're willing, go back to yer players and we'll stage a protest before the game on Sunday. We'll refuse to step into the photograph or half of the team will step in. We want to know quite clearly leaving this room that we have yer support on this." Jesus Christ, the whole place was buzzing. This is it. The whole country would be watching and a big bold statement was going to be made on Sunday.'

The GPA EGM had been held in camera and no statement on a planned protest was issued to the media, but word quickly reached the county boards in Cork and Kilkenny. Their intelligence was faultless. On Monday night Bertie Óg Murphy arrived at Cusack's house in Cloyne armed with every relevant detail from the discussion in Portlaoise. Cusack was one of the two or three most influential players in the Cork dressing room and would have been seen as the prime mover behind the GPA on the hurling panel. Murphy pleaded with him not to proceed with the protest. Cusack couldn't give him an answer.

At training the following night tensions increased. Landers had been the Cork captain when they won the All-Ireland in 1999 and had been outstanding in the defeat against Limerick in the 2001 championship, but during the first half of 2002 he was on and off the team, his form undermined by injuries and work commitments. He wasn't going to be fit enough to take his place on the panel for the league final, but he was at training in Pairc Uí Chaoimh that Tuesday night when a grenade went off in his lap.

'There was a bit of banter going on behind the City End goals,' says Landers, 'and then John Meyler [Cork selector] turned to me and said, "Take a good long look around this place. It'll be the last time you'll see it." He was dead serious, and straight away my heart sank into my stomach.'

He let it sit. There was a team meeting later to discuss the

league final and when the match had been dealt with Fergal
Ryan informed Bertie Óg Murphy, on behalf of the players,
that a protest was being planned. Immediately Murphy
referred to a letter he had received from Dessie Farrell, head
of the GPA. The letter requested that Cork players be released
from training to attend the GPA EGM and it also said that
'under no circumstances did he [Farrell] want to disrupt
Cork's preparation for the championship'. 'And Bertie Óg
said, "Ye stepping out of the photograph is upsetting my
preparation,"' Landers continues. 'He was right, because
from the word go that year the subs and the team had been
in every photograph. There was never a photograph with just
the starting fifteen that year. He made a very valid argument
which basically put us on the back foot because we didn't
want to upset Bertie Óg, to be fair to him.

'I actually brought it up then that we felt certain [young]
players were being victimized. I knew of players that got
phone calls [about joining the GPA] and I said, "Not later
than an hour and a half ago one of your selectors threatened
me." Bertie Óg said, "What are you on about?" I said, "You
can ask Meyler there now."'

Meyler didn't deny it and Murphy was scrambling for a
second, searching for the appropriate diplomatic response to
a situation that was becoming crazier by the minute.

It was clear that the panel was not nearly as united about
the league final protest as they would be about the strike six
months later. Alan Browne, the longest-serving player on the
team, had more reservations than most. He wasn't a member
of the GPA and he was opposed to GPA involvement in any
dispute between the panel and the county board. He didn't
want a disruption of the team photograph and he felt that the
panel were being rail-roaded into this action by the most
fervent GPA members in their ranks. After training that

night Browne and Landers discussed an alternative. Browne suggested that players walk in the parade with their socks down and shirts out, and Landers liked the idea.

'A decision was made on behalf of the whole Cork panel to stay out of the photo, and I felt that was wrong,' said Browne in a *Sunday Independent* interview in August 2003. 'They'd [the six players who attended the EGM] made a decision for a panel of players who were not consulted. I came up with the idea of the shorts and socks. It's a protest, and the county board get fined. Let fellas who want to do it, do it . . . I don't think they [the tactics] were thought through and there were people outside of Cork making decisions for the Cork hurlers . . . I never fell out with anybody but you just did not have the same relationship with players. I don't know if there was talk behind my back but certainly fellas were colder towards you.'

Seven of the starting fifteen went ahead with the protest, but Browne was one of those who didn't. That's where the coolness came from. 'He was the fellow who suggested it,' says Landers, 'and he was one of the fellows who didn't do it, which really annoyed the players. In fairness, Alan tried to find common ground between Bertie Óg's situation, whereby he didn't want the photograph upset, and our situation, where we wanted to make a statement. I asked him was he willing to go ahead with it and he said he was, but when it came to the league final he didn't do it. Later on in the year, as we were to discover, Alan became a very strong member of the strike and he was at the top table at the press conference.'

Landers had conveyed the changed plan to Kilkenny's Andy Comerford but he couldn't muster any support and came under enormous pressure to back away from any planned protest. Charlie Carter and Brian McEvoy were only subs for the league final and D. J. Carey wasn't on the panel at the time because of injury, so Comerford was isolated from his most important GPA allies on the panel. He was Kilkenny captain that year, which made it even more difficult for him to step out of line, but he held firm and led the Kilkenny team in the parade with his shirt out and socks down.

The protest didn't meet the fevered expectation of the EGM but it was something. A start.

The match was hectic. After seventeen minutes Cork were ten points down, but with seventy minutes nearly up they were a point in front; two late points for Kilkenny determined the outcome and the Cork players faced the recriminations. In the minds of the Cork hurling public the protest had caused Cork's defeat. In the eyes of the Cork hurling public there was no picture bigger than that.

Cork stumbled on. They lost to Waterford by a point in the Munster semi-final and beat Limerick by a point in the qualifiers. Management organized a day in Kerry in the interests of team spirit and it turned out to be more fun than the players had expected. Talk of the GPA went quiet and an implied truce produced a contrived peace. Morale was low.

'The rot had started before the Waterford game,' says Landers. 'It was only a matter of time before the beams in the roof came down.'

Against Galway in the second round of the qualifiers the house collapsed. Galway wiped them off the field in Thurles, winning by nine points at their ease. Fergal McCormack had made his championship debut against Limerick in the sixteen-point defeat in 1996, but he ranks the Galway match as the lowest point of his Cork career. 'At least,' he says, 'in 1996 we went out to play Limerick expecting to win. Against Galway there were no expectations. The preparation was so poor and the morale so low that it would have been a miracle if anything other than a defeat happened. It was all little things. I remember we were collected in Mitchelstown that day, myself and the Newtown boys and Neil Ronan. Meyler came along and gave us a T-shirt. "Throw that on there, lads." At the side of the road he wanted us to take off our fecking stuff that we were wearing and throw on our T-shirts. You'd have to be there to appreciate exactly the feeling.'

The way Landers tells it, what happened next came out of the blue. A month after Cork were eliminated from the championship Cusack appeared on a local radio show hosted by Neil Prenderville. The GPA chief executive Dessie Farrell and the former Kerry footballer Pat Spillane were the other guests, and the topic for discussion was player welfare. Cusack recognized his opportunity.

In the course of his interview a strained but diplomatic silence was publicly shattered. He accused members of the county board of intimidating young players on the issue of GPA membership and he highlighted a couple of basic welfare issues. There were serious deficiencies, he said, in the amount of training gear given to the players by the board, and he outlined a situation where the board had ceased to pay for gym membership for the Cork players. On a long rap sheet, these were sample charges. He also said that the county board was being run by one man [Frank Murphy] and that he was surrounded by 'yes men'.

The interview was conducted live on the morning of Friday 16 August, and was replayed in full the following evening. The local papers didn't pick it up until the *Cork Evening Echo* ran it on their sports pages two days later.

Inevitably there was a firestorm of reaction. Landers quickly came out in support of Cusack's comments, along with five other players, and agreed to appear on Prenderville's show too. Some delegates were up in arms at the county board meeting that Tuesday night but the players refused to be cowed. Alan Cummins called for the Cork management to resign and Kevin Murray backed him, suggesting that nine of the panel wouldn't play in 2003 if the current management remained in place.

Cusack and Landers quickly realized the gravity of what they had started and decided to take legal advice from Diarmuid Falvey, a friend of Cusack's with a solicitor's practice in the centre of Cork city. Over the next four months Falvey would be a central figure in the background to every move made by the Cork hurlers in the lead-up to the strike.

On the first Monday of September the GPA's chief executive Dessie Farrell attended a meeting of the Cork panel in the Vienna Woods Hotel outside Cork city. By then the number of GPA members on the panel had swollen to more than twenty and the undisguised presence of Farrell at the meeting enraged elements of the Cork establishment. Farrell addressed the meeting and then left. In his absence the players set about organizing themselves.

'We made a mistake there insofar as it got misconstrued in the media that it was a GPA meeting,' says Landers. 'It wasn't a GPA meeting, it was a Cork players' issues meeting. I remember Liam O'Tuama [Glen Rovers board delegate] saying at the board – and he was quoted in the papers – "We don't need anyone from Dublin coming down to sort out Cork issues." The GPA were there in the event of support being required, but this was Cork players' issues.

'We had a flipchart and in the centre of it was written "Cork players' issues", and we said, "Right, what's wrong with ye?" Selectors, expenses, training, jerseys, gear, food, holiday fund, tickets, gyms – all these things came out. "Right, lads, let's prioritize it," and we had a show of hands. I'd say if anyone had mentioned a strike at that stage the meeting would have broken up. But fellas were enthusiastic and they knew what they wanted.'

Twelve players were nominated by the panel to deal with the county board and they went into training. They assembled in Falvey's office and he simulated the cut and thrust of a hostile meeting with the county board. He coached them and tutored them – a kind of verbal callisthenics.

Before the meeting, then, the players were primed. Everything had been discussed, right down to what they would wear: on a show of hands they decided to wear suits. 'There was a big deal made out of it, wearing the suits,' says McCormack. 'Not to be intimidated by them. To go in there and mean business.' For the first meeting the eleven county board representatives were dressed casually. For the second meeting they wore suits.

Joe Deane was asked to be chairman of the players' group and it took him two weeks to accept the position. The others were convinced that he was perfect for the role. Unlike Cusack or Landers, who had already been confrontational and outspoken in the media, Deane wouldn't be seen as a divisive figure. 'Who was going to think ill of Joe?' says Landers, his clubmate with Killeagh. 'Joe was the darling. But he was also strong enough and independent enough to know the difference between right and wrong. If we were doing the bollocks there's no way Joe would have taken the position. He was fantastic – incredible.'

Going into the meeting, ten of the players had a topic on which they had prepared a brief. Landers and Cusack, however, deliberately stood back. 'Myself and Donal had no brief in there,' says Landers. 'We were just watching, and if there was a requirement to jump in, we'd jump in. We knew what the issues were. That was our strategy. They were expecting myself and Donal Óg to be doing all the talking and leading the sheep to the slaughter. We weren't. All the players were behind this.'

The first meeting began with tea and scones and ended in stalemate. The players reckoned that the county board had used it to gather as much information as they could about where the players stood and what the players planned. However, the spin that the county board put out was that the meeting had centred on the composition of the Cork management. Nothing was further from the truth, but it was a clever spin from the board's point of view. Selectors are an issue in every club, every year, and in GAA society there is little tolerance for the notion of players dictating who their team selectors should be.

The players were unhappy with members of the Cork management but they had to handle that issue carefully in public. Since Cork won the 2000 Munster final they had played in five championship matches and lost four of them under three different managers; at least two of those games had been lost from winning positions, while the Galway performance was regarded by the Cork public as completely unacceptable. With their stock so low the players couldn't be seen to be targeting team management as the principal cause of Cork's decline. Bertie Óg Murphy had resigned as manager after the championship and this was a source of genuine regret for the players, not least because the selectors who remained had been the problem in the first place. So they framed their position carefully: they said that they weren't refusing to play under the existing management but would prefer not to. It was a delicate exercise in semantics. The underlying reality, however, was clear to everybody. There was no future in the status quo.

At a second meeting with the county board early in November everything came to a head. The board issued the players with a written response to their range of welfare demands. The players asked for a ten-minute break to consider the document and were gone for the guts of an hour. 'Our response was, "Jesus Christ, they're treating us like desperate eejits altogether,"' says Landers. 'Wayne Sherlock said, "Lads, I'm going home. Fuck this. There's no point in doing anything. Who the fuck do they think they are?" He was going home because of his disgust at the response, not because we'd get nothing. We rang Diarmuid [Falvey] and asked him what we should do. So Diarmuid said, "Go in and quiz them as much as you can and get as much information out of them as you can and see was there any bit of a budge on them." So we went in and discussed each of the issues and obviously there was some heated debate.'

A battalion of county board officers were ranged across the top of the room, almost matching the players' delegation in size. Frank Murphy, though, was the key figure. This was his office, his turf. Elected officers came and went but he had been the full-time secretary for more than thirty years and he was the pulse of the county board. To take on the board the players had to confront Murphy. His poor attendance at training as a Cork selector had been one of the minor issues on the players' agenda. It turned into a flashpoint.

'We were trying to be calm and cool,' says McCormack, 'and I said, "In this day and age players put in an awful lot of time and effort to get off work early and everything else and it's important for people on the other side to give the same effort. Fifty per cent attendance at training isn't good enough for anyone, be it a player or selector. Frank, unfortunately, we have hardly seen you." He came straight back. He's the most intimidating man you'd come across. He'd put you back in your box if you let him.'

Murphy exploded. He highlighted his record as a selector

on sixteen All-Ireland winning Cork teams and outlined his heavy schedule of GAA commitments – meetings, functions, matches. Seán Óg Ó hAilpín had been designated to handle the selectors issue and he didn't shirk his responsibility. He spoke plainly, and Murphy came back again.

'Frank said to Seán Óg, "The players are putting words in your mouth," and then I stepped in,' says Landers. ' "Frank," I said, "not alone are you insulting everybody here, but you are insulting Seán Óg's intelligence. He has gone to college, he's a well-educated man, and I'm sure you know, Frank, none of us would put words in Seán Óg's mouth if he didn't want to speak himself." He tried to intimidate Séan Óg by barking at him, but Seán Óg came in very strong.'

It wasn't long before Kevin Murray got involved. He accused Murphy of being a negative influence in the dug-out during matches, of making derogatory comments about players and getting other selectors worked up. He made particular reference to the 1999 All-Ireland hurling final when Murphy wasn't a selector and Murray was one of the substitutes sitting nearby as Murphy 'screamed' at the Cork selectors to make changes before half-time. Eventually one of the Cork selectors had told him to 'fuck off' and pointedly refused to sit in the dug-out for the rest of the match, despite the spilling rain.

Murphy raised the issue of hostile remarks Murray had made about him in a local newspaper during the summer. Murray said that he had no problem repeating them, 'one to one', outside the room. Murphy let the invitation pass.

At one point in the meeting Cusack's incendiary radio interview from the previous August and his reference to a county board full of 'yes men' came up in the exchanges. Two of the county board officers sitting at the top table were clubmates of Cusack's from Cloyne: Willie Ring and Gerry

O'Sullivan, Diarmuid's father. It was Ring who made reference to Cusack's disparaging remarks, without identifying him by name. Cusack was furiously taking notes during the meeting and, like Landers, had no intention of speaking unless called upon. But he couldn't be seen to back down from a challenge.

'I was sitting next to him,' says McCormack, 'and he was wondering, "Will I say it? Will I go?" And I says, "Go on, go on, drive on." He's an unbelievable speaker and he just dismissed him. "I presume you're talking about me?" he said.'

Landers remembers it as one of the key moments of the meeting. 'Donal Óg said, "Willie, you know you're a yes man, and I'm telling you straight to your face now that you're a yes man." It was fairly hot and at that stage the line was clearly drawn.'

Other issues came up in turn. Browne made a vigorous contribution about the gym situation. The facilities in Pairc Uí Chaoimh were unsatisfactory and the access which players had enjoyed to the gym in the Silversprings Hotel on the outskirts of the city was cut off during the summer. The board treasurer, Pierce Murphy, said that they had been unaware of players using the hotel's gym until a bill arrived a few months earlier. This response drew spontaneous laughter from the players. Access to the hotel's gym was so structured that members of the football panel signed into one book and members of the hurling panel signed into another when they arrived. A spokesperson for the hotel said that the service had been withdrawn because the county board was 'no longer' willing to pay for the facility, which clearly indicated that previous payments had been made.

During the meeting Frank Murphy continued to say that three or four of the players were leading the others by the nose. His attempts to divide and conquer were futile. After a meeting that had lasted nearly four hours the players had gained nothing except a clear sense of the battle that lay ahead.

The attitude of the board only drove them closer together, although they had known the value of unity from the beginning. They had organized themselves for a long campaign and built structures to take the shelling. The scale of the operation was extraordinary. In the weeks after the September meeting at the Vienna Woods Hotel every member of the panel was contacted once every three days by a central committee of six players. When the strike loomed closer the frequency of contact became daily.

Cusack has a diary in which every day of that time in his life is logged – meetings, debates, phone calls. He was at the head and the heart of it. It spread into every hour of every day.

'I'd say it was Donal Óg more than anybody else that got the thing going,' says McCormack. 'For him it was a really ballsy thing to do. He was really risking his inter-county career, for someone who was young and looked like he could be there for a long number of years. When he got his point across we realized, "Why not? Why can't we say our piece?" Donal Óg must have made thousands of phone calls organizing meetings.'

Cusack has censored his thoughts in public on that whole period. He had no wish to pick at the scab and reopen the wounds. When he did speak it was about regrets: wounded friendships; the unintentional hurt caused to Bertie Óg Murphy, Dr Con Murphy and the team trainer Teddy Owens. He has spoken freely, though, about the togetherness of the panel because that was their sword and their shield. Constant communication was their means of making everybody feel relevant and included. 'If the players had anything to report, anything at all,' said Cusack in 2003, 'if anybody was on to them, we documented it and kept it on file. We just had to head everything off. We didn't want to leave anybody isolated. At that stage we had nobody else but ourselves. And we did stick together, nobody can deny that.'

By the last week of November that unity was critical. The board wrote to the players one last time, conceding nothing and indicating no prospect of any concessions. As the players gathered in the John Barleycorn Hotel they knew that the time had come for a radical response.

'When we got the letter from the board that week,' says Landers, 'we said, "Right, lads, the show is over. We're getting nowhere; they think we're not serious. We do one of two things: we stand up and be counted or fold, and it will be ten years again before something is done.

'The attitude of the board the nights that we were at the meetings was the defining thing. It was, "Fuck ye. We're the board and we're not going to be told what to do." We never went in there with an attitude that we would be telling them what to do. We went in there with what we felt were reasonable requests that could be met by the board – and as it transpired, anything we were looking for other counties were actually getting. So the twelve fellas met and we decided, "Yes, we're for a strike." The panel came in afterwards and we went through where we were.'

Some of the younger players had reservations, fearing that their futures with Cork might be jeopardized. Wayne Sherlock, captain of the team that year and one of the negotiators, voiced his concern too. 'We said to the players,' says Landers, '"This might mean standing down from inter-county hurling for twelve months. How do you feel about it?" Wayne Sherlock didn't want to do that. He said, "I want to hurl, I don't want to miss any opportunities – but I'm willing to make a sacrifice for everybody else." '

Landers spoke up to soothe the nerves of the younger players. This was all for them, he said. His own career was nearly finished. He reckoned he had one year left in his legs but given his prominent role among the militants he doubted he would be given that year. Kevin Murray was in a similar position. He had become an increasingly marginal member of the panel but he too had been highly visible in the media throughout the controversy and sensed that his days with Cork were numbered. He endorsed what Landers said. They had something to lose; the young players had everything to gain.

It was the key moment of the meeting. From there, attitudes hardened. 'We were sick of meetings,' said one player at the time. 'Fellas wanted action. The mood of the meeting was vehement and definite. Fellas wanted to go bald-headed for it.'

A letter was drafted giving notice of the strike, and it was signed by every Cork player present in the hotel. Corner-back John Browne and sub goalkeeper Bernard Rochford were both abroad at the time, but they were contacted and they requested that their names be added to the document. The mandate to act was unity.

One out, all out.

Fewer than twenty-four hours after the decision to strike was taken, a press conference was called in the Imperial Hotel in the centre of Cork city. Seven players sat before the media: Cusack, Landers, Deane, O'Sullivan, Alan Browne, Ryan and Ó hAilpín. The mix was carefully chosen. Browne and Ryan were both from Frank Murphy's club Blackrock, and Browne was a well-known GPA sceptic. Deane and Ó hAilpín would both be perceived as model inter-county players with stainless reputations. Cusack and Landers had an intimate knowledge of all the issues, and O'Sullivan had a huge profile in the game and was a darling of the Cork supporters. As a delegation it had everything.

The media were given a detailed document containing the players' grievances and what the board's response had been. In the course of the press conference Ó hAilpín offered this summary: 'As players we put in a lot of time and sacrifices and at the end of the day it would be no harm to be respected for the efforts you put in. The county board have come back with this answer. It is just basically abysmal.'

Cusack told a story of the chaos that surrounded Cork's home game against Limerick in the 2001 championship. Cork players had to drive through the crowd-clotted streets leading to Pairc Uí Chaoimh less than an hour before the throw-in after a Garda escort had failed to show up at Pairc Uí Rinn, where the panel had assembled to go through their warm-up. There was further mayhem at the ground where all of the dressing rooms were already occupied and the Cork panel were forced to assemble in the gym area. There are no toilets in the gym, and rather than using the public toilets, fighting the crowds streaming to their seats on the way, the players urinated in the corner.

The press conference received huge coverage on RTE's main news bulletins that evening and for the board it was a public-relations disaster. They refused to comment directly but it was known that they were furious at what they saw as serious breaches of a confidentiality agreement they had entered into with the players where both sides agreed not to discuss the negotiations in public. The players said they had warned the board that this confidentiality would be waived if talks broke down. In the Imperial Hotel that Friday evening all the old rules were torn up. This was a new game no GAA team had ever played before.

At first the players didn't know what the public's reaction would be. 'There were people in my club who said to me, "Ye'll be fucked out and they'll get thirty more players in,"' says Landers. 'That was their attitude and that was the attitude of the board as well. But I think what the board learned was that there was no other player in any other club that was willing to come in against the players.

'I have no problem saying that there were fellas in my club pro the board. I have no problem saying that in every club you had people who were pro-board. I went into my own club and explained the situation as best I could. I would say that my own club didn't give me support, but it didn't go against me either. If they were put to the pin of their collar I don't know what their response would have been. But what was heart-warming was that within three hours of the strike being called we had phone calls from clubs that had called emergency meetings and gave us their support. I won't mention the clubs now in case that would ever affect them, but we got phone calls from about seven clubs.'

The board immediately realized that they would have to join the public-relations battle. Speaking on local radio the following Monday morning, the county board vice-chairman Jim Forbes invited all elements of the media, local and national, to attend the county board meeting that Tuesday night. The board then brought the meeting forward by half an hour to accommodate the *Irish Examiner's* copy deadlines. According to Forbes they wanted the meeting to be afforded the same coverage given to the players' press conference.

At the board meeting the executive indicated some concessions and were at pains to illustrate reconstructed lines of communication with the players. But the board still refused to bend on serious issues. Under questioning from a handful of plucky delegates the county board showed no sign of conceding anything that might contribute to their defeat.

Wednesday's *Cork Evening Echo* ran with a lead story on its front page under the headline 'It's Sorted'. It conveyed precisely the mood which Tuesday night's county board meeting had sought to create. Pat Horgan, the board's PRO, went on radio and television expressing his belief that a resolution was imminent. The board had made concessions and extended a hand of friendship; how could the players resist it?

To the players, that *Echo* headline articulated everything that was dangerous about the consensus they believed had swept Cork on Tuesday night and Wednesday morning. As far as they were concerned the battleground was smaller but the conflict continued. The board needed to be seen to be talking to the players, but it was never their intention to bow to diplomacy. Every concession announced at the board meeting that Tuesday night had been won by militancy, and it was this realization that galvanized the players to continue.

One sub-plot perfectly captured the attitude of the board. In the final weeks before the strike was called, while negotiations and correspondence continued, players were chased by the board for money owed on match tickets. Some of the money had been outstanding since Cork's All-Ireland winning season in 1999. The board had every right to ask for the money, but with ticket allocation such a live issue in the negotiations and tensions so high between the board and the players, why pursue this now? It was a crass miscalculation and a clumsy attempt to assert their power over the players. At the time, though, they knew no other way. Unused to their authority being challenged, they were unable to summon the humility from which every compromise ultimately springs.

The annual convention of the Cork county board was

scheduled for the following Sunday. The board was anxious for quick progress and a tender public embrace between both sides in the dispute. On Wednesday night the players decided that the board could wait. And sweat.

In the meantime the strike escalated. The board's big PR play was about to be buried.

The timing of events had caught the Cork footballers slightly on the hop. When Donal Óg Cusack was interviewed by Neil Prenderville back in August, lighting the long fuse which exploded with the strike, the footballers were preparing for an All-Ireland semi-final against Kerry. By the time Cusack's comments had been picked up by the local media the footballers were in a state of concussion after an eighteen-point whipping. While Cusack's colleagues on the Cork hurling panel raised their voices in a chorus of support for his public stance against the county board, the footballers felt unable to speak. They didn't feel any less aggrieved at their treatment by the board and they shared all of Cusack's anger, but that week they felt cowed and beaten up and they didn't feel that the Cork public would countenance any complaints from them. But soon they found their voice. In an article in the *Sunday Tribune* that October Ronan McCarthy and Ciaran O'Sullivan, the two most prominent and committed GPA members on the football panel, went on the record with stories of county board pettiness and penny-pinching.

Five days after the hurlers announced their strike and twenty-four hours after the county board meeting designed to contain the blaze, the footballers came out in solidarity with the hurlers. They too were withdrawing their services.

It should have been a straightforward decision, but it didn't unfold like that. Most of the football panel had been members of the GPA for at least four years, but their membership didn't necessarily reflect any great conviction or latent militancy. When McCarthy went looking for players to join him at the GPA EGM in Portlaoise he struggled to get a couple. 'I think if the hurlers had needed twenty fellas to go to that EGM they'd have gone,' says McCarthy. 'I remember going around trying to get fellas to go to the EGM and they wouldn't go. They were happy to let somebody else do it. They were a weak bunch of individuals, to be honest with you, compared to the hurlers. I was very impressed with the hurlers. They had good leaders, fellows who were willing to put their names up in lights and pay the consequences, and I thought the team rowed in behind them very well.'

The footballers had two meetings to discuss their position, one of which was addressed by two of the hurlers and Diarmuid Falvey. Then they left the room and allowed the footballers to arrive at their own conclusions. 'It got hairy at one stage,' says McCarthy. 'I remember at one stage thinking, "Jesus Christ, we're going to walk out the door here and say to the hurlers, 'Lads, we support ye, but we're not backing ye.'" I remember we were heading that way at one stage. A statement of support, but we're not going out on strike ourselves.

'At that stage I reared up big time. I said, "Look, lads, I'm five or six years listening to fellas complaining about the county board – this, that and the other thing." About how they weren't being looked after properly and how it's terrible. And I said, "This is a once-in-a-lifetime opportunity that you don't turn your back on." I remember one player saying, "At the end of the day we were only here to win an All-Ireland." I said if we don't actually prepare properly and have things done and organized properly we're not going to win that All-Ireland – and the hurlers have actually proved that point since. When it went to a vote it was unanimous enough, but I would have felt they were weak enough about it.'

It surprised McCarthy because he knew that his impatience with the board was shared by everybody in the room. Little things always seemed to be handled badly. A whole series of paper cuts on their fingers. He remembers the 2001 Division Two League final. Free gear was handed out to the match-day panel of twenty-four on the week of the game. Mark O'Connor, one of the longest-serving players on the panel, had been there all through the league but he was injured for the final, and because he wasn't among the named twenty-four he wasn't given any free gear. Misjudgements and indignities such as that were repeated and multiplied.

'There was pettiness over meals, pettiness over phone bills. You were going training three or four nights a week and the boys were quibbling over pennies. I remember we played London away one time – I think it was a McGrath Cup final – and you got an itinerary for the trip, and down at the bottom it said that the players were not permitted to swap jerseys. If I went thinking about it I could come up with a hundred examples. I remember we went to Westmeath for a league match up in Mullingar. They wouldn't stop in Mallow for breakfast because of the cost of it and when we got to Mullingar all they had for us was soup and sandwiches. Some fellas had left west Cork early that morning and had been travelling for five or six hours. I was one of the fellas who went out that day and queued in the carvery and bought my own lunch.

'I think the important thing about the strike – and maybe it was never said – but I would certainly have felt that the players had responsibilities too. I don't know about the hurlers, but with the footballers a lot of them would have had a poor attitude. There's no point in asking the county board for gear and looking for the right foods and facilities and this kind of thing when they were going to be out in town at three o'clock in the morning, shit-faced, three or four days before a match. And I mean there was no doubt it was going on. I could see it from the county board's point of view as well. On the football panel there were a number of fellas who, if I had been sitting on the side of the county board, knowing what I knew, I would have been reluctant to be forking out money on them.

'I remember coming out after the All-Ireland semi-final against Kerry in Croke Park – and this will tell you what some of the footballers were like. There was a free bar upstairs and we were called to the bus because we were heading for a train. Next thing a load of players came down and their hands and their bags were full of bottles. The boys' mentality was because it was free they were going to get what they could. I would feel I've a balanced view of what was acceptable and what wasn't, and I wasn't being anti-board just for the sake of it. I could see what they were dealing with too.'

In any case the footballers joined the strike. McCarthy, O'Sullivan and team captain Colin Corkery fronted a press conference in Jury's Hotel and they hitched their wagon to the train. They were criticized in some sections of the media for jumping straight to strike action without entering negotiation. But it was already clear that strike action was the fast track to progress. Why wait?

The pressure on the county board was enormous now. The most powerful county board in the country had lost control of their own players. They were suddenly powerless.

At some point the penny dropped. Quiet negotiation continued between Joe Deane and Jim Forbes and some progress was made, but a comprehensive resolution was going to require significant concessions from the board and a public climb-down. The players didn't see it coming. And then it arrived.

A meeting between the players and the board was arranged for the evening of Friday 13 December in the Silversprings Hotel on the outskirts of the city – five footballers, five hurlers and members of the county board executive. The players met at half five, an hour before the scheduled meeting, and both panels were asked to be in the hotel at nine o'clock to discuss the outcome. The players expected movement but not closure.

Shortly after the meeting began, though, the hurlers knew that everything had changed. The entrenchment and antagonism which had characterized their other two meetings with the board were absent. The mood was conciliatory. The board had abandoned the pursuit of victory and had come to broker a peace.

'I'd been dealing with the board for years,' says McCarthy, 'and it was a huge culture change for me. They were willing to discuss and engage on issues you wouldn't have got near them on before.'

Diarmuid Falvey accompanied the players into the meeting, and at first his presence excited some hostility from the board. The players, however, had alerted the board to his intended presence in a letter they had sent days earlier and they were adamant that he should stay. 'Basically,' says Landers, 'it was a case of, "Do ye want the meeting to go ahead now or will we just continue to strike?" They said, "Okay so". ' The meeting lasted more than four hours but in all that time Falvey's presence was the only issue that resembled a flashpoint. 'Their attitude was very positive, genuinely very positive,' said Cusack at the time, 'and we'd be as suspicious as anyone. With the pro-player attitude they brought to the meeting it was very easy to do business.'

The players won. The board had tried to play hard ball and lost, ending an unbeaten run that stretched back beyond memory. On a range of issues – medical support, gym membership, gear allocations, post-training meals – the demands of the players were met. The county board refused to accept a supporters club, at least not in name. In other counties supporters clubs had become very powerful and the Cork county board weren't prepared to risk any dilution of their own power. Instead they agreed to the establishment of a Cork Teams Support Fund which would run major fund-raising activities and reap the acknowledged goodwill of the corporate sector in Cork. The fund would provide for Cork teams at all levels and would be separate from the players' fund and the holiday fund. It was agreed that a player would be one of only two signatories on all cheques drawn from the account as a safeguard against the board draining the fund for day-to-day costs that should otherwise come from their own resources. Essentially the players were being offered a partnership in the enterprise.

'That was incredible, unbelievable,' says McCarthy. 'When you hear the Cork county board talking about corporate Cork you know that something serious is going on.'

The concessions continued into the fine detail. The hurlers were told that they could buy six hurleys from a hurley-maker of their choice at the start of the year with the tab being picked up by the county board. Any hurleys broken during the year while playing or training with Cork would be replaced at the board's expense.

The package the negotiating teams brought to their respective panels was accepted immediately and unanimously. Shortly before 11.30 p.m. applause was heard from the room where the players were gathered. The strike was over.

★

Within two years Cork were All-Ireland hurling champions again. One of the county board concessions during the strike meant that the incoming manager Donal O'Grady was allowed to pick his own selectors. More than that, he was allowed to pick a selector from his own club, St Finbarr's, breaking a code which had existed on Cork selection commit-tees for decades. His successor, John Allen, was given precisely the same privileges, no questions asked.

The team sent out by O'Grady was the best-prepared in the history of Cork GAA. O'Grady's training and Cork's outlook were defined by the belief that as inter-county hurlers they were a group of elite athletes. Such a label involved a leap in how the players perceived themselves and implied responsibilities too, but the strike had already shown that they were ready. O'Grady wanted to treat them as professional sportspeople and he wanted them to behave as if they had that status. It wasn't enough to be on time for training; you had to leave yourself enough time to prepare yourself for training. If training was at seven the masseurs were ready to give rub-downs from half five onwards. If you had a stressful day at work or an issue to iron out with the county board liaison officer you were expected to clear those things off your plate long before training started. O'Grady would be on the field at six and a lot of the players got into the habit of presenting themselves on the field at half six. Arriving at a quarter to seven with just enough time to get changed was unacceptable.

Everything was ordered. They had a complex and finely choreographed pre-match warm-up routine that ran for nine minutes, devised in consultation with the players, guarantee-ing them all sixty touches of the ball. There were ice baths after training and meals that met the requirements of manage-ment and the needs of players. On his laptop computer

O'Grady analysed videos of matches and prepared packages for players to watch, containing anything up to twenty clips of footage. The players had personalized training gear that was laundered after each session and laid out in their place when they arrived for training the next evening. In Cusack's speech to the GPA EGM before the 2002 league final this was one of the conditions that he said every panel should aspire to. Here was the culture that the strike had conceived and delivered.

The players' strike had been an accidental by-product of the hurling revolution, but it wasn't divorced from it and it wasn't the end of it. Because of the revolution the wheel kept turning at a quicker pace than ever. In the mid-1990s Cork were lapped at the back of the field; ten years later they were in front again, playing a new game. It was the only way back.

The old game was dead.

Index